For Heather, who makes
our visits with "Harvey" so
much fun!
                    Much love,
                         Mom
Christmas 1999

"Perfectly Delightful"

"Perfectly Delightful"

The Life and Gardens of
HARVEY LADEW

Christopher Weeks

THE JOHNS HOPKINS UNIVERSITY PRESS
Baltimore & London

The Johns Hopkins University Press
2715 North Charles Street
Baltimore, Maryland 21218-4363
www.mail.press.jhu.edu

All material in this book was graciously provided by the Ladew Topiary Gardens, Inc.,
except for those items that were provided by the following sources: Horst
(photographs on pp. 167 [top], 204, 213); Frank Magro, literary executor of the late
Sir Osbert Sitwell, Bart. (portions of the poem "Rat Week" on pp. 133–34); Middleton
Evans (Plate 5); Theresa Airey (photographs on pp. 2, 176); John A. Robbins Jr. and Bill
Nelson, map on p. 64; Peggie Phipps Boegner and Old Westbury Gardens, Inc.
(photographs on pp. 28, 39, 189); Joan Wyndham and the National Portrait Gallery,
London (the painting of Renishaw on p. 157); Sotheby's, Inc. (Plate 17); *Country Life*
Picture Library (photographs on pp. 141, 146, 151); *Vogue* and Conde-Nast Corp., Inc.
(photographs on pp. 61, 204, 213); *Town & Country* (photographs on pp. 107, 109);
Maryanna Skaronsky (photographs on pp. 97, 245).

Library of Congress Cataloging-in-Publication Data will be found
at the end of this book.
A catalog record for this book is available from the British Library.

ISBN 0-8018-6112-8

Contents

Acknowledgments

It might seem that working on a book of this complexity must perforce involve the talents, cooperation, and encouragement of a great many people. But that statement would be wrong. For the truth is, preparing this biography of Harvey Ladew could not be called "work" at all: it was pure pleasure. I only hope that those who worked—no, frolicked—with me in the Elysian fields of Ladewiana these past few years agree.

First among the players must come Sibyl Brown, Elizabeth Constable, and Leith Griswold, without whose vision, dedication, and plain hard work the Ladew Topiary Gardens would not exist. Back in the 1960s it was they (and their husbands) who talked to Mr. Ladew about creating a nonprofit foundation to ensure the garden's survival, and it has been they who, in various capacities, have gently guided the garden's existence ever since.

In 1987 Mrs. Brown, Mrs. Constable, and Mrs. Griswold—the garden's three graces—"retired" from the day-to-day operations of the board and turned the office of president over to Martha Robbins. She, in turn, has passed the gavel on to Jean McCausland. I owe these women, too, a deep bow of gratitude, for they, and "the three graces," continuously and unflaggingly supported and encouraged me during the years that went into researching and writing this book.

Everyone associated with the gardens made certain I had total access to the mountains of primary source material stored in the Ladew house: Harvey Ladew must have had a historian's love for documentation, for he saved everything: I found thousands of photographs and scores of albums, as well as guest books, address books, seed and plant catalogs (and orders), hundreds of pages of his uncompleted autobiography, "Around the World in Eighty Years," drafts of his magazine articles, and untold scraps of paper bearing his random thoughts on topics ranging from garden design to packing for his next Florida winter.

I also owe an impossible-to-repay debt to Patricia Corey, Mr. Ladew's surviving niece. Acting solely out of love for her Uncle Harvey, Mrs. Corey graciously showed me the Long Island he knew, patiently read (and corrected) drafts of the manuscript, and treated me to delicious meals both in her own dining room and at Uncle Harvey's favorite Piping Rock Club.

Many others who have helped the gardens flourish have helped me in my project as well. While every corporate trustee, every member of the board of directors, and every consulting committee member unhesitatingly gave support when—or before—asked, I would like to single out a few, recognizing the baleful certainty that someone will be left out. Thus I gratefully acknowledge Alice Ober and Pattie Penniman, who have gained international renown for the garden's education programs; Barbara ("Bunny") Hathaway and Susan Russell, who have kept the gardens themselves as glorious as they were when Harvey Ladew himself clipped and weeded; John Robbins and John McShane, whose dedication to preserving the physical fabric of Ladew's house has rewarded them with countless hours of battling flaking paint, leaky pipes, and quirkish cooling systems; finally, Eleanor Weller Reade and Achsah O'Donovan, whose sense of beauty and ability to find just the right chintz have guaranteed that the interiors of Ladew's house remain as attractive as they were when *Town & Country* lovingly photographed them in 1935. Deep bows are also happily given to Lena Caron and Jennifer Shattuck, successively the foundation's professional directors, who put up with my nagging about scrapbooks, saw to it that reimbursement checks arrived promptly, and enthusiastically but subtly worked to see that thousands of day-to-day potential snags got removed before they arose.

Many, many others associated with the gardens also assisted me in diverse ways. These kind souls include Karen Babcock, Nancy Boyce, Mayo Bryan, Monty and Rita Byers, Sally Crosby, Ned Daniels, Ann Deford, Bibber Dow, Jim and Theo Easter, Polly Forbes, Barbara Gallup, Wendy Griswold, Dee Hardie, Annie Huber, Dee Huddles, Harriet Iglehart, Peter and Joan Jay, Charlie Keenan, Phil Krach, Eleanor Schapiro, Tim Vadas, Jane Viele, Michael Wettach, and Heather Wilhelm.

Thanks are certainly due to Eileen Rehrmann, former Harford County executive, and to Arden Holdredge and Janet Gleisner of the Harford County Department of Planning and Zoning, who, knowing the importance of the gardens to Harford County, provided me with the time to write much of the text. In addition, I wish to acknowledge Maggie Pugliese at Sotheby's and Camilla Costello at *Country Life* for helping to obtain permission to reproduce material that so aids in understanding the story of Harvey Ladew. I also (and perennially it seems) thank Robert J. Brugger of the Johns Hopkins University Press for being the perfect impresario, confidant, and friend. In addition to his many other contributions, Bob placed the manuscript in the hands of Grace Buonocore, the perfect—and most patient—editor.

A heterogeneous cast of characters also assisted in a variety of ways. Alphabetically they include Jim Abbott, Dr. Ann Aker, Bob Armacost, Bob and Lucinda Ballard, Nan and Paul Barchowsky, Julie Baxendell, the duke of Beaufort, Lady de Bellaigue (Royal Archives, Windsor Castle), Helen Budd, Mary Helen Cadwalader, Brodnax and Mignon Cameron, Margaret Carver, Joel Cohen, Sean Culton, Eleanor Davies Tydings Ditzen, Rosemary Donner, E. Beck Dorsey and her son, John, John Eggen, Dennis Fiori, David P. Fogle, Melora Freeland, S. Kyle Glenn, Randall Greenlee, Mallory Hathaway, Pete Hathaway, Richard Horst, Ray Jezierski, Peter Lang, Frank Magro, Michael Makley and Andy Kreuz, Len Melish, Harold Orlans, Dorothy Patterson (Delray Beach Historical Society), Ben and Seth Ranneberger, Garner Ranney, Lois B. Reed, David Roszel, the late Vlasta Schmidt, Eldon Scott, Rick Scrabis, Bonnie Shriefer, Sir Reresby Sitwell, Bart., Michael Staz, Mimi Tilghman, Susan Tobin, Mike Trostel, Mario and Betty di Valmarana, Giles Waterfield, Maurice and June Weeks, Sam Westrick, and Bo Wiley.

Finally, I am delighted to offer a bouquet to Julia Duryea Sprigg Cameron, who introduced me to the wonders of Ladew's gardens in the first place.

A Note on Sources

Harvey Ladew left a wonderfully self-documented life, including hundreds of letters to his sister, Elise Grace, and scores of pages of an unfinished autobiography tentatively titled "Around the World in Eighty Years." The quotations in the text are taken from this material unless otherwise noted; the date of each letter is given if known. These documents may all be found in the archives of the Ladew Topiary Gardens (LTG) in Monkton, Maryland; readers interested in exploring Ladew's rich life are encouraged to make arrangements to peruse the material during normal business hours. Shortly after Ladew's death in 1976, a committee headed by Martha Frick Symington collected and edited a few of his autobiographical notes and published them under the title *Random Recollections* (Monkton, Md.: Ladew Topiary Gardens, 1981); I have quoted from this booklet a good deal and give brief citations as needed. In addition, the posthumously published autobiography of Ladew's great friend Billy Baldwin, *Billy Baldwin Remembers* (New York: Harcourt Brace Jovanovich, 1974), contains a full chapter on the topiarist; I have quoted extensively from it, too, and give brief citations as appropriate.

"Perfectly Delightful"

PROLOGUE

"Mr. Ladew, alone, designed the gardens"

Harvey Ladew lived long enough to see his gardens at Pleasant Valley Farm become famous. In 1968, at age eighty-one, he was pleased to write his sister, Elise Grace, that "*2,000* people came this year" to Maryland to visit the place. "You may be interested in reading some of the letters people whom I don't know have written telling me how much they like the garden. They come from Delaware, Philadelphia, Virginia, Washington, Texas, California."[1]

Harvey S. Ladew at his best—"Fox Hunter Extraordinary," declared the Baltimore Sunday Sun Magazine *in the fall of 1957.*

The enchanting world that is Pleasant Valley—22 landscaped acres divided into fifteen "garden rooms"—contains a diversity that would be hard to credit to anyone but Harvey Ladew, a rare and unusual man who embraced a seemingly impossible breadth of diverse interests. This living work of art becomes playful where the fountains splash; grows stately where the allées sweep into the dark grandeur of the surrounding forests; and relaxes into simplicity where the wild-flower-filled meadow drifts down from the rear of the house. It has a place for every mood and leaves the visitor with an enduring impression of its maker's serenity, sophistication, and wit.

Writing to his sister in May 1971, Ladew encouraged her to make a visit soon. Late spring, he told her, found the garden at its best, with the first roses, "the large tree at the back of the house dripping—not with rain but with big, heavy blossoms of my white wisteria," and iris. "Harvey had the most marvelous collection of iris," one friend recalled with a sigh. "During the season when that was in bloom, it was just a beautiful spot. It just swept down the center—this ribbon of iris on either side and down the middle."[2]

While the iris garden dazzled with its riot of hue, other sections impressed

Ladew's magnificent house and gardens—the stunning, contrapuntal view toward the house (above); the vista from the library arcade across the Great Bowl to the topiary allée (facing page).

"Perfectly Delightful"

through more subtle use of color. The apple orchard, for instance, contains dozens of fruit trees underplanted with scores of azaleas. Ladew chose shrubs that bloomed in all shades of pink, white, and pale mauve to complement the delicate colors of the apple blossoms. Indeed, when trees and shrubs bloom at the same time, it seems as if one is watching two gently blushing clouds, wafting along on parallel paths, one forever 10 feet above the other.

Ladew laid out other color-theme gardens, as well. There is the Yellow Garden, a magnificent sloping space roughly 50 feet wide and 250 feet long, centered around a swift-moving stream that prismatically reflects and fractures the garden's colors, transforming them into sparkling golden flecks. There are the Keyhole and Victorian Gardens, whose regal splashes of old rose, burgundy, and mauve turn the relatively small spaces into ballrooms of magnificence. And there is the Pink Garden, a difficult V-shaped area that twinkles all summer with every imaginable shade of pink: from the little girl pinks of single roses and tulips to deep, almost somber, pink of late-season sedums. In less capable hands these awkward spaces would have become apparent afterthoughts; at Pleasant Valley, Ladew made them small works of art.

And, of course, there is topiary. Winston Churchill's "*V* for Victory" and top hat recall Harvey's favorite statesman; seahorses symbolize his beloved Florida retreat; the *Man Walking a Dog*, à la Henry Moore, represents Ladew's nod to modern art; and, best of all, the lifesize hunt scene, in which a pert yew fox perennially outpaces two riders and a pack of five panting hounds, will endure forever as a clipped yew homage to the sport that became a lifelong obsession.

For decades Ladew suspected he had made Pleasant Valley special. "I think I have managed to create something beautiful and worthwhile in my life," he wrote in the 1960s. The ladies and gentlemen of the press certainly told him he had. Over the years his house and garden provided copy for reporters from *House & Garden* (and its French counterpart, *Maison et Jardin*), *Vogue*, *Sports Illustrated*, *Town & Country*, the *Washington Post*, and the *New York Times* ("acres of topiary splendor. Every inch of these gardens has been designed by Ladew personally"),[3] as well as two cover stories for the *Baltimore Sunday Sun Magazine* (September 22, 1957, and July 18, 1965).

Garden clubs and gardening tourists strove to outdo each other in praise: "One of the loveliest country places in America," wrote the organizers of the 1960 Maryland House and Garden Pilgrimage. "Mr. Ladew, alone, designed the gardens and topiary hedges which are considered the finest expression of topiary art in this country, vying in beauty and artistic design with many world-famous gardens in Europe." The Garden Club of America, meanwhile, reckoned that "the gardens' lasting impression is of the *joie de vivre* of their creator. Here imagination, inventiveness, and ingenuity have been coupled with a sculptor's hand and eye and a horticulturalist's knowledge of plants. Boundless good humor and fun find expression in each of the many and varied separate gardens. The zest for life so evident at Pleasant Valley Farm is infectious."[4]

Individuals distinguished in the horticultural world from both sides of the Atlantic joined in these paeans: "I can't tell you how much I enjoyed seeing your many little gardens, all so different and charming," wrote Henry Francis du Pont from Winterthur in May 1956. "As for the Swan hedge, it is a marvel of ingenuity and beauty." "I thought your garden was one of the most magnificently designed I have ever seen (& I have seen most of the great gardens of England)," wrote Diany Binny, whose own Kiftsgate Court in Gloucestershire ranks among the greatest of Britain's horticultural treasures. "If I was not married with children," Binny continued, "I would offer my humble services to you as gardener as I can't think of greater pleasure than working with somebody who has got such a great conception of beauty and design."[5]

Official blessings came in 1971 when the Garden Club of America, whose members had honored Ladew in 1964 with the title member-at-large ("in recognition of his landscape artistry"), awarded him the prestigious Distinguished Achievement Award for "creating and maintaining the most outstanding topiary garden in the country without professional help." "Mr. Ladew has through the years shaped and clipped the topiary himself," wrote Sibyl Brown in nominating Ladew for the award. "The proof of the excellence of these gardens . . . is that they all communicate with each other harmoniously."[6]

Aware, as he told one friend, that he had "adopted the most evanescent of art forms,"[7] Harvey devoted the last decade and a half of his life to ensuring that this truly distinguished—and truly fragile—work of art be preserved for the public. "I'd love to have them come and visit my garden," he told a reporter for the local weekly, the *Ægis*. "I created it for people."[8] This struggle provided a positive outlet for him during times that otherwise found him troubled by money worries (real or imagined), servant problems, ill health, and, as he wrote his sister in 1967, a general feeling that "America is going to HELL." Of course, Ladew being Ladew, he quickly added, "Luckily, as you know, I never worry—and I am happy—only a little sad at the change in our once lovely nation."

He had been fretting about his finances at least since 1947. That October 21 he wrote his sister, "You do not say if you are leaving me something to support me in your will and it looks as though I will need it—and I am sure I don't want to end up in the poor house. Well, maybe I will be so old and ga-ga I won't know what goes on."

Servant problems worried him the most—even more than his own failing health and (imagined) financial crises. In the early 1960s he found himself without domestic help for the first time in his life. He told his niece Betty Blagden that he lived "in this maison for over a week last year with not *one* servant—not even a 'cleaning lady' to come for a few hours." He added, "I will *never* do that again. I had to cook and try to make up my king size bed—and I couldn't make it up—was about to phone Abercrombie to send me a sleeping bag." In 1964 he wrote to his Maryland friends Ben and Leith Griswold, "I don't think I can go on looking for servants. [Last year] I had three drunken maids all bearing references from Vanderbilts, Whitneys, etc. The last maid was brought back in a taxi after St. Patrick's Day—she had completely passed out and the taxi driver had to drag her down the path. I had to telephone the police to come and remove her! I can't stand this sort of thing much longer." He later had to dismiss one chauffeur "when he brought a WHORE back to spend the night. That was trop fort! He said, 'She is my cousin' and I said 'That is even worse as it is *incest*!'"[9]

By the late 1960s, his body—banged about by years of hard riding and high living—began to fail him, even as his good humor endured. Anticipating the end, in May 1967 he wrote his sister to ask, "Do you believe there is a place called Heaven with a lot of saints (who would certainly be awfully dull) and Angels flying around? I don't—but anyway, there it is. I feel sure they wouldn't let me in." In November 1968 he wrote to say, "I told my doctor that I lived on a liquid diet all the time. Soup, milk, Scotch, and gin. He said he thought the diet had agreed with me—but I said I *didn't agree with him*!" Ladew philosophically added, "One can't reach the age of 81 without being a bit damaged. I am perfectly happy. I do not take the world or life seriously."

In the face of all this, his struggle to create a legal mechanism for saving his horticultural masterpiece seems poignantly gallant. More than once, as he might have phrased it, he came close to throwing in the trowel. "I tried very hard to do something about it, but got no help," he wrote his friend Benjamin H. Griswold III in 1963. "So, finally, I really have ceased to care what happens to this place." Later that year he wrote Griswold to thank him for offering to help him in trying to leave his house and garden to Maryland. "Lots of people we both know have often said, 'You *can't* let this beautiful garden be destroyed'—but they have done nothing to help me." He concluded with a bit of false bravado, saying, "Actually, I no longer care what happens to the place—though I have tried to economize to endow it for years. Grace & Co. advise me to go ahead and spend most of my principal and I mean to outdo Elsa, Perle, and Mrs. Cafritz in giving balls and large entertainments. Plan to invite 200 of my most intimate friends to make a trip around the world in four large jets—each plane would have a celebrated French chef. Of course, you and Leith will be invited." He concluded sourly, "Really I no longer care if the topiary I have worked on for 35 years is bulldozed and the place is sold off for ranch-type houses."

Awed by the perfect beauty of his garden, and frustrated by his apparent inability to ensure its survival, he wondered, "How did I ever do anything like this?" Indeed, how did he, born into wealth and privilege in Gilded Age New York, find his way to a backwater corner of rural Maryland? After half a lifetime spent hobnobbing with the world's rich and talented, living as the houseguest of a maharajah, taking a camel caravan across Arabia (with travel tips kindly provided by T. E. Lawrence), weekending in the stateliest of Britain's stately homes, hosting a Belgian prince, matching wits with Edna Ferber, Cole Porter, and Gertrude Stein (in English) and Jean Cocteau and Colette (*en français*), what caused him to take up spade and pruning shears and fashion this truly great creation, certainly by any standard among the most important gardens ever made in America?

I

"I loved seeing all my young relatives"

"I wish you wouldn't use my middle name, 'Smith,' when you establish the foundation," Harvey Ladew wrote his attorney friend Nicholas Penniman, then roughing out plans for incorporating the Ladew Topiary Gardens. "It's such a boring, common name and I have no idea where it came from."[1] That somewhat casual remark says much about Harvey Ladew. No one ever called him—or his relatives—"boring" or "common." In fact, he took distinct pleasure and pride in his *un*boring and *un*common family, relishing their adventures, marveling at their ready wit and imagination, admiring their independence and their blithe disregard for the opinions of others. While that might sound like a sort of willful eccentricity, it wasn't. It was simply that various generations of Ladews, Wallses, and Graces blissfully refused to be ruled by others.

In part, certainly, Harvey Ladew's restless independence came from his lively curiosity. As Billy Baldwin, his Baltimore-born, intimate friend of many decades, wrote, "Harvey loved everything you could imagine you might if you had all of his money. He had delicious food. He was wildly interested in the theater, and music as well. He drew and painted extremely well and kept a wonderful diary that was never completed."[2] No wonder Ladew refused to submit to the standards of others. No wonder he led his "perfectly delightful" life (to use one of his favorite phrases) solely according to his own, colorful lights. No wonder he designed and planted personality-radiating gardens that have intrigued the cognoscenti for three generations.

Harvey Smith Ladew II, "gardener, sporting art patron, and good companion" (as the *Tatler* dubbed him), was born into the fluid yet definitely upper strata of New York society at his parents' house, 3 East 67th Street, on April 6, 1887. He retained an interest in the city, its attractions, and its people the rest of his life: he treasured its opera and theater and maintained a series of much-visited pieds-à-terre. His last flat was at 155 East 49th Street, a chic address one block east of the Waldorf-Astoria. He asked his friend Billy Baldwin to decorate it. "He spared no expense," Baldwin has written of that job. "The atmosphere and the things he had in it made you think that you were in a great London flat. It was an absolute knockout."[3] By 1967, though, when he was plagued by ill health and lack of servants, he turned against New York. He referred to it as "Filthy Fun City," and he decided to sell "that dirty little apt." "I never go to the theater any more and I hate the poisonous air and crowds."[4] Even so, he did maintain his membership in his two favored clubs, Brook and River. He also kept a few accounts for emergency purchases: in 1967 he wrote his sister to buy some special "green velvet ribbon at Bloomingdales or Altmans" and explained, "You could charge it."[5]

Aware of the cushion that the certainty of great inherited wealth gave him, he wrote that that certainty "may help to explain the very amusing and happy life that followed."[6] His own natural—if sometimes trenchant—wit must have helped, too. For instance, he was once pleased to note that Brooke Astor had "sold that horrible place" in Rhinebeck. "When Vincent died Brooke said she was going to bury him under the croquet court where he had spent his happiest hours and I said, 'Well, then, Vincent will be dead on everyone.'" (A devotee of "naughty" puns, he also liked to tell "the story about the old girl who went on the garden tour to Hawaii and she said 'We were wined, dined, and lei-ed everyday!'")[7]

The lifelong bachelor developed an interest in his family early on and retained an interest in and fondness for his immediate relatives. At age eighty-one, when most people and events in the world irritated or depressed him, he took time to write his sister, Elise, to tell her, "I loved seeing all my young relatives, especially [niece] Pat and her new house which is really lovely and exactly right for today."[8] Throughout their long lives he and Elise, his only sibling, remained extremely close. According to Billy Baldwin, brother and sister shared "the same passion and wonderful taste in houses. Her great rambling house in Westbury was simply one of the most personal and fascinating houses in Long Island." Baldwin also felt that brother and sister weren't merely emotionally close; they "were remarkable look-alikes" as well, adding that if she "had grown a moustache, they really could have been mistaken." Moreover, he wrote, brother and sister "never walked—they trotted, leaning forward almost like the Tower of Pisa." "You always felt their balance would fail them and they would crash headlong into a building or tree. If you walked behind them down Park Avenue, it was an odd sight to see the movement of their trotting round bodies."[9]

Ladew voluntarily became something of a family historian, and in this avocation he was aided by his lifelong fondness for photography. He purchased his first camera in the late nineteenth century and maintained a keen interest in the art form all his life. Indeed, his niece, Pat Corey, recalls that in the 1930s Ladew managed to acquire one of the world's first "subcompact" cameras, a tiny machine that could function while hidden in the palm of one's hand. "Uncle Harvey just loved that little camera," she said. Later, in World War II, the U.S. government used cameras like it for espionage work—"but Uncle Harvey had one of the first ones!"[10] His Maryland residence still contains mountains of photographs and other papers recording and documenting his ancestors' doings—their business ventures, travels, romances, and (especially) their parties. This almost childlike love of mechanical toys in any form continuously surfaced. In 1949 he wrote his sister that he had "just invested in a new record changing attachment" that played "those big new records" through any radio. "It will play twelve records so the music can go on for, I believe, five or six hours without having to touch the machine. . . . I think it is wonderful."[11] Then, late in life, he grew keen on portable tape recorders, especially one that "plays the radio and also does tapes," given him, he enjoyed telling one and all, by Baron von Radovitch: "He's the head of Moët et Chandon Champagne."[12]

Ladew's childhood found him in the middle of New York's Gilded Age at its most gilded. He watched society's comings and goings with his customary bemusement, refusing to be impressed while keeping a good ear for particularly resonant names. Edith Wharton probably would have placed his father's side of the family among the city's "new money," while putting his mother's among the "old." In effect, this gave young Harvey an entrée into both worlds, which probably contributed to his easygoing acceptance of much that would have horrified

Young Harvey Ladew's New York. Looking up Fifth Avenue from 46th Street around the turn of the century, one may see the twin spires of St. Patrick's Cathedral in the background and Harvey's mother's carriage, pulled by one gray and one brown horse, in the foreground.

(or at least surprised) one camp or the other. He himself remembered the mixed feelings he experienced when he cleaned out his parents' town house after it was sold. "I went up to the attic," he wrote, "and found a box containing some of the toys and books we had owned. It made me sad to think how much we had once loved the old dolls and other superannuated toys. Among the books I found a small paper-covered one which was the list McAllister had made of who were members, in his opinion, of the '400.' I looked it over and thought it was so ridiculous that I tossed it into a scrap basket with the toys. I knew the descendants of most of these people and knew that many of them had not been in any society—except Mr. Lyndon Johnson's Great Society—for very long. It made me think of an Englishman who met an American at his club in London. During their conversation, the Englishman, in an attempt to place the American, asked him if he knew any of the Vanderbilts. 'Oh yes,' the American answered. 'We knew them when they were Vander-building.'"

A Fortune from Leather

Ladew's paternal wealth came from the leather business. His grandfather, the first Harvey Smith Ladew, was born in January 1826 in the town of Olive, Ulster County, New York. (The hamlet was originally known as Ladew Corners.) This Ladew's father was a tanner and obviously someone of means, for, according to the *New York Tribune*, he grew successful enough to provide "a good education" for all his ten children.[13]

Somewhat forgotten today, tanning ranked as one of New York's great nineteenth-century industries. Centered in what was affectionately termed "The Swamp," an area just south of the Brooklyn Bridge along Frankfort, Pearl, Houston, and Cliff Streets, the city's leather factories turned out the belts that made the nineteenth century run. To get a sense of how the industry grew, the number of hides inspected in New York skyrocketed from 265,000 in 1827 to 1,168,000 in 1847 and 4,420,000 in 1867. According to 1890 census figures, that year 200 New York tanneries produced $20.6 million worth of leather, and 257 shoe factories turned out $23.6 million worth of shoes.

Harvey Smith Ladew I chose to follow the family business and entered the tanning world in Ulster County. In 1847 he joined the firm J. B. Hoyt & Company, established in 1846 by Joseph B. Hoyt and one of the largest such concerns in America. (Ladew and Hoyt cemented their ties by marrying sisters.) In 1868 Ladew was sent to Maryland to oversee tanning operations at Hoyt's Flintstone Tanneries in Allegheny County; while in the Free State, he purchased the Cumberland Tannery for Hoyt in 1870. The following year, in recognition of his Maryland successes, Ladew was transferred to the company's main factory, in New

"Perfectly Delightful"

York City, and was made a general partner in the firm, along with Daniel Fayer-weather and Hoyt himself.

In 1884 Hoyt retired to his estate, Hoyt Hall, near Stamford, Connecticut, worth an estimated $3 million.[14] That year the firm, headquartered at 28 Spruce Street, was reincorporated as Fayerweather & Ladew. Its plant covered ten city lots; the main building, 236–46 Eldridge Street, was six stories tall and 150 feet deep and boasted an eight-story, 159′ x 168′ wing on Houston Street. Fayerweather & Ladew took pride in tanning its own hides (as opposed to buying tanned hides from others) "at tanneries in the bark regions of the Middle States, where oak grows with the best bark,"[15] and owned eight such establishments in Pennsyl-vania, New York State, Maryland, and Tennessee. Ladew himself had charge of these distant factories and visited them "regularly in rotation every few weeks." He and his wife had two sons, Edward R. and Joseph Harvey, both of whom found employment in the family business; Edward acted as superintendent of dis-tant plants while Joseph made a home for himself in the business department.

On March 7, 1888, H. S. Ladew went to work as usual in the morning. That evening, "he attended an auction sale of pictures. He became somewhat excited as the sale went on," suffered a stroke, and died on March 9. This "genial" man, "of pleasant manner [who] at once made friends with all whom he came in con-tact," also had "a generous nature and . . . on various occasions used his well-earned wealth in works of charity and philanthropy."[16] At the time of his death, his firm "was far in advance of all the leather houses in the extent of their wealth and the magnitude of their business."[17] The exact extent of Ladew's wealth is un-known, although when his partner, Fayerweather, died in 1890, he was worth an estimated $6 million.[18] (One should multiply these sums by 20 to get their 1990s equivalent.) It is known, however, that Ladew lived well. In 1887 he bought a house for himself at 871 Madison Avenue. The property fronted the east side of the avenue for 32′3″ and had a depth of 63 feet. According to H. S. Ladew's notes, scribbled on Hoyt & Company letterhead, he spent $65,552 on the building and $27,000 on the lot; he budgeted $15,000 for furniture for the new house (includ-ing $209 for a burglar alarm) and a further $30,000 for stables. Harvey Ladew remembered his "grandmother Ladew's" residence "on the corner of Madison Avenue and 68th Street" as "a large brown-stone house with a good size conser-vatory" opening onto the dining room. "I am a bit nostalgically sad when I pass it today [c. 1960]. It contains several shops, and the basement has been converted into what they advertise as a 'Whamburger.'"

In 1882, H. S. Ladew's eldest son, Edward, married Louise Berry Wall at her parents' New York residence, 43 Park Avenue, located in the heart of the city's "old-money" Murray Hill neighborhood. Louise Wall and her family brought a hefty strain of good humor and fun to the sober-sided Ladew clan. Harvey La-dew, only son of Edward and Louise Wall Ladew, recognized this and wrote that his "two grandmothers could not possibly have been more different." Whereas the elder Ladews attended strictly to business, "grandmother Wall had always been very social, and had travelled abroad a great deal. She was very handsome and always very 'elegantly' dressed by Pacquin, or some other famous French dress-makers; she wore some lovely jewels . . . [and] always entertained a good deal."

Ladew termed his father "successful as a man." If that meant that Edward Ladew enjoyed "manly" sports, the statement seems certainly true, for Harvey remembered his father as "an expert shot and a keen fisherman." The senior Ladew had something of a romantic past, too. In 1968 Harvey sent his sister a "book about (Lady) Emerald Cunard and her infamous daughter Nancy"; in the accompanying note, he explained that he "only met Emerald, who was a famous hostess, once": "I was coming out of Claridge's after lunching there, and so was she and she said 'Aren't you Harvey Ladew?' I said, 'Yes, I am.' And then she said, 'I'm Emerald Cunard and I was in love with your father when we were young.'"[19] The son, however, did not share his father's outdoor interests: "He took me along with him duck shooting or on fishing trips," Harvey recalled. "I hated freezing in a small boat and disliked the whole thing." (Billy Baldwin wrote that "Harvey's idea of exercise consisted of a mild game of tennis.")[20] Edward Ladew did, however, pass on one trait to his only son, namely a love of good food. Harvey remembered "our cellar in New York" always contained a large barrel of oysters, some wild ducks curing, and "live terrapins strolling about the cellar floor."

All that activity occurred in the basement of 3 East 67th Street, the large house Edward Ladew built for his family just around the corner from his parents' Madison Avenue residence. The household would consist of Mr. and Mrs. Ladew, son Harvey, daughter Elise (born 1890), and a shifting number of servants. Harvey described it as a "comfortable brownstone from which [he] had a good view of Central Park." Although the Ladew house has been demolished (its site now serves as access to a modern apartment building's underground parking lot), the three houses to its immediate east, numbers 5, 7, and 9 East 67th Street, have survived. One assumes the Ladew house was similar in scale and style to these neighbors. None of the remaining houses is a copy of any of the others, but one may say with safety that each is—and presumably #3 was—comfortable. They all rise five stories above ground, probably four main floors and a servants' attic. All three seem to have a European-influenced *piano nobile* plan, whereby the grandest rooms are located on what Americans call the second story. Otherwise, all exhibit the eclectic design styles favored by well-to-do New Yorkers of the period—a bit of Gothic revival here, a classic revival cornice there, with carved plaques, shaped terra-cotta trim, and balustrades and urns squeezed in wherever they could be squeezed in. Parenthetically, one should note that houses farther east in the block have survived, too. They evince the easily detected hierarchy among New York buildings of the time, since they are one story lower and sport less elaborate trim than the more desirable dwellings closer to Central Park.

"Perfectly Delightful"

Harvey Ladew's birthplace, 3 East 67th Street, has been demolished (it stood at the extreme left), but it presumably resembled the surviving eclectic houses on the block.

A room-by-room inventory (c. 1900) of the Ladew house's furnishings allows one to create a precise picture of the house in which young Harvey grew up.[21] (The furnishings may sound downright bizarre in the 1990s, but they represent the height of 1890s chic; again, one should multiply these figures by 20 to get their present-day equivalent.) One found a billiard room, wine cellar (with $200 worth of goods in it), laundry, kitchen, basement hall, and furnace room on the lowest level. On the story above, one found the front parlor with "2 tiger skins" worth $350, a quantity of bronze and ceramic figures, a "Russian bronze card receiver" ($25), a *lot* of curtains—"3 prs. lace curtains, 3 prs. red plush curtains, 2 prs. Moorish portieres"—"2 antique opium pipes, $25," and, wonderfully, "1 bull fighter's suit, $200." Next door was the "middle parlor," which must have functioned as something of a music room, for it held a piano ($350) and a "plush piano cover, $30," a mandola, a mandoline, a "gilt music stand, $150," and "1 pr. castanets" (value of castanets: zero). The middle parlor/music room also contained two fur rugs (one black bear, one leopard), some Dresden, Sèvres, and Royal Worcester vases and figurines, a "gilt cabinet" containing a Sèvres tea service, "4 china bon-bon boxes," a statue called *Secret Love* on a marble pedestal (together worth $1,000), and a dozen paintings including de Beaumont's *Temptation of St. Anthony* valued at $3,000, easily the most valuable work of art in the house, and a painting Harvey eventually inherited. Acres of fabric must have lent a somewhat dark, mysterious air to the room. Could any sunlight at all have pierced the "1 pr. pink lace curtains, 1 pr. pink plush curtains, 1 pr. pink portieres, 1 pr. blue portieres, 1 punk [*sic*] portiere"? The front hall (with, among other treasures, a tall case clock, an umbrella stand, and an unnamed "plant") connected the two parlors with the writing room, butler's pantry, and dining room. That last contained a mix of the expected—glass and china valued at about $3,000, a tapestry ($100), table, chairs, and sideboards—and the unexpected: "1 organ, bench, cover, and music" in all worth about $550.

Upstairs one found a sitting room (with furnishings valued at $1,000), "water pantry," dressing room, and bedroom furnished, in addition to bedding, with a "gun case containing 17 guns, revolvers, fishing reels &c" worth $2,000; up more stairs and one came to a sewing room, quarters for Harvey and his sister, a "back room and bath room," "store room," and a sort of catch-all space for the mistress of the house: "wardrobes, dresses, furs &c of Mrs. Ladew, $1,000." Finally, on the top floor, came the servants' rooms with furniture valued at $300. In all, the house's furnishings weighed in at $53,199, or a bit more than $1 million 1990s dollars.

"I HAVE READ, READ, READ ALL MY LIFE"

Harvey enjoyed a boyhood in turn-of-the-century New York which was at once typical yet different from that of his peers. He attended a series of private academies before graduating from the Cutler School, class of 1906. He deemed himself a mediocre student at best, but he did credit his schools with instilling a love of literature in him: "I have read, read, read all my life," he wrote his sister in 1970. Indeed, a fondness for books forms one constant in his life. As a young man he kept a diary noting what he had read month by month. His list for December 1918 suggests the catholicity of his taste, for he completed *Pepette le bien aimé*, *Les transatlantiques* by Abel Hermant, and Arnold Bennett's *Self and Self Management* and had trudged halfway through Boswell's *Life of Johnson*. The following month he continued to plug away at Boswell while starting and completing Mistral's *La reine Jeanne*, Martial Douel's *Au temps de Patrarque*, a trio of Goldsmith's works

Billy Baldwin later called Harvey and Elise Ladew "remarkable look-alikes," even for brother and sister; here they pose about 1900.

(*The Vicar of Wakefield*, *The Good Natured Man*, and *She Stoops to Conquer*), and *The Gentle Grafter* and *Cabbages and Kings*, both by O. Henry. He continued to buy books and read into the 1960s, when he was in his eighties and not always in the best of health. In December 1960, for instance, he received catalogs from Bernard Quartich, Ltd., in London, A. Grandmaison & Cie. in Paris, and the Paperbook Gallery in New York; from the last he ordered a collection called *Forbidden Limericks*. (His disappointed catalog annotation observes, "These limericks aren't erotic, just dirty.")

The senior Ladews moved to Europe each year for several months and always employed a tutor to teach Harvey and Elise the language of the country they were visiting. Consequently, both children grew up multilingual. Late in life, Ladew wrote his sister that he had just finished a "long life of Balzac," whose books he loved. "You SHOULD read good books—like, for instance, Balzac's Le Pere Gorriot," he scolded her in 1967: "You would find them very amusing and interesting and you would be reading something more worthwhile than Biographies of Royalty" (which she apparently favored). Continuing, he impishly asked, "[Have you] ever read that the Empress Elizabeth of Austria went away and hunted in England for years when she found out that the Emperor had syphilis? They don't tell you things like that in the average biography!" Even as he entered his eighth decade, he was pleased to note, "[My] Italian is excellent now. I am through 'Hell' (Dante) and half through 'Purgatory,'" and he was able to "jabber away at a great rate" to his two Italian servants. "Too bad Dante is not alive today," he added. "He could write a *hell* of a good book on America as it is at present."

In her later years, Grandmother Wall lived with the Ladews at 3 East 67th Street and also accompanied them on their yearly trips abroad. Harvey remembered her as "an inveterate sightseer [who] dragged [him] through every famous Museum and Palace in Europe." She was evidently inclined to give her only grandson free rein (or at least to look the other way), for Ladew recalled a favorite game—"quite exciting and rather dangerous"—he developed on these trips. While in the throne rooms of palaces, he would wait until the guide finished talking and the group started to move on to the next room. "The moment all had disappeared, I would make a quick dash for the throne, sit on it for a brief second, then rush off to join the tourists." It pleased him no end to be able to say, "I feel sure that I have sat on more European thrones than any living person." It certainly seems worth pointing out that he said "join the tourists," not "join the *other* tourists"; he evidently had a sense of being someone special even as a little boy. He later wrote that he valued those trips abroad: "I feel I learned a lot that I could not have known about in school. For instance, I can order breakfast in five languages."

Ladew's love of literature—and, one assumes, a somewhat precocious nature—earned him a great treat when as a boy he was allowed to call on the best-selling author Elinor Glyn. Writing in the 1970s, one scholar observed that in order to get a sense of the cultural life of Edwardian-era Europe, "it is necessary to read the novels of Elinor Glyn and to realize that *Three Weeks* sold five million copies." That book tells the tale of a Balkan queen who receives her lovers while clad in diaphanous garments and lying on a tiger-skin rug. And although it's easy to dismiss the book today (its plot "must rouse the mirth of twelve-year-olds"), readers "were unsophisticated in 1908. Mrs. Glyn received immense acclaim and was invited to stay in the Court of St. Petersburg. Princes and princesses felt it intriguing to meet her."[22] And so did young Harvey. "When the day arrived, I was a bit nervous but made my way to the Plaza Hotel where she was staying [in] a lovely big room overlooking Fifth Avenue and Central Park. There were many vases of flowers about, doubtless from many admirers of her celebrated book. I looked about for a tiger skin, but alas there was none!"

When Glyn appeared, Ladew judged her "no longer young but still good looking in a rather strange way with fiery red hair." "I told her how much I admired her book and that I hoped she would write another one." Glyn offered him some of her favorite tea and entranced the youthful caller by telling him, "'I have

"Perfectly Delightful"

it sent to me every year by caravan across the Gobi Desert? Of course I was very much impressed." To his surprise, Ladew came across his favorite childhood author some twenty years later when he found himself sitting next to her at a luncheon in London. "I reminded her that we had met and that she had been very kind to me. 'Do you still have that wonderful tea sent to you across the Gobi Desert?' I asked. 'What on earth are you talking about?' she said and I decided it was better to change the subject."

Ladew thoroughly enjoyed associating with the literati. His guest books brim over with names such as Cornelia Otis Skinner, Terence Rattigan, and Sacheverell Sitwell. He also enjoyed telling about the time he and his friend Charles Towne, editor of the *Smart Set*, ran into another Ladew crony, Edna Ferber, who had just returned home after plastic surgery to reduce the size of her nose. "Charlie said, 'Edna, I see you've cut off your nose to spite your face.' That was a dangerous thing to say to anyone as witty as Edna but I never heard her reply." Ferber later wrote him, "It was pleasant to hear from you, dear Harvey. I find myself, to my surprise, living at the Savoy-Plaza Hotel, for this winter at least. Next summer, when you are sweltering in Maryland, it would be so pleasant for me if you and Marian [Hall, a noted decorator] could come up to spend a weekend with me at my house in Connecticut. Don't you think you could manage that? I do hope so."[23]

Then there was the time a friend took him to a party given by Dorothy Parker. "I had never met her but had greatly enjoyed her clever writing. At the time Hattie Carnegie was suing Dorothy for a large dressmaking bill and the papers were full of the story. The party was held in a large hall Dorothy had engaged and we went in through an entrance decorated with large placards with amusing bits of writing. One of them read, 'You owe all this to Dorothy Parker. She owes it all to Hattie Carnegie.'"

Young Harvey also attended weekly dancing classes ("[where] I was a much better scholar . . . than at the several schools I went to") as well as painting and sculpting classes at the Art Students League. Louise Ladew also hired a sculptor ("some of whose work is in the Metropolitan") to teach her son how to create three-dimensional works in stone, clay, and papier-mâché. These lessons continued on the family's European sojourns. For instance, in Vienna one winter, Mrs. Ladew found a young painter "to give [him] lessons and take [him] through museums and galleries and private collections." Harvey truly liked Vienna—"what a charming, gay, fun-loving city; I still thrill to happy memories: light music, laughter and dancing everywhere"—but not "the horrible, guttural" language. "I learned during the war they turned an inoffensive little four-letter word—tank—into an unnecessarily long, clumsy word, *Strumpansserkraftwagenabteilung*!"

Ladew gained his first artistic success in 1905 when he was chosen to draw the cover for the Cutler School's publication, "Fortnights." He continued to paint and draw all his life. "I immediately started a new picture that I have been longing to paint ever since I left Paris," he wrote his sister from Florida in 1949 some-

This sketch by a teenage Ladew of Caruso and other notables reveals the young man's interest in drawing and music.

what tongue in cheek. "It is very strange and weird and is called 'Salon d'un Surrealist.' I have designed a special frame for it which will be made when I return to New York and, the moment you see it, I know you will send someone to try to buy it for your collection of early Ladews—and how right you will be to try to acquire it, as I feel it will cause a sensation in the art world." He excitedly wrote her that he had "about a half dozen other ideas" for pictures. "I do not intend to go to Palm Beach for I could not do any serious work if I am up half the night."[24] For decades he designed his own party invitations and Christmas cards and never missed a chance to ink out a little something. In 1967 he received an invitation to a party which read, "Please wear a black tie and a sombrero"—"I answered it on a sheet of paper. I had drawn a 'self portrait.' I was nude wearing a black tie and a sombrero but carrying a large bunch of flowers." Retaining his interest in sculpture, the following year he wrote his sister, "I am finishing a small statuette of a

"Perfectly Delightful"

mermaid taking a *bath*—in a *bath tub*. She has a cigarette in one hand and a cock-tail in the other! I think you will find it amusing."[25]

Just as he appreciated the effect of a piece of sculpture, so, too, did he enjoy experiencing the three-dimensionality of buildings. He visited Venice on and off for a half century and always made time for a sojourn to the mainland to marvel at the villas of Palladio. "Elsa [Maxwell] and I are going to motor to Vicenza to see the Palladian architecture," he wrote his sister in 1947. "Wouldn't it be nice to have Jim visit us in . . . Venice and he could study Italian architecture at first hand in one of the finest buildings—also see the Palladian architecture in Vicenza near-by," he wrote in 1949.[26] The garden he would create in Maryland certainly re-flects this love—and understanding—of architecture, of the thrill of moving from small to large spaces, of the delight one can take in the interplay of solid and void, light and shadow, of the importance of strong design, and of the value axes and cross axes have on structure: in other words, how a garden is experienced as one walks through it.

Harvey constantly urged his sister to join him in fun-filled self-expression: "Go ahead and paint—like Grandma Moses. Use your own taste and imagination and try to get attractive colour effects," he wrote her in 1947. "Oil paint is much easier than water colours. I have another wonderful suggestion as to a teacher. There is the nicest old Frenchman that Mary Rogers and I took lessons from. He is perfectly *charming*," Ladew enthused. "His name is Monsieur Jacques Maroger. Later you might graduate to a killing class he has with Mrs. Hearst, Jessie Don-ahue, Margaret Duke—but don't let that frighten you." He reassured his sister that M. et Mme. Maroger had both stayed with him in Maryland and she need not be "terrified" of him. "He was in charge of all the cleaning and repair of the paintings at the Louvre," Harvey wrote to Elise to complete Maroger's resume, "and he used to make the design for the modern Gobelins tapestry. I KNOW you will like him." Certain of what was important, he added, "M. Maroger has a very good sense of humor and is a dear old fellow." In a later letter he confessed, "actu-ally I don't like his painting very much as it is too classical and has not enough life in it." Nonetheless, he commissioned a portrait from Maroger; that canvas, which shows Ladew resplendent in his hunting pink, still hangs in the sitter's Maryland house.[27]

Interestingly, while Ladew kept up with current literature (early on he urged his sister to read *Catcher in the Rye*—"VERY amusing"—and Sartre held a decades-long fascination for him), contemporary painting left him cold. He liked to paint takeoffs on the works of Dali to show how easily anyone could grasp that man's style, and he minced no words about Spain's other modern master, writing in 1947, "I do not like Picasso at all. Think he is just bluffing." But if he had no use for Picasso's cubist canvases, he did confess to liking "the very early things," add-ing, "He draws wonderfully."[28]

Not only did his childhood in New York instill in him a love of painting and sculpture, but it also made him something of a theater bug, and he reminisced, "I hardly ever missed a good Broadway play. I loved all Clyde Fitches plays. I loved all Belasco plays and the wonderful actors and actresses he developed. I never missed a Ziegfeld Follies or Weber & Fields." In 1900 he started a scrapbook of all the plays he saw that year. It ran to fifty-nine pages and includes theaters from Europe to New York to Havana. He self-confidently wrote brief critiques of the performances, and it is clear that even as a twelve-year-old he had developed a good, critical eye: in Havana's Teatro de Tacon, for instance, he saw "Acts from the operas Aida, Sonambula, and Boheme" and deemed the evening "very peculiar but never-the-less very interesting"—adding in a world-weary way that the acting "was as good as it might be expected to be in Cuba. All the chorus girls were about forty years old." In New York his family took him to see *Cyrano de Bergerac*, and he found "Coquelin perfectly great as Cyrano!" He noted further, "Sarah Bernhardt has not as much acting to do in this play but she was splendid too. She did not look old at all from where we sat."

He developed a fondness for opera in New York, although not all his early visits to the Met proved successful. For instance, he wrote that his parents lived next door to a Mrs. Gould. During those years, the schoolboy Ladew and "an extremely good-looking and attractive" classmate often found themselves asked to accompany Mrs. Gould "and some other older woman" to the opera. This was partly because "Mr. Gould never appeared" on the scene ("but I have since heard that he had another family of seven children") and partly because Mrs. Gould knew how much the boys loved opera. Ladew said, "[I] would have enjoyed this immensely, except that this is what always happened. The group would gather at Mrs. Gould's for dinner served to us by a footman in black satin knee-britches and with powdered hair."[29] Unfortunately dinner took so long that they "always arrived about ten minutes before the curtain went down on the first act. . . . The lights went on, diamond tiaras and jewels flashed in the golden horseshoe, box-holders waved to each other," and Ladew tried to imagine what he had missed. "After the entre-act, the lights went down and the curtain rose on the second act. When the curtain rose on the third act we rose from our seats—and DEPARTED! I was infuriated but I have an idea that Mrs. Gould did not greatly care for music. Then we usually dropped in to one or two private dances before kissing each other good night." Philosophically, Harvey wrote that he could accept these evenings because he had "plenty of opera on [his] own."

As was true of painting, he retained an interest in opera all his life. In 1967, while planning a visit to his sister in New York, he wrote that he hoped she would take him to hear Caballe again. "She is much too fat but I have *never* heard such a voice. And I would like to hear Birgit Nilsson in *Die Walkure*"; three years later he wrote, "I'm looking forward to seeing you June 1st—and to hearing Joan Sutherland's beautiful voice, which is the greatest I have ever heard." And in his sometimes grouchy later years, when he felt that America was "going to hell," he

"To Harvey—LOVE—The Duncan Sisters." Ladew spent his life entranced by all forms of theater from opera to vaudeville, as this image of the two once famous vaudevillians suggests.

threatened to move to Europe and take a suite at the Madrid Ritz, a hotel he chose partially because it would be easy "to go to the Scala in Milan—Bayreuth, Salzburg."

But his New York childhood didn't consist just of operas and oil paint. There were also games in the park with other boys: "prisoner's base" and "bicycle polo" were favored, and he recalled that roller skates played "quite a large part" in his life in those days. "I used to skate to school carrying a hockey stick to use as a brake."

There were also horses. Ladew wrote that he inherited a love of horses from his parents, but especially from his mother, "in whose life they played a very important part." Actually, Edward Ladew seemed to have little use for horses at all and left "the entire management of the stable and the selection of horses" to his wife. Harvey recalled that he grew up with ponies and horses. "A shaggy little donkey was my first quadruped. My sister and I took daily drives behind him in a little governess cart complete with governess. He was not stubborn in any way as his kind are reputed to be and he trotted contentedly along at a brisk pace. New York in that time was a city in which the horse was king." Louise Ladew, who "loved to show horses," was also "an accomplished whip, having taken lessons in driving both a four-in-hand and tandem." The Ladews kept a private stable on Lexington Avenue to house their horses and carriages. These wheeled vehicles, "painted dark green and black and always highly polished," included a one-horse brougham ("which my mother used on her shopping expeditions"), a larger two-horse brougham (used for going out to dine or to the theater), a Victoria, a sleigh, and Edward Ladew's "light, rubber-tired road wagon."

Although Harvey Ladew's parents didn't ride for sport, when their only son turned twelve, they insisted he start taking riding lessons from Stanton Elliot, "an English dealer and a successful exhibitor of both saddle horses and hunters." But if the senior Ladews encouraged Harvey to learn to ride, they refused to let him jump, for they considered that "very foolish and dangerous." Young Harvey also developed a special fondness for the elegant horses of New York's mounted policemen. He pointed out one particularly good-looking animal to a visiting "horse-loving young Virginia woman, whose life was spent mostly at race meetings and in the hunting field." The horse was so handsome the visitor "couldn't resist going up to the policeman and saying, 'Officer, can you tell me how that horse was bred?' The embarrassed officer blushingly answered, 'In the usual way, I suppose.'"

Elise Ladew as a youngster in one of the family's carriages.

"Perfectly Delightful"

From Long Island Sound to the Sea of Japan

In 1893 Edward Ladew, who had inherited a controlling interest in the family leather business, talked his brother into joining their father's company with other concerns to form the United States Leather Company, a conglomerate made up of many quasi-independent firms. (Edward Ladew's share brought him $2,375,240.72; Joseph realized $1,765,163.28.)[30] Both brothers served as directors of the new company and maintained an active interest in it. But office work did not keep them from their true vocations, travel and just having fun.

The year he helped incorporate the leather conglomerate, Edward Ladew, described in one newspaper article as "short, fat, and jolly, rich and loves to spend money,"[31] bought a country place on Long Island for his young family near the fashionable village of Glen Cove. (He also built a leather factory near the town.) The property, called Elsinore, consisted of about 132 acres improved, as Harvey later wrote, by a "perfectly hideous," large, white-painted frame house "covered with carefully cut yards of gingerbread," with a large, second-story chapel "decorated in the Gothic style" and all crowned by a clock tower "in which a set of chimes boomed out the hours." The Ladews bought the place from the estate of Samuel L. M. Barlow, a co-owner of the Cunard lines; the house had actually been built for an English actor surnamed Burton, which may explain the undoubted theatricality of the place.

Although the house made Harvey Ladew shudder ("to improve its architecture, it would have been necessary to tear it down and build another"), he did relish the site—"on a high hill overlooking an enormous stretch of Long Island Sound" and boasting a half mile of shoreline. Ladew recalled the sound fondly: "We swam in it several times a day. I do not remember that anyone had swimming pools for the water was clean. We fished from our bathing house which was built out from the beach."

He also loved Elsinore's gardens, which included "many fine pieces of various yew from England and Ireland and other rare plants, not often seen in American gardens." Laid out in the highly formal manner of the day, the gardens featured a wisteria-embowered pergola leading to the front door, large stone urns planted out with yuccas and salvia, and boxwood-edged beds. There was also an elaborate series of lofty greenhouses, again typical of late Victorian taste. Two contained grapevines (one for white grapes, one for black), one contained palms, yet another hothouse flowers to provide winter bloom for the house. ("My mother went in for flowers and won many prizes with them at the New York shows.") These provided young Harvey with his first experience in horticulture. And while he later rebelled against the period formality, he had to know about palm houses and pergolas and bedding out so he could rebel against them.

Beyond the landscaped areas, the working farm boasted stables, cattle barns, pig pens, and chicken coops, and it was in these outlying areas that the two Ladew

The Ladews' country place, Elsinore, near Glen Cove, Long Island. Note Mrs. Ladew's formal gardens with cannas and other tender plants grouped around the urn.

children developed their lifelong love of all animals. The estate also contained its own quarter-mile track where the family exercised and trained their famed trotters.

Edward Ladew, a keen sailor, no doubt selected Elsinore for its location adjacent to the Long Island docks of the New York Yacht Club. There he anchored his ship, the *Orienta*, on which he commuted to his office in the city (at 159–65 East Houston Street), boarding after dinner and then quietly sailing to town at night so he had time to sleep and have breakfast before docking in lower Manhattan. The *Orienta* held no charms for Harvey, though. He dismissed his father's vessel as "not especially big," although he admitted there were "four nice cabins and good accommodations for the crew." Perhaps his lack of enthusiasm for the ship was due to his being a "very bad" sailor. "I can recall many rough days, when I was miserable, during short cruises to Newport or Bar Harbor." He never did develop a fondness for sailing, and in later years, when he spent months hunting in Europe, he always returned to America braving the new-fangled airplane and sent his valet home across the Atlantic on a Cunarder.

Beginning in the 1890s, winter usually found the Ladews in Florida, a place

Harvey "always loved." Actually, the family could be considered "Palm Beach Pioneers," since the community itself dates from the late 1880s, when retired oil executive Henry Flagler began constructing a railroad down Florida's swampy east coast. Harvey Ladew truly witnessed the complete transformation of south Florida from a vast emptiness to one of the premier resort areas in the world. "Miami was hardly on the map in those days," he wrote of his early visits. "It is amazing to think of Miami today, with its towering line of hotels and business buildings presenting a skyline akin to New York and its skyscrapers."

Flagler constructed two large frame hotels at the then southern terminus of his new railroad on a strip of sand between the ocean and Lake Worth. His six-story Royal Poinciana, with rooms for twelve hundred guests, opened in 1894; the second, the Breakers, opened in 1896. Flagler had both of them painted in his favorite shades of white and lemon yellow and thus began Palm Beach.[32] Flagler also built a few cottages on the grounds of his two hotels, and Ladew's future kinsman Michael Paul Grace leased one of these. One of Grace's granddaughters

Elsinore's formal parlor. To improve the house, wrote a critical Harvey, "it would have been necessary to tear it down and build another."

recalled that her family's "first winters were spent in his rented cottage," which she described as "a large, shingled house, standing in a row of identical houses."[33] Each hotel contained a cavernous dining room. According to Ladew, these were

> the only places to eat in town until along came Jim Bradley, who started a big gambling establishment on the shore of Lake Worth in 1898. One had to be a member of the "Club" to be admitted as gambling was forbidden—though everyone knew what was going on. Bradley's restaurant was famous and the food was unsurpassed. Though everyone knew it was a gambling house, the police were supposed to be ignorant of the fact. However there were occasional raids on the club which had somehow been warned that the police were coming to inspect it. When this happened the gaming tables were reversed and all the chips gathered up so that, when the police appeared, the room had an innocent look and the gamblers were sedately dancing to Mr. Bradley's excellent band.
>
> Bradley provided the delicious food at a ridiculously small price but made a great deal of money in return on the winnings at the roulette tables. As he made large contributions to various Palm Beach charities, the police closed their eyes on the illegal gambling and after Mr. Bradley's death the popular citizen was honored by a life-size bronze statue which still stands by the driveway near the former gambling rooms, where the Four Arts building is now bringing much culture—art, lectures, music—to the city.

This, then, was the Palm Beach of Harvey Ladew's youth. "In the beginning, before planes carried me there in a few hours, we took the long overnight trip to get there—but it was worth it. The train carried us right to the door of the Royal Poinciana Hotel. How wonderful it was to get to lovely summer weather after leaving New York in snow storms. There was golf, tennis, and a mule-drawn 'Horse Car' that carried us a short distance from the lake to the enormous Breakers Hotel and the ocean bathing. On Washington's Birthday there was always a big ball at the Poinciana or Breakers and then we all made our way home, having engaged accommodations on the train well ahead. Of course there were no planes in those days and no one would have thought of motoring back in the cars of the day which were continually breaking down and having punctured tires."

Reminiscing, he found it "amusing to look over many old photos of early pioneer days in Palm Beach, especially ones of the beach. The bathing suits we wore are unbelievable and, of course, there was no thought of such a thing as the new topless suits for girls. Far from such a thing as that, the girls were all modestly dressed in long skirts and wore black stockings; even the men were fully clothed in long trunks and shirts."

Henry James, who visited Palm Beach in 1904, found the life there "all most agreeable and diverting," and young Harvey would have agreed. He recalled, "In those early days there were very few automobiles about. We all rode bicycles and enjoyed doing it." Other people got around in three-wheeled wicker chairs propelled by a driver peddling while sitting on a seat behind. Ladew added that "these odd machines were very popular with young couples who were driven by discreet [servants] through what was called 'The Jungle.' The jungle disappeared long ago but it really was a jungle and it went from near the Poinciana to what is now Worth Avenue."

According to Ladew, "Along a path in one part of the jungle there was a small muddy pond where really large alligators were fenced in. This was called 'Alligator Joe's'; [he] would put on a show in which he entered the pond to wrestle with an alligator and ended the performance by drawing the angry creature to shore. It took a very skillful fellow to do this without getting badly bitten during the act and as all newcomers wanted to see it, Alligator Joe must have made quite a good income during each winter." Other entertainments sound equally simple and innocent: "several baseball games during the season between teams of guests from the two hotels which caused great excitement. There were a good number of yachts and trips to Nassau and fishing parties and much bridge after dinner. Perhaps a silent movie now and then; one went to see poor Pearl White facing torture and death but always escaping miraculously at the crucial moment."

As Palm Beach grew in popularity, "a group of rich men built a very beautiful movie theater and at times Zigfield [*sic*] would bring his company down and use the house as a theater," Ladew wrote. "Quite a few of the Zigfield girls married and settled down in Florida and many of their descendants still live there. (The builders of the theater had their own permanent seats as one might have a

Harvey Ladew (right) and friends digging into the sand at Palm Beach, c. 1915. Fifty years later he laughed that the bathing suits they wore were "unbelievable."

"I loved seeing all my young relatives"

*Palm Beach, c. 1914, and Ladew's future friends and relations (*foreground left to right, *Hubert, Michael, Peggie, and Ben Phipps) display the latest in Florida transportation: bicycles, tricycles, and peddled wicker chairs.*

box at the opera.)" In the 1960s, Ladew attended a "most amusing" benefit party. "The performers were all Zigfield Follies girls who had married and lived in Palm Beach or nearby. Though they were now quite ancient, they put on a very good show wearing some of their original Zigfield costumes, singing the old songs and doing dances they had done years ago in some of Mr. Zigfield's shows. At one point the m.c. asked if there were any grandchildren of the performers in the show and quite a number of hands were raised in the audience—causing roars of laughter."

Edward Ladew died in 1905. He had placed his fortune, an estimated $2.5 million, in a trust, the income from which would go to his widow until the two children had turned twenty-five; then the income would be divided into thirds; at her death, the capital would pass outright equally to Harvey and Elise. Somewhat stifled during her marriage (recall that she loved to ride but her husband didn't; she loved to garden while he loved to sail), Louise Wall Ladew truly came into her own in 1905, when she took over operations at the Glen Cove factory. According to a contemporary newspaper article, she built one hundred "pretty little houses, most of them cement cottages," for factory workers to create "a little city of our own here in the valley." Moreover, in just a few years she had increased the firm's business by $1 million. There certainly weren't many women of her social position who took up managing a factory, and she naturally attracted the attention of the press. One story—"How Mrs. Ladew Made a Million Dollars as a Factory Boss"—notes that as "the only woman among 800 men," Louise Ladew's "personality stands out all the more remarkably. She dominates them all."[34] This might be taken as further evidence of the family's disregard for convention, a trait Harvey certainly inherited.

Louise Wall Ladew, that wizard of the leather business, died in 1912, the year after daughter Elise's debut. Harvey and Elise, now fully financially independent, continued to live at Elsinore—and quite happily, too, it sounds. "We were young, life was wonderful. . . . The house was always full of friends."

Once freed from the restraint of overconcerned parents, the young Ladews took up hunting seriously. "How lovely Long Island was in my boyhood," Harvey wrote. "There were country lanes and dirt roads to ride. There were still many farms with large fields to gallop over and tempting fences and sheep hurdles to jump." He learned to jump on an old retired polo pony named Fireworks. "We did not get on too badly," Ladew wrote, and after a month or so of practice he felt able to take Fireworks to "the next Meadow Brook meet which was to be held at the Piping Rock Show Grounds," not far from Elsinore. Present that day were Ambrose Clark ("looking as if he had stepped out of a sporting print or a Leicestershire hunting field"), Mr. and Mrs. "Hal" Phipps, and others who greatly influenced Ladew in later years. The outing proved only a modest success, Fireworks not being especially cut out for the hunting field, since he was not able (or willing) to jump anything higher than 3½ feet. But then Ladew's friends Joe and Molly Davis "took pity" on him and lent him "a wonderful old hunter" named Nimrod—"there was no mightier hunter in the Meadow Brook field than he. Anything I have ever learned about jumping a horse is due entirely to what Joe and Nimrod taught me." Ladew then bought a horse of his own from the Davises. He described his new possession as the best jumper he ever owned, notwithstanding the animal's unprepossessing appearance—"a rangy, flea-bitten, grey gelding," he lovingly called him. Elise Ladew, too, quickly became a fixture with the Meadow Brook. She even took up racing, and her brother particularly remembered one "Ladies Race" at the Piping Rock Club which Elise won. There was nothing amazing about that, except, the doting Harvey wrote, of the dozen or so "girls in the race," Elise Ladew was the only one to ride sidesaddle.

The year after Louise Ladew's death, Joseph Ladew (Edward's younger brother) invited Harvey and Elise to join him on a round-the-world cruise. Harvey wrote that his uncle was the true sailor in the family and lived only "to buy one yacht after another; each time a larger one. He thought anyone having a yacht

Elise Ladew, 1903. The skilled young horse-woman grew famous for winning races riding sidesaddle.

should have it built so that it could be used by the Navy in case of a war." Uncle Joseph's ship buying climaxed when he commissioned the *Columbia*, a 436-ton, 180-foot-long floating palace that cost $175,000 and required a crew of thirty.

This was the vessel the family boarded in Naples for the 1913 cruise. It is not clear why they boarded in Italy, not in New York, but so many things about this cruise still mystify. The yacht steamed through the Mediterranean to Alexandria, thence through the Suez Canal to India, where the party's real adventures began. In Bombay they were greeted by a Captain von Muller, commander of the German warship *Emden*. Ladew wrote, "[Von Muller] felt it was his duty to have a look at a ship that might have belonged to the American navy, but, when he met our party, he must have changed his mind, unless he thought we were all spies. At any rate, he invited us to tea on the *Emden* the next day and my sister and I accepted, being naturally very curious to see a German warship." The entire party then left ship for sight-seeing: a special chartered train took them to Delhi and to

"Perfectly Delightful"

visit the prince of Baroda, among the subcontinent's grandest rulers. Harvey alone also spent a few days as the houseguest of the somewhat notorious maharajah of Kapurthala. (Harold Acton, a future acquaintance of Ladew's, wrote that in the hedonistic Venice of the 1920s, "a phalanx of dancers would waggle their legs among multi-colored fountains," competing with "the Princess of San Faustino's sleek satellites in exhibitions of solo Charleston" for the attention of "Prince Jit of Kapurthala.")[35]

After reboarding in Calcutta, and "disregarding schedules,"[36] they sailed on to Singapore, then to Bangkok to pay a call on the king of Siam, then up the coast of China to Japan "at the right moment to see the trees in the full glory of their blossom." In June, the group left Tokyo for Vladivostok, where they had chartered a private car to join the Trans-Siberian Railroad. But on June 11 the Japan-

Harvey's Indian host, the maharajah of Kapurthala, during Ladew's tour in 1913.

"I loved seeing all my young relatives"

ese navy seized the *Columbia* at the port of Wakayama, on the Inland Sea, midway between Kobe and Nagasaki. The event became headline news throughout the world: "Ladew's Yacht, New Yorkers Aboard, Seized by Japanese," screamed the *New York Times*; "*Columbia* Carrying Party of Society Leaders on Oriental Cruise, Enters a Forbidden Port and Is Held by Officials"; "Entire Sailing Party Placed under Arrest."[37]

While possible internment in a Japanese prison made a rather ignominious end to the trip, Harvey Ladew loved to tell of his arrest the rest of his life. Although he regretted not having taken a diary on the cruise, he did take a special camera, called an Eastman, which he used to document his adventures on and off ship in roll after roll of film. "You point the thing and you have two speeds," he recalled in 1970. "You choose the speed and the lens just revolved" to produce a panoramic image. The Eastman took only black-and-white photographs, but Harvey had some hand-colored in Japan—"so beautiful, don't you think?"[38]

The young Ladews also continued their Florida winters. Their party going was much publicized, and Harvey and Elise found themselves featured in several newspaper and magazine articles. In one, for instance, dated March 8, 1914, and entitled "Outdoor Dancing at Palm Beach," the writer described a costume party given by William Thaw IV and Howard Phipps at which one William Lawrence Green appeared "in an apple colored wig and an evening gown of a lighter shade," while "Elise Ladew wore tango trousers, with costumes of Turkish effect." Another story describes how "Miss Elise Ladew and her brother, Mr. Harvey Ladew, entertained their friends with a moonlight ride through the jungles in wheelchairs and a dance in the coconut grove"; another chronicled "a dinner for fifty members of the dancing set in the Poinciana Grill" given by Harvey and Elise.[39] Sometimes their Florida entertainments took a horsey turn. Ladew recounted how "Jimmy Cooley, who wrote a delightful monthly article on sports for *Town & Country*, and who hunted with [the Ladews] regularly," told him that "he had been asked to start a drag in Miami, Florida—of all inappropriate places!—for the benefit of guests at the new Coral Gables Hotel. His description of the drag was very funny and he said it was laid through tomato fields and orange groves. At the end of each drag, he said, he always came in covered with tomato and orange juice—so he decided to give it up."[40]

"THE KING OF THE DUDES"

Much as Ladew enjoyed all his relatives, it was Louise Wall Ladew's brother, E. Berry Wall, born in 1860, the toast of Deauville, who became his favorite. "To say that my uncle was an extraordinary character," his admiring nephew wrote, "is to put it mildly." Harvey Ladew judged his "Uncle Wall" to be "quite a different person from [his] Uncle Ladew. The only way in which they were alike is that

Visiting Peking in 1913, Harvey took this panoramic photograph of the famed Forbidden City with his "Eastman" camera.

they were both spendthrifts." For a few years in his youth, Wall worked in his own Wall Street stock-brokerage office. But it didn't take him long to think the matter over and formulate what became his lifelong credo, a design for living which his nephew later embraced: "A man who inherits a comfortable fortune is foolish to work. He should leave business to the industrious fellows who need the money." So he retired from the world of commerce at age thirty and "for the rest of his long life Mr. Wall did nothing but live on his income, wear bright clothes, go to the races, and drink champagne," according to the bon vivant's obituary.[41]

No shirker from the limelight, Uncle Berry became a frequent and favorite subject of reporters covering the international social scene. To the journalists he was, and would be all his life, "The King of the Dudes." (A somewhat disapproving reporter, the same man who wrote up Louise Ladew's success at the leather factory, described meeting the businesswoman "at the horse show, . . . accompanied by her pretty young daughter, Miss Elise, her twenty-two-year-old son, Harvey, and by her dilettante brother, E. Berry Wall.") Nephew Harvey, in fact, gave his uncle the perfect prop, a red chow pup that grew to be beloved by caricaturists.

Harvey's lifelong fascination with the celebrated boulevardier once took physical form, and it did so in a manner that sums up an epoch: a costume party thrown by Elsa Maxwell and memorialized in the panting prose of New York gossip columnist "Cholly Knickerbocker." "It will be many moons before New York Society again raises high-jinks at such a fantastically successful party," the chronicler told his readers. "And my topper is off to Elsa—she certainly knows her stuff!"[42] Guests had to dress as their favorite contemporary, and, judging from the in-jokes and choice of subjects, the gala must have taken place around 1930.[43] George Gershwin came as Groucho Marx, Beatrice Lillie as Clifton Webb, and when Mrs. Vincent Astor arrived as the princess de Polignac, she "was greeted with cheers"; Ladew's friend Kitty Miller arrived as torch singer Helen Morgan, Sarah Jane Sanford appeared "as her brother, 'Laddie,' in polo attire" ("it really

"I loved seeing all my young relatives"

Harvey, on the right, promenading along the Riviera in the 1920s with his Uncle Berry and Aunt Lomie Wall. One can almost hear the monkey fur of Aunt Lomie's coat rustling in the breeze.

was an inspiration"), and Emily Vanderbilt Thayer came as the Prince of Wales "in a more formal moment." One might have thought that Cecil Beaton would have taken the cake for his impersonation of Mercedes de Acosta. (Knickerbocker deemed the effect "grand," for Beaton had gone "to the trouble to make himself up like the aesthetic Mercedes and even had that lady's highly painted red ears and tri-corner hat.") But Beaton's outfit paled when Harvey Ladew appeared dressed as Berry Wall: that caused "a sensation"—"Could anything be more marvelous?" Knickerbocker wondered. "And where did Harvey find that Chow dog?"

Berry Wall, like his mother (and, indeed, like his nephew), abandoned frivolity and became deadly serious when it came to matters of dress. In fact, Wall's obituary told of one reporter who wrote, "Berry Wall was actually wearing last year's clothes." Incensed, Wall summoned the upstart and waved in front of him "a letter from a Fifth Avenue tailor agreeing to provide him with ninety pairs of trousers every three months during the current year." Uncle Berry bought his shoes and hats from Poole in London. "He had a fondness for very loud checks and brilliantly colored Ascot ties," Harvey recalled; he also favored lavender-colored spats. His ties—often made of silk the same color as his chow's fur—came from Charvet in Paris, a firm that "also manufactured his high collars which rose to his chin." Although Harvey Ladew wrote that "those collars must have been frightfully uncomfortable in a warm American summer," one has the feeling he rather wished he could have worn them, too. He admiringly added that "just as Queen Mary stuck to the same kind of hat," Uncle Berry "wore those starched collars all his life, long after anyone else would have wanted to be seen in such an oddity. The collar, of course, made him very conspicuous and the subject of many caricatures." But Wall could be innovative in his clothing, too, and Harvey recalled that his Uncle Berry often told him "that he wore the first dinner jacket that had ever been seen in America. He appeared in it the first time at a 'Hop' in the United States Hotel in Saratoga, where he went each year for the racing season. It caused quite a stir."[44] Indeed it did, and, according to Ladew family lore, the

When Elsa Maxwell threw a dress-as-your-favorite-contemporary party in the early 1930s, Harvey chose to come as his Uncle Berry—complete with red chow pup. "Could anything be more marvelous?" wondered the columnist "Cholly Knickerbocker."

maître d'hôtel "told Uncle Berry he would have to leave since he was not properly dressed."[45]

The Fifth Avenue Easter Parade stood as something of a perennial highlight in Uncle Berry's life, and the possibility of being photographed wearing his best did not diminish his pleasure in the event. Nephew Harvey recalled that while his "very beautiful and charming aunt was always simply but becomingly dressed," it was "Uncle Berry who was always featured in next day's papers." Not every Easter outing proved successful, however, and Ladew loved to tell of the time "one of the strongest pillars of the church" had asked him and Uncle Berry, both Presbyterians, to share a pew in St. Patrick's Cathedral for holy service. The pair agreed (they could always join the parade later) largely because "there was to be very wonderful music that day and a great soprano from the Met had offered to sing." Complete unfamiliarity with the Catholic service and with Latin ("an added complication") might have undone lesser souls, but not Harvey and his uncle. They decided to watch and copy those around them: "When they stood up we stood and when they sat we sat." Everything went smoothly until at some point the congregation again stood. Uncle Berry, thinking the service had ended, took his top hat from under the pew (where he had put it for safekeeping) and placed it on his seat. "Unfortunately the service was not over and everyone sat down again," Harvey wrote. Uncle Berry landed smack on top of his prized topper, "which went off with a fairly loud bang." "Everyone looked at us." Ladew recalled that his uncle became "dismayed and distraught," not because he had interrupted divine service but because he had ruined the hat he expected to wear (to applause and general delight) in the Easter Parade: "How could he possibly step out on Fifth Avenue without a hat and face the photographers who were sure to be waiting for him?" Chagrined, the two men sneaked out "a side entrance leading to Madison Avenue" and crept home. Ladew typed up that tale, intending to use it in a book he planned to call, with a nod to T. S. Eliot, "Mishaps in the Cathedral."[46] But the book, like Uncle Berry's stroll in that year's Easter Parade, never materialized.

In 1916, having "spent two, tidy small fortunes," Uncle Berry expatriated himself and his wife to Paris, thanks to subsidies from Harvey and Elise.[47] (He did make one return trip to America, in 1928, "but when he realized he would have to deal with Prohibition," he fled in "indignation and disgust" and "hastened back to Paris.") "In those days," Ladew recalled, "one could live much better in France and for less money than in America." The Walls took an apartment in the Hotel Meurice, perhaps not everyone's idea of budget accommodations. There Uncle Berry fell in with a set of agreeable cronies who populated what his nephew called "the French racing world." In 1928 Uncle Berry officially opened the social season by winning a thousand dollars in a bicycle race: "Riding a bicycle through the streets of Paris was nothing to a gentleman of a mere sixty-eight who had danced until four o'clock in the morning," one admiring reporter opined.[48]

At some point in his career, Uncle Berry decided he had grown too fond of hard liquor and vowed to drink nothing but Champagne. A steady diet of Champagne—starting with a pint each morning for breakfast—suggests a man who took his victuals seriously. Thus, one should not be surprised to learn that Uncle Berry had a dish named after him, and in Edwardian-era recipe books, one finds, along with dishes such as peach Melba and chicken Tetrazzini, steak Berry Wall. The ingredients for four people are:

2 lb. beef steak 1½ inches thick
2 t. butter
½ t. dry English mustard
1 t. Worcestershire sauce
1 t. minced parsley
salt and pepper to taste

It sounds simplicity itself to make: one broils the meat (three to four minutes per side) while blending together the other ingredients. Then with a sharp knife one makes five or six crisscross incisions on one side of the steak and spreads the incised side with the butter/mustard/Worcestershire mixture. Finally, the whole thing gets placed under the broiler for another minute.

Harvey Ladew spent as much time as he could with Uncle Berry in France and is known to have visited him in Monte Carlo during the winters of 1925, 1927, 1930, and 1931. He also wrote that he went with Uncle Berry to the Cafe de Paris the first night Vernon and Irene Castle danced there: "They were totally unknown and at the time quite hard up. But the great success their dancing made did not depend on any expensive, fabulous gowns Irene wore. She was young, slender, lovely looking and had designed her own simple costume of bright grey chiffon trimmed with wide grey fur—on her exquisitely poised head she wore a simple Dutch lace cap. When 'les Castles' danced they seemed to literally float over the floor and they and the 'Castle Walk' which they introduced created an immediate sensation."

Ladew grew nearly as fond of Uncle Berry's wife, Aunt Lomie, whom he remembered as being "very beautiful. Many artists painted portraits of her." In 1947, after the Walls' death, Harvey wrote his sister urging her to "bring Lomie's lovely painting by Madrazo over to hang it" in Elise's Long Island house. "She has on a blue satin gown and, as she was very beautiful, I think it would be a great decoration and a very dignified family portrait. I *know* I am right about this." Lomie Wall had studied singing with Marchesi and Jean de Rezke and Harvey felt, "The reason I have always loved music is because she sang to me often accompanying herself on the piano or guitar." Ladew's own niece, Patricia Corey, also recalled that Uncle Berry's wife "had a beautiful voice. She could mesmerize a room when she played the guitar and sang."[49]

Harvey recalled that, "added to all this, [Aunt Lomie] had a great sense of humor." She probably needed it to live with a character like Uncle Berry. In addition to the other "colorful" facets of his personality, he evidently had a great fondness for *les femmes*, and nephew Harvey wrote that when he spent three mornings in 1947 cleaning out his uncle's effects at the Meurice on the old man's death, he found, among the "stacks of Menus from Gala parties" and signed photographs of King Alphonso of Spain, the king of Sweden, "and from celebrities ranging from Lily Langtry to Lily Pons, Lindberg, General Pershing, and Franklin Roosevelt," a bundle of "really killing" photos of his "uncle's old girls: chorus girls, all in tights." Harvey viewed those last images scientifically and judged their subjects "rather plump [with] fat legs which their tights showed off nicely. Theirs was evidently the type of beauty popular in those days"—but, equally evidently, not the type that held any attractions for *him*!

When war broke out in 1914, Uncle Berry and Aunt Lomie decided to abandon France for Spain and headquartered themselves at the Madrid Ritz. The couple asked their favorite nephew to join them, which he eagerly did. "I loved Spain," Harvey wrote, "especially the Prado Museum." He also loved the Madrid social whirl. Through his aunt and uncle, he met "and became great friends with" the Casa Torres. "[Their] daughter, Blanquita Casa Torres, now [c. 1960] the Duquesa de S., is the mother of the beautiful Queen Fabiola of Belgium. Blanquita was a debutante and had been brought up with the young Infantas. She went to all the big balls and parties and took me with her." He had especially fond and vivid memories of one ball given at the palace of the duke of Medinaceli for the king and queen of Spain. "The ladies were all in beautiful gowns and wore tiaras and lovely jewels," he wistfully wrote. "The gathering made a wonderful picture which I will never forget. When the Royal pair were announced, a line of footmen, in the Medinaceli livery, descended one of the staircases to meet them, carrying lighted silver candelabra. Of course, champagne flowed."

"THE SOCIETY WEDDING OF THE YEAR"

In April 1914, shortly before the Great War began, Elise Ladew married William Russell Grace. The newspapers fell over themselves covering the event. One dubbed it "the Society wedding of the year"; another felt it "outdid anything ever thought of by George Eliot."[50] The bridegroom joined the Ladews to one of the world's great fortunes, whose beginnings can be traced to James Grace and his wife, Ellen Russell. It seems necessary to go into these associations at some length, because the Graces and their spouses tended to "completely adopt each other's families, [and] they really had little need for friends," as a Grace descendant has written.[51] And since Harvey Ladew's beloved sister married William Russell Grace, she, and by default he, became part of that extended family.

Prominent Irish landowners, James and Ellen Grace moved to Peru in the

Margarita Phipps (née Grace) and Ladew's sister, Elise, then Mrs. William Russell Grace (right), attending an auction of polo ponies, c. 1930.

1840s, where they established vast copper, sugar, and shipping interests.[52] The couple prospered and their firm "became the leading house on the west coast of South America." James's eldest son, William Russell, joined him in South America. In 1864, William Russell Grace, suffering from ill health, moved to the United States, where he was made head of the firm W. R. Grace. He bought an estate in Great Neck, Long Island, and, somewhat surprisingly, entered the brawling world of Tammany Hall and was elected mayor of the city of New York. Elise Ladew married his eldest son and namesake.[53]

To get a sense of how shocking Louise Ladew's factory management must have seemed at the time, Peggie Phipps Boegner has written of her own mother's complete—and expected—lack of concern for financial affairs: "With her upbringing, it would have been astounding had Mother ever interested herself in the stock market or even in her will," "Mother," née Margarita Grace, being a first cousin of Elise Ladew's husband.[54]

The Grace men and their in-laws, while attending to business when necessary, also became some of the greatest sportsmen of their time. And while they took part in the usual sports such as golf and shooting, their true love—almost obsession—lay with horses, specifically with polo. William Russell Grace II, Elise Ladew's bridegroom, made his estate, the Crossroads, near Westbury, Long Is-

---

"I loved seeing all my young relatives"

39

land,[55] the epicenter of the polo world. Indeed, in announcing his engagement, the New York papers deemed it appropriate to describe the groom-to-be as a "polo enthusiast": "Every year he holds a polo tournament at Great Neck, where he has a fine polo field, and in the fall he holds a race meet."[56] And although Harvey Ladew never felt tempted to mount a polo pony and do battle with his kinsmen, he did share their love of the game. His sister did, too, and frequently accompanied her Grace in-laws to matches.

"A special train carried a contingent represented by the Vanderbilts, the Goelets, the Harrimans, and others of the 400," a reporter enthused about the Ladew-Grace nuptials. In addition, "all the employees of the big Ladew leather factory," accompanied by fife and drum, "lined up around the veranda . . . so that the entire town might do homage to Princess Elise, as they called this young woman whom they had known and claimed since her childhood." Then came "the sound of a bugle horn far down the road and presently the red coated members of the fashionable Meadow Brook Hunt Club rode into view. The hunt had ended on the Ladew estate, and the horsemen repaired to the ceremony, bringing their hounds with them."[57] The wedding ceremony itself took place outside under an old apple tree, "which dropped white petals" on the bride and groom. Then, after an afternoon of tangos on Elsinore's lawns, the young couple left their three thousand guests for a honeymoon in Europe.

They also left a happy but desolate Harvey: "I could not live here without my sister," Ladew told a newspaper reporter on Elise's wedding day. Thus he "turned the key on the big rich country place forever."

"Perfectly Delightful"

"Happiness comes in absorption"

When his beloved sister, Elise, married William Russell Grace in April 1914, Harvey Ladew found himself with no intimate day-to-day family ties. His father had died in 1905, his mother in 1912, and now his sister, with whom he had always lived and traveled, had gone to make a new home for herself and her husband. He also found himself in quite comfortable circumstances financially, since he had gained control of his share of his father's fortune on April 6, 1912, the day he turned twenty-five.

Thanks to travels with his family and an inborn love of reading (and, no doubt, encouraged by relatives such as Uncle Berry Wall), he also found himself with widely varied avocations. He later wrote that he could not "imagine going through life without a great many hobbies." Concentrating on a single interest struck him as being "very dull." Continuing, he said he "realized at an early age" that he would "probably never be a Tilden, Bobby Jones or Paderewski, Velasquez, Culbertson, Nimrod, or an Isaac Walton"; but it never stopped him from "going right ahead and having a lot of fun." Even among the horsey set, he realized that the people he liked best "did not have one-track minds," or as he called them, "race track minds."[1] So there he was with no family responsibilities and blessed with good health, a deep, manifold curiosity, and a sizeable private income. Virtually anyone today, placed in those agreeable circumstances, would resolve to set out and treat oneself to a very, very good time.

And that is precisely what Harvey Ladew did. He created a milieu for himself into which, to quote Ellen Terry, "only beautiful things were allowed to come," and he populated the stage that became his life with an extraordinary cast of friends. Indeed, his longtime friend Billy Baldwin, dean of American interior decorators, made a telling point when he wrote that "one of Harvey's eccentricities was that he was not interested in society, per se. He was interested in all kinds of people." The pages of Ladew's guest books and scores of surviving letters certainly bear this out, for they reverberate with names such as T. E. Lawrence, Beatrice Lillie, Elsa Maxwell, Cole Porter, Horst, Anthony Hail, Jessie Donahue, Moss Hart and Edna Ferber ("two of his best friends, who stayed with him during the triumph of *Showboat*"),[2] Richard Rodgers, Van Truex, Sacheverell Sitwell, Clifton Webb, Terence Rattigan, the duke and duchess of Windsor, Harold Acton, and the Duncan sisters (famed vaudevillians), as well as the perhaps more expected entries from the *Social Register*, *Burke's Peerage*, and the *Almanach de Gotha*. That heterogeneous group did, however, share one quality: *accomplishment*. They could be movie stars or interior decorators or playwrights or hostesses or cabaret entertainers—or even a Baltimore socialite who captivated a king and earned a niche in history as "the woman I love." The point was they all excelled at something. And it seems at least an inferential tribute to Ladew's own charm that so many, varied people chose to befriend him.

Hunting with the Meadow Brook

Harvey Ladew evidently decided to establish his own residence the minute his sister announced her engagement, for in May 1914 he sold the family place in Glen Cove, Long Island, and purchased 4½ acres of land in the nearby village of Brookville. He then hired architect James W. O'Connor to design what was described as a "large, roomy" house. He named his new residence the Box and moved in that fall. Even though there wasn't much acreage around the Box, Ladew managed to indulge in his love of animals. In addition to a small stable, he created quarters for other livestock, and an unidentified clipping from that time gives the glad news that "Harvey S. Ladew won the honor of raising the fattest hog at the Nassau County Fair with a porker that weighs 750 pounds."

He chose to live in Brookville principally so he could be close to the Meadow Brook Hunt. In the early twentieth century, Brookville (along with the contiguous communities of Westbury and Glen Cove) formed the heart of Long Island's hunting country. The polo-playing Phippses lived at Old Westbury House; the Piping Rock Club was nearby; and the Meadow Brook's riders could freely gallop over the farms that filled that still rural part of the world. Ladew's first hunting friends were Joe and Molly Davis. This couple had lent him his first jumper, Nimrod, and they would later introduce him to the joys of hunting in Harford County, Maryland. In the years just before the First World War, the Davises rented a cottage at the entrance gates of a large estate. "I loved the cottage and the cheery breakfasts we had before starting out," Ladew wrote. "It was usually still dark when we arrived at the meet and we could not see the pack as it approached us but their eyes were a hundred tiny phosphorescent spots which glowed weirdly at us from the lights of our car. It was all new and terribly exciting to me and I will never cease to be grateful to Joe and Molly."

Ladew also grew close to the *bon viveur* Ambrose Clark, an heir to the Singer sewing machine and Kimberly-Clark thread fortunes. Clark and Ladew both took

Ladew titled his 1924 watercolor of a hunt with the Meadow Brook The Finest View in America.

pride and pleasure in the "unmistakable English cut" of their hunting clothes and the gleam of their boots, which both kept "polished to shine like mirrors." The elegance of Clark's 500-acre Westbury estate, Broad Hollow, equaled his sartorial splendor. He used the forty-two-room main house, with its two-story Greek revival portico, circular stair hall, and Adamesque stained-glass dome, for nonstop entertaining. Lunch parties for five hundred were the norm and always bore the strong flavor of the field, with menus featuring wild game, stuffed pigs, and squab. Since Clark damned automobiles as "the invention of the devil" and banned them from Broad Hollow, he commuted from Long Island to Manhattan in "his four-in-hand, with a footman and bugler in attendance."[3]

A fiercely competitive huntsman "whose passion in life was horses" ("he raised, trained, and rode them from sun up to sun down until the day he died"), Clark let nothing distract him once on the trail of a fox. Ladew remembered one hunt when Molly Davis had been thrown from her horse. "While she was lying on the ground, still dazed and cautiously moving her arms and legs to see if any bones had been broken, Brose Clark came galloping full tilt towards her. 'Are you hurt, Molly?' shouted Brose as he neared the recumbent figure. 'I don't think so,' Molly answered faintly. 'Well then,' he shouted again, 'roll out of the way so I can jump that fence.'"

The Meadow Brook Hunt had already acquired an illustrious history when Harvey Ladew became active in its affairs, and it numbered Theodore Roosevelt among its earliest members. Roosevelt's biographer Edmund Morris wrote that TR initially considered hunting "effete and un-American," but in 1885 the future president decided to give it a try. He found that it contained the "stern and manly" qualities he demanded of a recreational sport and became a regular rider. On one memorable Saturday, the hunt met at Roosevelt's Sagamore Hill "and after the traditional stirrup cup set off over particularly rough country." According to Morris, "Roosevelt, riding a large, coarse stallion, led from the start. Careless of accidents which dislocated the huntmaster's knee, smashed another rider's ribs, and took the skin off his brother-in-law's face, he galloped in front for fully three miles. Eventually his exhausted horse" fell trying to jump a stone wall, throwing its rider and causing Roosevelt's left arm to snap beneath the elbow. "Yet he was back in the saddle as soon as the horse was up, and rushed on one-armed [with] the blood pouring down his face. Washed clean that night, his cut face plastered and his arm in splints, he presided over the Hunt Ball as Laird of Sagamore."[4]

Ladew's experiences with the Meadow Brook reflect his jovial personality just as much as that "stern and manly" ride reflects the Rough Rider's. Ladew recalled, for instance, "One day 'Dotsy' Nicholas was thrown from her horse during a fast run. It happened that among those out there was a new member of our field who had quite a reputation as a Lothario in Broadway's most Bohemian set. 'Dotsy' had never met him, but she was very grateful when he helped her [back] into the saddle. Later she said to a friend—'I must say "Mr. X" was very kind; when I had that fall he stopped and picked me up.' 'I'm not at all surprised,' the friend remarked. 'I've always heard he was very good at picking up fallen women.'"

Ladew's first halcyon days living on his own suffered a slight setback on May 30, 1915, when his new house caught fire and burned to the ground. On the 29th he had gone over to his sister and brother-in-law's to celebrate the birth of their first child and spend the night. But in the early morning, the telephone rang with the news—"Your country house is afire and can't be saved!" He raced back to the Box only to find a mass of flames with firemen and servants scurrying to salvage what they could. Suddenly, Ladew spied one fireman carrying a radio. Never one to miss a chance for a party, Harvey turned the machine on, and as music played and his house burned, he and the firemen sat down to a picnic of coffee and sandwiches, and, as one local newspaper incredulously reported, "A good time was had by all."[5]

When America entered the war in 1917, Ladew, then living in Madrid with Uncle Berry and Aunt Lomie, returned to New York to enlist. His relatives suggested he "give the matter some thought" before offering his services. Determined to do his duty, however, after some investigating he found a Lt. Lejeunne, who "was getting up a liaison company of French speaking citizens." And since he had spoken French before he "knew a word of English," he decided that was the outfit for him. He applied, was accepted, and was sent to Washington with the rank of second lieutenant.

Filled with thoughts of romantic espionage work, Lieutenant Ladew eagerly awaited his first assignment. Finally it came: translate a list of things for the field kitchen (*la cuisine roulante*, he recalled) from French to English. He balked and

told his superiors that he "knew very little about kitchen utensils of any kind." They remained adamant, however, and he managed to produce some sort of translation, which "the officers seemed satisfied with." His next project proved more ambitious, for orders came to translate the handbook on the *soixante quinze* gun, "the most prized weapon in the French Army." Although he didn't think that task quite suited him either ("I said I knew even less about cannons than I did about kitchen utensils"), his superiors insisted. So he set to work and found "lots of small illustrations of the various parts of the *soixante quinze* that were a bit hard to put into English." Harvey plugged away, and when he had somehow completed the project, he received a citation from the French government.[6]

After his successful translations, Ladew asked to be sent to the front as a reward for jobs well done. He eventually received his wish and was ordered to France, but, just as he was about to leave for the trenches, he came down with pneumonia and found himself "shipped off to Mrs. Whitelaw Reid's hospital, which had been made from an artists' colony she had built" on the Riviera. After several weeks in bed, but still weak, he was released and waited out the duration of the war recuperating in sunshine and warmth.

With peace restored, Ladew returned to Long Island and bought a 23¾-acre working farm on Hegeman's Lane in Brookville for ninety thousand dollars. The property was improved by a two-story frame farmhouse built about 1780. Although he initially intended to keep the place simple and use it only as a hunting lodge, his imagination took over, and he set about transforming the modest dwelling with the aid of architect O'Connor and interior decorator Elsie Cobb Wilson. The three turned the unassuming house into a showplace important enough to draw the attention of the national press. Critic Charles Keefe, for instance, featured the made-over residence in the prestigious tome *The American House*, published in 1924. ("Sometimes I wonder if you realize what a wonderful brother you have," Ladew wrote his sister in 1967. "Every house he has ever owned has appeared in magazines.") In all, praised one critic, "from modest beginnings by unpretentious means," the old house had "gracefully been converted into a perfectly appointed seat for autumn hunting activities."[7] The five photographs and two floor plans of the Box in Keefe's book (Ladew reused the name "the Box" for his new house) show a rambling, shingle-covered structure basking in a garden full of hollyhocks. A roomy sun porch and conservatory marked one flank, a full-length entrance porch and a smaller side terrace another, and a deep sleeping porch yet another. (That last detail had become the rage in early-twentieth-century American house design; the magazine *House and Garden* noted approvingly in 1914, "The number of sleeping porches constantly increases.") "A very pleasant and homelike building," Keefe wrote of Ladew's new/old house, "with an old-fashioned garden and a pleasant setting."[8]

The interior of this "Headquarters of a Hunting Sportsman" (as *Town & Country* headlined its story on Ladew's lair) featured horses as the dominate decorative motif, with "an unusual whip rack," a collection of stirrup cups, a hooked stair rug with horses in profile, and "framed needlework pictures of the chase which most . . . would travel far to see." Ladew also created a pine-paneled bedroom based on one he had seen at the newly opened American Wing at the Metropolitan Museum of Art, and a "ye olde" dining room with rough plaster walls, random-width pine floors, exposed oak ceiling beams, an oak refectory table, and lots and lots of pewter. "The whole establishment exemplifies the interest and personality of the owner himself," *Town & Country* purred. "No wonder the result is so satisfying."[9]

Horses dominated the outside of the place, too, as Ladew actively entered into the equine-breeding business.[10] To accommodate his growing herd, he built a series of barns, stables, and show grounds that would be the scene of many successful charitable enterprises. (It was in the stable yard that he began the topiary hunt scene that ended up in Maryland, as is discussed in Chapter 4.) He com-

"Perfectly Delightful"

The Box, Ladew's lair near Brookville, Long Island, as it appeared in 1925: "a perfectly appointed seat for autumn hunting activities."

pleted the grounds with a tennis court ("cleverly secluded by a thick hemlock hedge"), a hefty-looking wooden pergola, and a pool "with a minute pavilion" where one could change "or play backgammon between swims."

Ladew also started a kennel at his new place, where he bred prizewinning wire-hair fox terriers. The fox terrier craze typifies the nature of Ladew's enthusiasms: although it—and many later projects—proved short lived, in the beginning he gave it his all, no doubt agreeing with the credo of his great friend T. E. Lawrence, who wrote that "happiness comes in absorption." (Patricia Corey suggested that her uncle left so many projects incomplete "because he had such a great sense of vision. He could *see* what the end would be and didn't see any reason to spend the time and trouble actually getting there.")[11] According to a period newspaper clipping, Ladew bought his dogs in England, "chiefly from the Duchess of Newcastle," whose Notts strain had "produced more winners than any one or several kennels." Not content with blue-blooded bitches from coroneted breeders, Ladew set to work on his first known magnum opus, a proposed definitive history called "The Fox Terrier Now and Then." The book never progressed beyond a few crudely typed pages, but researching and planning it excited him greatly for many months.[12]

That, then—manor house, garden, stable, kennel, tennis court, and swim-

Ladew (center) *at the height of his 1920s fox terrier phase.*

ming pool—formed Ladew's headquarters as he Charlestoned his way through Long Island's hedonistic Gatsby era. It was the 1920s, a time, in the words of his friend Osbert Sitwell, "of saxophones and strident pleasures," and Ladew, of course, merrily placed himself in the thick of it, always with a twinkle in his eye, always willing to laugh at himself. The *New York World* chronicled one of his parties, "the famous pony dinner that rivaled Harry Lehr's celebrated monkey banquet." Apparently, Ladew summoned forty friends to Hegeman's Lane to mark some recent victories at the Piping Rock Horse Show. When the celebrants "assembled in the dining room, even Berry Wall, that sophisticated member of society, gasped with surprise," for "it was young Mr. Ladew's own idea to have the ponies as guests and to have box stalls built for them where they could munch oats from silver buckets and quaff water from golden-hooped pails" and have their palates cleansed with sugar plums gently fed to them by "grooms in livery." When the two-legged guests had recovered from that spectacle, they sat down at a "damask covered banquet table in the form of a horseshoe. Near the curves of the table on either side were the box stalls of hard wood garlanded with roses and bedecked with blue ribbons won by the occupants." Continuing, the reporter observed that "the table equipment, made to order, was symbolical of the occa-

"Perfectly Delightful"

sion. The silver salt cellars were miniature feed boxes. The golden celery holders were replicas of hayracks, and all the glassware was engraved with delicate little scenes of the field, the road, and the course." Then, suddenly, "the great doors at the side of the dining room were thrown open and three of the tiniest ponies were led in by grooms. When they had been led away there was a moment of complete darkness and then as the lights flashed up, periwigged servitors stood behind the chairs with the favors—gold mounted riding crops and silver stirrups."[13]

In retrospect, such frolics only formed a warm-up to the social climax of Long Island's giddy 1920s, the visit of the Prince of Wales, who steamed into New York Harbor on the *Berengaria* in September 1924. (Perhaps coincidentally, Noël Coward also visited Long Island that summer, arriving in New York from England on September 17, 1924, on board the *Majestic*. A recent biography of Coward called New York the "fashionable destination that year": "it offered enjoyment beyond the restrictive English laws" partially because "moral laxity was not uncommon.")[14] Residents of Long Island's North Shore "stretched their imaginations to the fullest in an effort to lure the future King of England to their parties."[15] Ambrose Clark even built an oak-paneled ballroom onto his house— just in case the need should arise. Clarence Mackay probably threw the most magnificent of these galas. Ladew found himself one of several hundred invited to enjoy dinner at Mackay's French Renaissance–style chateau before the ball began. While the owner of the Box deemed the party too much of a good thing ("there was too much music and one would have liked a little respite with, perhaps, soft music by which to eat the delicious food and drink the wines"), the guest of honor had nothing but praise for his "American hosts who spared no expense in demonstrating the splendour of a modern industrial republic." The prince wrote that he had never attended a party that featured "not one but two orchestras, the stars of popular Broadway revues, and two dance bands directed by the great Paul Whiteman."[16]

But hunting and polo—not dances and dinners—were the reason for the royal visit. As the prince noted in his autobiography, "the international polo matches between Great Britain and America were to be played at the Meadow Brook Club . . . and I crossed the Atlantic to watch the games and see something more of the country." The prince spent a good deal of time in Westbury, and it pleased Ladew to write that the English visitor played polo on his brother-in-law Russell Grace's field in Westbury. Uncle Berry, who wouldn't have missed the proceedings for the world, recalled that one of the Graces' three daughters "asked the Prince of Wales, after she had climbed on his lap, 'Sir, why do you always fall off your horses?' Everyone caught his breath, but the Prince only smiled. 'I don't fall off, my dear,' he answered. 'It's the horse that falls down.'"[17]

The prince also wondered if he might go out with the Meadow Brook for a hunt. Of course he might. He would need a horse, though, and the club's master of foxhounds (MFH) asked Ladew to lend his prize jumper, the Ghost. (Plate 1.)

Watching the hunt on Long Island in the 1920s. Harvey with E. F. Hutton and Hutton's then wife, Dorothy.

Ladew, who had met the prince in England and called him "one of the hardest riders to hounds" he saw ("and that is saying a lot"), readily agreed. But then the prince's equerry, "Fruity" Metcalf, told Ladew that the prince "insisted on hunting in a snaffle: no curb bit." This threw Ladew into paroxysms of terror, for he felt that the horse wouldn't cooperate if he had an unusual type of bit in his mouth: "It was the worst morning I ever remember. I was a nervous wreck." He recalled, "We were hunting on one of Meadow Brook's biggest countries. The fences were exceptionally high and very solid. . . . [But] every jump he made was perfect. We had a good fast run and the prince was delighted with the morning's sport." After the hunt, Ladew recovered his nerves with "a breakfast which consisted mostly of several stiff drinks of scotch."

Then came the polo matches, and although the American team won them,

"Perfectly Delightful"

two games to none, the prince left Long Island much impressed with "the fine homes with well-kept lawns and swimming pools." Compared with the creature comforts Americans took for granted, the luxury to which he was accustomed in Europe "seemed almost primitive." In sum the visit convinced him "America was a country in which nothing was impossible." He continued his North American tour on to Canada and wrote Ladew, on September 22, 1924, from his private railway car, Balmoral, to thank him "very much" for mounting him that day with the Meadow Brook Hounds. "I enjoyed it so much, and could not wish for a better ride than 'The Ghost.'" He then added, in longhand, "Hope you'll be over hunting in England next season."[18]

That Meadow Brook hunt launched a forty-five-year friendship between the prince and Ladew. It also certainly added to the American's glamour. As the weekly gossip sheet *Town Topics* ("The Journal of Society") noted in its September 18, 1924, edition, "so friendly" had Harvey Ladew become with the Prince of Wales "since that personage set his tan suedes on American soil" that the American's stock among eligible debutantes rose higher than ever: "which is saying much, for Harvey is still considered young, good-looking, and well endowed with the world's goods."

The visit even enriched Ladew financially. News of the successful royal hunt spread quickly, and offers to buy the Ghost poured in. All he had to do was name a sum. Ladew told one would-be buyer, "'I will take $10,000,' in those days a practically unheard of price for a hunter." The figure proved acceptable, however, and the deal was closed. (A few months later in England, Harvey ran into the Prince of Wales, who said that he'd heard about the sale and joked, "Don't you think you should give me a commission?")[19] Ladew then organized a party to celebrate his windfall, and in honor of the horse that made it all possible, he asked his guests to come dressed as ghosts. ("Some of the costumes, though rather gruesome, were very clever and amusing.") With Halloween nearing, Ladew thought it appropriate to illuminate the grounds around his house with lanterns in the shape of jack-o'-lanterns and fill the trees with figures of ghosts in filmy draperies. "The music was good [and] champagne corks popped until dawn."

DOUGLAS FAIRBANKS'S CHRISTENING
AND A RHINO NAMED MARY

Not all of Ladew's Long Island frolics involved royalty of the European variety. Indeed, some of his fondest memories involved escapades with those who might be called kings and queens of the stage and screen. Actors and actresses held a lifelong fascination for him, and he was often pleased to tell that as a boy he had been taken to the christening of Douglas Fairbanks Sr. ("What funny things we remember.") In middle age he became an early follower of the Venice

Film Festival, and his guest books show that he was constantly playing host to the likes of Beatrice Lillie and Clifton Webb.[20] Finally, in old age, while contemplating expatriation, Ladew consoled himself about a possible move to Switzerland with the fact that he already knew Charlie Chaplin and his wife, who had a chalet in that country. He recalled that in the 1920s he "spent a weekend with him" at a Long Island house party, and then on Monday they "both went down to the steamships to see Gertrude Lawrence off for Europe."

During his Brookville days, his friend Dorothy di Frasso, the American-born wife of the Roman count Carlo Dentice di Frasso, called on Ladew with silent-screen sensation Rudolph Valentino in tow. That visit, though, did not prove as successful as the Prince of Wales's, principally because Ladew found Valentino a bit de trop: "deficient in education or manners" and arriving with a "red Morocco leather suitcase with gold fittings." In fact, Harvey's horrified English valet claimed to recognize Valentino as the gardener who had worked "at Mrs. Bliss's house almost next door" to them. To di Frasso's surprise, Ladew didn't even find "the Sheik" handsome—"just a fairly good looking Italian peasant." Valentino evidently didn't shine at conversation, either, for after the visit, Ladew caustically attributed the actor's success in pre-talkie films to the fact "that he was silent."

A few years later, Ladew, having heard about "the strange new world, the movie empire," decided it was "high time" he explored it and met "some of its extraordinary residents." He realized he "could easily see all its marvels" because "there could not possibly be a better guide" to show him "all the wonders around HOLLYWOOD" than Dorothy di Frasso, who lived there part of the year.

Di Frasso, born Dorothy Taylor in Watertown, New York, "inherited some twelve million dollars from her father's leather-goods business," wrote their mutual friend Elsa Maxwell. A leather-based fortune formed one bond between Ladew and the countess, as did their restless personalities, and, Maxwell continued, di Frasso's "escapades and racy tongue provided feature writers with good copy for forty years." Di Frasso surrounded herself with a number of "interesting" friends; of these, by anyone's standards, Benjamin "Bugsy" Siegel must be reckoned among the more colorful. "Dorothy naively believed Bugsy was an innocent, overgrown boy," said Maxwell, "an opinion that was hardly shared by the business associates who later liquidated him." Once di Frasso asked Siegel (aided by "a weird assortment of grifters and cutthroats") to help her find a $300,000,000 treasure she heard was buried on an island off the coast of Costa Rica; another time, in what Maxwell dubbed "Dorothy's dizziest brainstorm," di Frasso and her husband introduced Siegel to King Umberto of Italy as "Bart" Siegel. The king, "who misinterpreted the nickname as an abbreviation for baronet, must have been baffled by the rather unconventional speech and mannerisms of Dorothy's protege. . . . 'He acted odd for a baron,' Umberto said. 'He tried to sell us dynamite.'"[21]

Anticipating adventure with a fun-loving contessa as his guide, off Ladew

"Perfectly Delightful"

Dorothy di Frasso (left), Ladew, and Kay Francis at Hollywood's Place Piquale nightclub, c. 1930. The contessa seems to be plotting another of her "escapades," which, wrote Elsa Maxwell, kept feature writers busy for forty years.

went to California. Ensconced in his hotel (one assumes it was the Garden of Allah or the Bel Air), he phoned di Frasso, who immediately ordered him to check out and move in with her. He did so and was happy until she told him, while "shaken with hysterical laughter," that another guest, the Italian "Count C.," had come down with some terrible disease and the entire house had been placed in quarantine. "No one is allowed out of it until they find out what his illness is," his hostess blithely informed a fuming Ladew. "Now that you are here, we can play gin rummy all day! You can't imagine how bored I've been." "My delight in seeing Dorothy," he wrote, "cooled off at this—and I am afraid I did not appear very enthusiastic."

In typical Ladew fashion, though, he decided to make the best of things: "after a few cocktails I felt better about the situation." He found much to admire in the house, which had been decorated by the legendary Elsie de Wolf, and in the "lovely garden." He even detected a pleasing bit of intrigue, for "the count was an Italian friend who had become enamored of a rising young starlet and Dorothy offered to put him up while he did his courting." This mollified Ladew, and he and his hostess settled down to an evening of gossip and "interminable games of gin rummy." They dealt so many hands, in fact, that Ladew wrote, "I do not know

now who ever came out ahead"—an unprecedented occurrence for one who took his cards seriously.

The next morning a doctor called, and it turned out that the count didn't have a mysterious disease after all—only flu—thus freeing Ladew to fling himself into the Hollywood whirlwind. He enjoyed the hobnobbing with the denizens of the movie colony, particularly "with the Richard Bartholomews, who were among Dorothy's best friends," but he suffered deep regret over not meeting his own favorite star, Gary Cooper. (Di Frasso explained to him that she and Cooper "had had a quarrel, though she had been greatly responsible for his success.") He spent one morning "riding with Clark Gable through the hills near Hollywood" and returned to "a good breakfast of scrambled eggs and bacon and waffles and maple syrup" prepared by Gable's wife. ("Both the Gables were very nice and I enjoyed my morning greatly.") Another day, di Frasso wangled an invitation to "the Hearst palace and its fantastic ranch." That proved a mixed success. Although Ladew admired the Gobelins tapestries, the paneled rooms, and the ancient Spanish chairs, he regretted that the newspaper magnate had cleaned the statuary that dotted the grounds ("a patina would have given them a softer look") and had some doubts about the swimming pool and its Greek temples. But he felt he understood it all when he learned that "Mr. Hearst only allowed paper napkins" in the main dining room.

Of course, he had to see the movie sets. Di Frasso had arranged "to have the fiery little Mexican star, Lupe Velez," show him around. They would visit the best, of course, MGM, then at its peak of glamour. Ladew wrote, "[Velez] arrived for me early one morning driving a large white Dusenberg which she told me had won first prize at the last motor show and had cost $15,000." His guide "dressed to match the car—in white slacks, a white beret on her flaming red hair, a white silk shirt, and rows of diamond bracelets on both arms up to the elbows." At the studio they saw Kay Francis and bumped into Gary Cooper after all. (He recalled, "I knew that he and Lupe had once had a romance"; so, though it pained him, he "discretely withdrew and looked elsewhere.") They also sneaked onto a set where Marian Davies was shooting a scene—"sneak" because Davies and Velez weren't then speaking. All went well until Davies saw Velez and cried, "Put that woman out—I will not go on until she leaves." Ladew added, "I must say that I was embarrassed."

After a couple of restorative cocktails, during which time Lupe proceeded to tell Ladew "what a bitch Marian was" ("The movie colony seemed to be a very scrappy lot of people!"), off they went to see the Tarzan set. This stop, too, proved eventful. Ladew met and liked Tarzan, Johnny Weissmuller, and enjoyed watching the filming. "The scene was supposed to show Tarzan springing out of the jungle and leaping onto the back of a rhinoceros and stabbing it to death," he recalled. Although rhinos "are thought to be one of the fiercest and most dangerous animals in Africa, Johnny's partner in the act proved to be anything but

"Perfectly Delightful"

Actress Lupe Velez never made it big in movies, but she did find one starring role—as Harvey's Hollywood tour guide in the early thirties.

fierce." Ladew, who loved learning that the rhino's name was Mary, wrote that when the trainer "tickled Mary's stomach, it made her lie down in the mud which she apparently liked. At this moment the trainer moved away and Tarzan suddenly emerged from the jungle and leaped on her back and stabbed her with a large, stage dagger." It was "cut, print" until "Lupe let out some loud hysterical screams and the furious photographers said that the whole scene had to be retaken as it was a sound Movie."[22] After the retake, Weissmuller ambled over to visit with the duo. "[Velez] asked him to join us and motor back to their home in the Dusenberg but he said he couldn't as he had an appointment." Ladew knew "that Lupe was very jealous of him," and the news of this mysterious "appointment" resulted in "a loud, angry conversation between them" which Ladew would not repeat. "She suspected a rendezvous of some sort."

In all, Ladew loved his behind-the-scene visit and his guide, whom he deemed "great fun and the sort of person one instantly felt one had always known." But alas, "Poor Lupe. Not long after I had left Hollywood she committed suicide." Looking back at the visit forty years later, he wrote, "I don't think I care to see Hollywood again. But it was fun."

Hunting with a Contessa and Hosting an Incognito Prince

Ladew often visited di Frasso in Italy, and if anything, these trips proved more memorable than his Hollywood sojourn. He recalled that in late 1925 she sent him a telegram, "Will you come to Rome and hunt with us this winter? You can have Mrs. B's bullet-proof bed." Mrs. B., he explained, was a married woman who once had a famous affair with an Italian prince. When the outraged Mr. B. caught the couple in flagrante in the di Frasso palazzo, the prince dived under the bed, which deflected the husband's gunshots. "Don't you think that's terribly funny?" He accepted, of course, and relished sleeping "in the beautifully carved 15th century bullet-proof bed."

Notwithstanding the somewhat frivolous phrasing of the invitation, Harvey took the hunting itself seriously. "Those were unforgettable days, completely different from fox hunting in any other part of the world," he wrote in an article for *Harper's Bazaar*. Hunting in Italy was special partially because of the names of the meets (he particularly liked one called Divine Amore), partially because of "musicians strolling about and strumming on mandolins," partially because of the "vendors of macaroni and roasted chestnuts," and partially because of the unique landscape, "a land of pale olive-green fields intersected here and there by deep ravines and topped with the occasional dazzling little shepherd huts. The broken lines of ancient aqueducts were often silhouetted against the horizon and now and then, in the far distance, there would be a glimpse of St. Peter's dome."[23]

He also enjoyed the heterogeneous nature of his fellow hunters. As he told his *Harper's* readers, there were cavalry officers, "looking very smart in their sky-blue uniforms, flowing blue capes, and highly polished black boots"; Italian aristocrats (and he grew particularly close to Count Lanfranco Rasponi, owner of the "beautiful Villa Fontallerta, high up in the Tuscan hills");[24] and the princesses Theodora and Margharita of Greece, "accomplished horsewomen" whose brother, Philip, would become duke of Edinburgh.[25]

While out one day, Ladew asked the huntsman, "a young Irishman named John Dix," what he thought of hunting in Italy. Dix replied that one day his "hounds were running a fox and in full cry when they suddenly disappeared from view." He explained, "I couldn't imagine what had happened to them and thought they must have been bewitched. After some little time I heard them again, still in full cry, but running *under the ground beneath me*! The fox had gone down into a subterranean passage with my hounds after him." Dix discovered that the passage was "part of an ancient town": "When I went down into it myself, crawling on my hands and knees, I found it to be a bricked tunnel with a floor of stone. This sort of thing does, I admit, add to the novelty of Italian hunting."[26]

On some nonhunting days, Ladew accompanied the cavalry officers to the nearby riding school, Tor di Quinto. "Here there were all manner of complicated

"Perfectly Delightful"

Harvey hunting near Rome in the 1920s: he particularly admired the cavalry officers ("looking very smart in their sky-blue uniforms") as well as the landscape, with "the broken lines of ancient aqueducts."

jumps," he wrote in his unpublished autobiography, including a steep hill called a *descente*, "which horses and riders were trained to slide down at an unbelievable angle." One night, possibly emboldened by wine, Ladew found himself "filled with great courage" and told his soldier friends that the thing he most wanted to do before leaving Rome was to ride down the *descente*. "They at once said they would be delighted to arrange it." The next morning he went to the school, a bit less enthusiastic but still game. He listened to instructions and then set out. Unfortunately, he forgot what he had been told: "[I] reverted to my old seat to such an extent that I was practically lying on the horse's back. It was great fun when one got used to it and I did it several times."

On other nonhunting days he visited the great Renaissance gardens in and around Rome. Many of these were not then generally open to the public, but with di Frasso as a guide, all gates were opened: she may have been a bit unconventional, but she was, after all, a contessa. "It is not necessary to be a student of garden-architecture to feel the spell of quiet and serenity which falls on one," as Edith Wharton wrote of those ancient pleasances, "but it is worth the student's while to try to analyse the elements of which the sensation is composed." It is known that di Frasso showed Harvey the gardens at her residence, Raphael's Villa Madama (noted for "the broad simplicity of its plan"), as well as those at the Villa Medici, famed for panoramic vistas of "the wide sweep of the Cam-

pagna and the mountains," and the Villa Chigi, with its boxwood hedges "termi-
nating in a semi-circle of statues, backed by an ilex-planted mount." These and
many others "all testify to what Rome's crown of gardens must have been" and
remain "full of suggestion to the student of her past."[27] Indeed they proved in
Maryland when, not ten years later, Harvey Ladew laid out his own hedged axes
in Harford County.

Sometimes Dorothy di Frasso arranged nonequestrian amusements for her
guest. One day, as Ladew wrote his sister, di Frasso told him he *"must"* go to hear
the Sistine Choir. "So we went to a concert they gave at the Vatican." Di Frasso
explained that when choir boys were young, "their families had a slight operation
performed on them which enabled them to keep their beautiful soprano voices all
their lives, so they earned money for the family singing in choirs and in opera. It
was nice for the family but the poor boys missed a lot of fun." At the concert he
and di Frasso attended, "the 'boys' were around 80 years old—bald or with white
hair." "When they let out high soprano notes from those old faces—noises that
reminded one of Callas or Joan Sutherland—it *was terribly* funny and Dorothy
was laughing and holding her muff over her face. I laughed, too—you couldn't
help it—though it was sad for the boys."[28]

Ladew kept up with many of his Italian friends long after those hunts. Rasponi often visited him in America, and Ladew and di Frasso maintained their
sometimes rocky relationship until she died. On July 7, 1968, Harvey wrote his
sister that di Frasso had asked him to ring in that new year in Las Vegas, where
Marlene Dietrich, Cary Grant and Clifton Webb were giving a party for her. "I
wanted to go very much but could not get a ticket on a plane. Poor Dorothy died
in the train on the way back and I would have been with her—so I am glad I did
not go."

As often proved the pattern with his enthusiasms, he decided to write up his
Italian hunting experiences. In the article, which appeared in *Harper's Bazaar*, he
traced the origins of the Roman hunt to 1836, when the earl of Chesterfield established the Societa Romana della Caccia alla Volpe (with Prince Don Livio Odes-
calchi as MFH) and brought over an English huntsman, a pack of Irish horses,
and some hounds.

The Gatsby era frequently found Ladew visiting Italy more conventionally as
a tourist. For instance, he spent a wonderful holiday in Venice in the 1920s with
his longtime companion the Belgian count François de Buisseret. A clutch of
romantic-looking photographs exist as testament to that stay: some show the
two men feeding the pigeons in the piazza; some show them riding in a gondola;
some have them posing in front of the Doges' Palace, the American looking
swarthy and mysterious, the Belgian blond, with an impossibly classic profile.

At some point, de Buisseret, attaché to his country's embassy in Washington,
introduced Ladew to Prince Charles of Belgium, second son of King Albert. The
music-loving prince had found himself center stage since World War I, when he

"Perfectly Delightful"

Ladew (left) and his great friend the Belgian count François de Buisseret. The date is the mid-twenties, the pose timeless.

had to flee to England after the Germans overran his homeland. Ladew's friend Harold Acton recalled that the London war years were "enriched by Prince Charles-Theodore of Belgium's performances" on the violin. "The emigrant Prince made the plight of Belgium very poignant to me and I felt a great sympathy for this flaxen figure from a Memling altar-piece." Acton was also touched by Prince Charles's "neat sketches of sailing ships at sea which expressed the homesickness he otherwise concealed under polished reserve."[29]

Prince Charles evidently found Ladew amusing and accepted his invitation to visit New York, but he insisted the visit be unofficial. He arranged to sail to America under the pseudonym "Charles de Rethy," and de Buisseret booked passage for them on a liner. The prince, "a tall blond lad of twenty-seven with a distaste for pomp," according to a contemporary newspaper account, enjoyed his anonymity and spent the voyage quietly playing shuffleboard and "chatting with the unsuspecting ship's officers." But on the last night out, at the traditional masquerade gala, the "decidedly handsome" prince borrowed a uniform from one of the crew, "and a Belgian woman recognized the regal face under his visored cap."[30]

Journalists in New York, of course, got wind of the impending royal visit and swooped in a pack to meet the ship. "Annoyed at the reception he received from newspapermen at the pier, the prince said, 'I'm just a tourist and want to be treated as American tourists are in my country. I'm here incognito as Charles de Rethy and I'd like to remain so.'"[31] Ladew, also waiting dockside, ushered the prince and the count through the mob and out to Brookville. He then did his best to treat Prince Charles to a quiet visit, but with little success. When, for example, he took Molly Davis and his Belgian guests to lunch at the Colony, "Cholly Knickerbocker" appeared on the scene and recorded "what a stir" the "handsome prince" caused. "He makes any of our movie heros look like Ben Turpins," Knickerbocker gushed, as "pearl draped necks were craned, lorgnettes were focused in his direction, and several of the more excited . . . forgot Emily Price Post's social dictates to the extent that they stared." Then Mrs. Cornelius Vanderbilt, "our unofficial hostess to visiting royalty," decided to "corral Prince Charles for a luncheon or dinner at 640 Fifth Avenue."[32] Despite such mishaps, the prince and Ladew remained close friends, exchanging Christmas cards and notes for years. At least once the prince and de Buisseret visited Ladew in Maryland, for *Town & Country* told its readers about the trip "King Albert's little boy" made to "Harford County, where Harvey Ladew [had] . . . taken up his residence." Their conversations, the magazine breathlessly reported, "were carried on in flawless French."[33]

Ladew undoubtedly did converse with Prince Charles in French, for, as has been noted, he spoke the language before he spoke English. As a child he had spent months each year in Paris, where he also frequented the theater. He particularly favored one "in Montmartre which was approached down a dark, spooky cobbled passageway" and vividly remembered one play set in "a lunatic asylum where the inmates suddenly overpowered their nurses, doctors, and guards and proceeded to torture them in the most realistic, blood-curdling manner. They would gouge out their eyes or burn them with lighted cigarettes as the victims screamed with pain." But that was long ago and far away, and a septuagenarian Ladew concluded, bittersweetly, "I doubt if I would enjoy this sort of thing at my present age."

During the 1920s he found another sort of Parisian theater. "I went to many plays at the Comedie Francaise and, as the lighter side of the theater appealed to me equally, I never missed the little revues in the Boulevards." He also witnessed performances of the Ballets Russes and recalled a sensational staging of *L'Apres-Midi d'un Faune* and Nijinsky's "revealing costume." He remembered that before the ballet was over, the queen of Denmark got up and left her box. Ladew thought she had gone because she was so shocked by the costume—as did Nijin-

"Perfectly Delightful"

sky: "so he wires her an apology. The Queen wrote back that she was not at all shocked and just had to go to the bathroom."

On less intellectual evenings he attended the Folies Bergeres, where his decades-long interest in Josephine Baker began. He recalled watching her in the 1920s when she "would make her descent in a majestic manner with practically no clothes on—just a string of bananas around her waist or a 'ceinture' of small ivory tusks, a lot of spangles and a coiffure of huge waving ostrich plumes." That image, he wrote, always reminded him "of the famous picture at the Armory Show, 'Nude Descending a Staircase.'" Baker, born in St. Louis, moved to France

Ladew first saw the singer Josephine Baker perform in Paris in the 1920s; this famous photograph of Baker, taken by Hoyningen-Huene (c. 1930), suggests why the singer held a decades-long fascination for Harvey.

and became the rage of Paris. Ladew was not the only person to find himself, as his photographer friend Horst has written, "as enraptured by the uninhibited pep and exuberance of her performance as by the beauty of her elongated brown body, her long, agile arms and legs, her neat, small head with its big eyes and blazing white teeth, and the exotic warmth and accent of her singing voice."[34] Baker's career spanned many decades, and Ladew eagerly attended a performance of hers at the Folies in 1949. In that show, he wrote his sister, Baker played Mary, Queen of Scots: "She wears clothes all through the show and has discarded the belt of bananas." The bemused Ladew finished the tale by noting, "AFTER they chop her head off she sings Gounod's Ave Maria! I thought she should have sung, 'Yes, We have no Bananas.'"[35]

"ENGLAND WAS MY UNDOING"

However much Ladew enjoyed his continental sojourns (and he did), he found his true spiritual home in England. Billy Baldwin, in fact, called his friend "practically a lunatic on the subject of anything having to do with England."[36] According to Baldwin, Ladew's Anglophilia grew so intense that the American took to bringing English toilet paper back to the States—to the general horror of houseguests. Baldwin wrote that their mutual friend decorator Ruby Ross Wood once begged, "Harvey, please, for God's sake, consider the feelings of your guests. . . . Buy some nice, soft American toilet paper!"[37] He never did.

He made his first prolonged visit to Britain in 1919. It was to be a season spent hunting, the first of twenty-one consecutive such trips, for he continued to devote the winter months to riding to English hounds until Nazi submarines rendered these visits impracticable. And a glorious season 1919 was, too, even though he later joked that "England was my undoing" because "the bad example of so many Englishmen of the leisure class enjoying life unconcernedly put an end to any thought I might have had of going home to work."

At first, he divided his hunting time among the Quorn, Cottesmore, and Belvoir, all clustered around the Leicestershire village of Melton Mowbray (or, more familiarly, "Melton"). Since the early nineteenth century "swells, hard-riders, beauties, and dissolutes" had made Melton a center of serious hunting, as devotees built a series of hunting lodges in and around town. They also made it a center of serious partying, since "the mad Marquess of Waterford" and some chums literally painted Melton red one night, giving rise to the well-known expression for having an extremely good time. By the 1880s the town had become a fixture on the social calendar: Melton in the winter followed by salmon fishing in Ireland; then London for "the season" and a summer of Goodwood, Cowes, and grouse shooting.

During the years Ladew knew Melton, its earlier rambunctiousness had, if

Hunting in the famed (and flat) Vale of Belvoir, c. 1925.

anything, intensified as "that air of unreality identified with the 1920s did not leave the hunting world untouched." The hunting lodges of the town, "already steeped with a certain rakish folklore, now blossomed in a new eminence." While "the yard of every lodge abounded with horses and grooms, the houses were filled with aristocrats, bankers, royalty, and bounders."[38]

Ladew had the good fortune to spend his first season as a houseguest of "Algy" Burnaby, the Quorn's MFH, at the Burnaby family's eighteenth-century seat, Baggrave Hall.[39] What better introduction could he have found? He deemed Burnaby "one of the best Masters the Quorn ever had. He was able to control his huge fields and did it after a fashion all his own." The Prince of Wales, who began his Quorn outings in 1923, echoed these sentiments, noting that "with a weather-beaten complexion, hawklike nose, piercing eyes, and the intellect of a statesmen, Algy Burnaby kept his hard-riding field under perfect control." The prince further observed that "in addition to providing ideal country for the chase, the hunts centering on Melton Mowbray formed a sturdy and cosmopolitan society. Inter-mixed with the local gentry . . . was a lively sampling of dashing figures: noble-men and noblewomen; wealthy people who had discovered that the stable door was a quick if expensive short cut into society; a strong injection of Americans from the famous eastern hunts; cavalrymen and Guardsmen; good riders on bad horses; bad riders on good horses; and last but not least the yeoman farmers."[40]

"Happiness comes in absorption"

Harvey Ladew's England

For his second English winter, Ladew decided to lease a cottage, Creaton House, in the village of Creaton. It was "small and old," and he "loved it from the start." The house itself had a tiny living room (but with space for a Bechstein grand), "an equally small dining room," and three bedrooms, all overflowing with "old and really good furniture" and "rare hunting prints." Although the grounds took in "only a few acres," Ladew found them neat and complete: "a small kitchen garden, a stable with six roomy boxes, a well-fenced field, a grass tennis court, and a rose garden which was, of course, never in bloom during my winter tenancy." Creaton House also came complete with its own staff, who lived in a separate service wing. There was a cook (Mrs. Brown), a waitress, a gardener (Mr. Brown), and "a 'between maid,' an appellation which intrigued" him greatly. "I soon learned that 'Tweenies,' as the English call them, are a sort of Cinderella. They do the most unpleasant jobs." Ladew's own gentleman's gentleman—the Irish lad Wilfred Sherin, who will figure into many of these 1920s adventures—and an American chauffeur rounded out the establishment. Ladew wrote of Creaton that in addition to a comfortable house, a pleasant garden, and a talented staff, late each day he could hear Evensong from the old church below. "What more could I ask for?" he wondered. "Absolutely nothing. I have never been happier. Before long I had settled down to the English hunting life and loved it more than anything I had ever done before or since."

Down-to-the-wellies Anglophile that he undoubtedly was, Ladew did balk at two stereotypical English penchants, their preference for warm cocktails and disdain for central heating. He recalled one house party where he was playing bridge with an Englishwoman who wondered if she could have a martini. He summoned the butler and put in the request. When the drink arrived, the Englishwoman took one sip of it and said, "Oh! It's so very cold! Mr. Ladew, *would* you be kind enough to take it over and set it by the fire for a few minutes?" He sometimes wondered if the cold rooms were intended to make up for the warm drinks. For, much as he loved Creaton House, he felt that his bedroom there "would have done duty for one of our modern deep freeze outfits." After suffering through his first frigid night, he asked Mr. Brown to turn on the furnace. "Nothing much seemed to happen in the way of heat," Harvey wrote, "though quite an amount of smoke and soot drifted lazily about the rooms and corridors." So he devised a solution of his own. He bought three small oil stoves, which, to his "English household's amazement," he had placed in a semicircle behind his chair as he faced the fire. "When I moved into the dining room, the stoves were brought in after me. They followed me upstairs when it was time to take a bath."

Ladew also hunted with the Pytchley, in Northamptonshire. "Far removed enough to hold its independence," the Pytchley offered more serious sport. "The Pytchley was not frivolous," one authority has written, notwithstanding the efforts of Ronald Tree and his wife, Nancy (on both of whom more later), "to introduce something of the Melton image into a rather conservative" hunt.[41] Ladew

Baggrave Hall, seat of the Quorn's legendary MFH "Algy" Burnaby and Ladew's home for his first English hunting season in the vicinity of Belvoir Castle.

remembered his first day with the Pytchley vividly. "It was quite unlike any meet of hounds I had ever seen in America. It certainly seemed pretty wonderful to me. I was jittery with excitement and expectation." All went well until they neared the end and came "to a wide, shallow brook": "people ahead of me had pulled up their horses and were fording it. My little mare, however, was still full of beans"—and so was Ladew. So they tried to jump it but, instead, landed in the middle, causing a tremendous splash that drenched "a tall, immaculately groomed man" trying to cross the brook on foot. "The air now rang with angry curses. Paying no attention to my apologies, he glared fiercely at me, shook himself like a wet terrier, and, as it would have taken too much time to stop and kill me, galloped off after the hounds."

His soggy victim turned out to be the earl of Airlie, and despite that unfortunate meeting, the two men became great friends. Airlie often visited Ladew on Long Island and in Harford County, and Ladew spent several holidays with "him and his charming wife at their haunted castle, 'Cortachy,' in Scotland."[42] Leith Griswold recalled one visit to Pleasant Valley which both men probably wished never happened. Ladew then employed an Irish butler, "a real Sinn Feiner," said Mrs. Griswold. The butler "hated the English—just hated the English. This Irish butler also drank rather heavily. Anyway, Harvey had ordered a roast goose for dinner. And this Irishman killed a skunk and put it on a huge covered dish and

"Perfectly Delightful"

came in and put this dead skunk in front of Lord Airlie. That caused quite a lot of consternation." But, she added, at Ladew's establishments, "things like that were very apt to happen."[43]

Fond as Ladew became of Creaton, notwithstanding its lack of central heating, it simply would not have been in his experiment-relishing nature to follow a set routine, however pleasurable, year after year after year. Consequently, he chose to vary his lodgings. One year, for instance, he stayed in Market Harborough and leased a second-floor flat in a small house that adjoined a pub called the Angel. Although he loved Market Harborough ("it was just the sort of little town Surtees characters might have lived in"), he felt that his pub-crawling neighbors left much to be desired, for smoke "from very inferior cigars" frequently "curled up through the ancient dark oak boards" that made his floor.

Kippered out of Market Harborough, he chose the village of Guilsborough for the 1928–29 hunting season, taking a flat that had been created in the second story of an abandoned schoolhouse. He liked his apartment, "which belonged to a woman of very good taste," and set out to do a good deal of entertaining. To his great satisfaction, one of his Guilsborough soirees was written up in the ultrasmart magazine the *Tatler*, whose winter pages bulged with the goings-on at Melton. During another of his Guilsborough winters, his Long Island hunting friend Molly Davis and her daughter visited him, and he gave a dance in their honor. He hired "the best band" he could from London, "the dinner was not bad, the champagne good, and there was plenty of it." He noted further, "All my friends liked Molly and her daughter," and he felt he could chalk up the evening as "a great success."

Ladew often celebrated New Year's Eve at Craven Lodge, once the private residence of a major general, who, down on his luck, had divided it into a series of rooms and suites for the hunting fraternity (and sorority), with ample stabling for guests' horses. One rented quarters for the entire season, and after the Prince of Wales leased a suite in 1923, Craven Lodge became extremely fashionable among the Melton set, "a snob's paradise," one hunting historian has called it. Guests at Craven threw "a party every week, and often these would be in fancy dress. The turn-out for the fancy dress could be sophisticated. A favourite amusement was to go in drag" or "as animals or circus figures."[44]

The American thoroughly enjoyed fancy dress in general and the Craven parties in particular. ("Harvey loved costume parties," Billy Baldwin wrote, "and he never missed an opportunity to give one or attend one. He had quite a supply of scarves and odds and ends, so he could dress up at the drop of a hat.")[45] Ladew's practiced eye appraised the costumes he saw at Craven as "very original—and sometimes rather daring." Nor did he voice any complaints about the evenings themselves, which often got a bit rowdy. He remembered one night in particular when a woman he called "Mrs. X" "had her clothes carefully ripped off while she stood in the middle of the dance floor, leaving her with a large picture

Ladew wrote that his "schoolhouse" flat was owned by "a woman of very good taste." This view of the pillow-filled parlor certainly looks comfortable enough.

hat, an old fashioned corset, and a pair of voluminous lace-edged panties above her black silk stockings." While she "was actually more modestly dressed than girls in modern bathing suits, the effect was very startling at the time." In fact, it so startled the Ambrose Clarks (then hunting in England) that they "refused to come to the next New Year's party." (Clark leased the nearby Warwick Lodge, where he stabled fifty hunters, "double the number to most yards.")[46] More sedate evenings featured other Ladew favorites, such as *tableaux vivants* and high-stakes card playing.

Some days Ladew motored over to Gloucestershire to ride with the Beaufort Hunt. During those excursions he frequently stopped off in Oxford "to see the lovely ancient buildings and a few friends who were studying there." He saw a good deal of one Long Island friend in particular, George Rose, "a nice boy with a very good sense of humor." The two laughed for hours over some of the university's more arcane rules. Of these, Ladew numbered as special favorites "No student shall walk along the streets of Oxford carrying a crossbow or spear" and "No student living within the walls of Oxford shall keep either a bear, badger, or wife."

During the 1920s, Oxford gained importance as much for its effect on the country's mores as for its contributions to scholarship. Until the Great War, English society had consisted of certain distinct and unbridgeable "sets," and "there

"Perfectly Delightful"

was little exchange between the sporting sets and 'the arts.'" Indeed, when Margot Tennant, with horsey antecedents, married the classical scholar Henry Asquith, it "appalled" the Leicestershire hunting world. By the 1920s, however, "this antipathy between sets grew less rigid," and "Oxford was largely responsible for this reconciliation of opposite cultures." The point being that both sets shared in the postwar euphoria and that neither group went there to work: "the essential was pleasure." The novels of Evelyn Waugh certainly capture that spirit, when people felt free to do anything "as long as it was 'amusing.'"[47]

That atmosphere fit Ladew like a well-cut dinner jacket, and he spent many a day (and night) in Oxford. He recalled that "Rose, a keen huntsman with the Meadow Brook," stabled "a pretty good jumper" at Oxford. One year Rose entered a steeplechase and invited his mother, who had a house in London, and Harvey to watch. Ladew and Mrs. Rose settled themselves by the water jump. All went well until George reached that point—he cleared the jump, but then came a big splash and both horse and rider "emerged dripping and covered with black slime." Ladew said he "had a flask ready for Mrs. Rose but [they] let George share it." He asked George "if he was all right," and the youth replied, "Quite. I was just diving for pearls."

Costumed revelers ring in the New Year at Craven Lodge, c. 1925. Ladew sits, where else but, front and center.

Another time Rose had arranged a lunch party for Ladew. He had also invited the expatriate American Henry "Chips" Channon. Ladew recalled that "one of the boys" he was lunching with described Channon as "a dreadful snob—and hated to be an American." Rose encouraged the impish Ladew to ask Chips what part of America he came from. "I did—and he said 'Chicago' and was furious at me." Harvey added, "Although I often saw Chips while I was in England, we never spoke." He later dismissed Channon as "a ridiculous person" but acknowledged him to be "clever in a way as he got to know every titled person in England." Channon also, notwithstanding his homosexual preferences, managed to marry one of the great British heiresses, Lady Honour Guiness, although she eventually divorced him.

On other nonhunting days, Ladew explored the English countryside and poked around antique shops. (Patricia Corey noted that her "Uncle Harvey loved finding treasures in out-of-the-way places—much more than at Christie's or Asprey's.")[48] He recalled one establishment in Market Harborough "that sold cast off furniture, old engravings, and pieces of Victorian china." One day, after digging through nineteenth-century bric-a-brac, he found "five small original oil paintings by Ferneley. They must have been painted of horses owned by a family who had lived in Market Harborough many years ago, for they were all framed alike." He "bought the lot for $200," and they still hang in his Maryland house.

He also enjoyed acting as guide to visiting American friends. When the Davises stopped to see him in Guilsborough, he decided to show them Oxford, which he "knew pretty well by then." Molly Davis expressed an interest in one of the university's colleges, and Ladew told her it was Magdalen, pronouncing it, as the English do, "Maudlin." Then his guest saw the word written and decided to pronounce it mag-da-lin, leading to heated words about the merits of English English (Ladew) versus American English (Davis). "About a week later," Ladew wrote, "we were in London at the National Gallery. Molly motioned me to come to her [and said], 'I just wanted to show you this painting of Mary Maudlin.'" Ladew laughed at that and later looked up the word in his dictionary. He found that one of the definitions was "Drunk enough to be emotionally silly," and he and Davis shared "a good laugh" about that, too.

This charming man was often asked for weekends at English country houses, whose fabric—and gardens—he scrutinized. He frequently visited the earl of Cardigan's Deene Park in Northamptonshire. Conveniently near the stylish hunts, Deene "added much to the history of frivolity" that characterized Melton in the 1920s. At about that time, for instance, there was an aged Lady Cardigan, "who waited scantily dressed on her balcony, and heavily roughed and painted, in the hope that a passing stablelad might take her for a comely lass."[49] Deene, built over six centuries and enjoying "a splendid panoramic setting, fine specimen trees, and a discerning choice of shrubs and herbaceous perennials,"[50] has been home to the Brudenell family since 1514. The Brudenells were made earls of Cardigan in the seventeenth century, and Deene's dining room contains portraits of the horses owned by the Lord Cardigan nicknamed the "hero of Balaclava," as well as "a painting of him leading the Charge of the Light Brigade."[51] On one of his visits to Deene, Ladew did not conceal his surprise when he encountered "a large glass case with a stuffed horse's head" in the entrance hall. His host, though, patiently explained that this was the head of the horse the then Lord Cardigan had ridden in the celebrated "Charge."

He also often visited the duke and duchess of Newcastle at Clumber, a grandiose Italianate mansion begun in the 1760s and added to continuously throughout the nineteenth century. The first time he stayed at Clumber, invited by the terrier-breeding duchess, he gasped at that "veritable palace which probably had fifty or more bedrooms. But it was, from an American point of view, lacking in bathrooms." He described how he awoke one night "and tried to prepare" himself for the unpleasant trip down the hall. "Then I suddenly realized that this would not be necessary if the mahogany stand contained the Pot de Chambre it had been designed to hold. I quickly opened the little door and there it was! But on withdrawing it, I found it had a brightly painted, gilded Newcastle crest painted on it and it seemed almost a sacrilege to use it. However I could not face the long walk down that chilly corridor." Although the house was demolished in 1938, "the date marking the end of an era in which such vast seats were still useable and used,"[52] the estate's 4,000-acre park remains much as it looked when Ladew knew it, and its ornamental lake, neoclassical temples, greenhouses, and miles-long allées would all reappear—in smaller scale—a few years later in his Maryland garden.

While Ladew was at Clumber, the Newcastles often took him to see nearby Renishaw Hall, seat of the Sitwell family. He liked the house but especially admired the grounds with their broad terraces, topiary obelisks, strategically placed ponds and lakes, box-edged flower beds, statues, sweeping lawns, and small, private yew-enclosed gardens; reinterpreted versions of these features, too, would appear at Pleasant Valley Farm. Ladew's friend Harold Acton, another frequent guest at Renishaw, termed the estate and its surrounding landscape "elegiac." "It is intensely English, with a charm that grows upon one," he said, adding, "This environment has enriched the poetry of the Sitwells, who were brought up here, within a dozen miles of Chatsworth, Bolsover, Clumber, Welbeck, and Hardwick Hall."[53] On one of these visits Harvey met and was befriended by his generation of Sitwells—Edith, Osbert, and, particularly, Sacheverell.

A recent article entitled "Making the Bourgeoisie Sit Up" in Ladew's favorite magazine, *Country Life*, called Edith, Osbert, and Sacheverell Sitwell "three of the most outrageous figures of 1920s artistic life."[54] Harold Acton, a friend of Ladew's and of the young Sitwells', met the "two tall fair-haired brothers" in Italy, where they reminded him of "eighteenth-century Englishmen on the Grand Tour, robustly languid, seeing everything of interest with alert shrewd eyes." He noted that the brothers "swerved aside from the beaten track, rediscovering forgotten painters and architects. Their quest," like Ladew's, "was agreeably devoid of any pedantry or system. They wandered at their own sweet will. And from a sunny winter at Amalfi or Algeciras they would bring fresh books to disperse the British fog. And they did so steadily for years, shedding a warm southern light around them."[55]

The Sitwells held enormous appeal for Ladew. As suggested, they represented the height of artistic chic. They also boasted an impossibly grand lineage, and Ladew never sneered at the combination of coronets and hefty bank balances. First, the father, Sir George Sitwell, came from an old "County" family who had lived on the same land since around 1200. They dwelt there in unostentatious comfort until the Industrial Revolution. Then, suddenly, they became enormously rich when someone discovered that thick veins of coal lay beneath their 7,000 Derbyshire acres. In addition, there was Sir George's wife, Lady Ida, who did not shy from reminding those around her that she could trace her antecedents back through the dukes of Beaufort to the royal house of Plantagenet.

During the 1920s, the decade Ladew met them, Osbert and Sacheverell shared a house fronting London's Carlyle Square. Acton remembered the city residence as a "shrine of eighteenth-century shell furniture, sailing ships of spun glass, humming birds under globes, petit-point screens, porcelain spaniels," and other ornaments "so many and so varied that at moments one felt one was in an aquarium . . . at others in an aviary." One assumes the brothers were amused in the 1940s and 1950s when they encountered similar decorative schemes at Ladew's Florida retreat.[56]

The mid-1920s also found the two Sitwell men rearranging their months in the country: Sir George and Lady Ida expatriated themselves to their eleventh-century Tuscan castle, Montegufoni, in 1925 and gave the family seat to Osbert, the elder son. In 1927, Sacheverell and his wife, Georgia, moved into a small country house, Weston Hall, in Northamptonshire, right in the midst of Ladew's hunt country. But they emphatically did not move there to ride with the Pytchley because, "despite their own sporting ancestry, the young Sitwells loathed" the vigorous outdoor life Ladew loved: "they never rode and detested the hunting and shooting set," dismissing them as "insensitive philistine snobs."[57]

That both brothers befriended the hard-riding Ladew suggests they were drawn to the many facets of his personality that lay beyond the paddock. There were the arts, of course. There was also what is today called "lifestyle." As the 1920s wore into the 1930s, Osbert, for example, began to spend more and more time "visiting the houses of the rich whose company he enjoyed. He was in many ways the perfect guest: a considerable raconteur; a celebrity on his own account; and what was known in the jargon of the times as 'a tame cat'—because of his known inclinations he could be a close, indeed an intimate friend of any woman, without the faintest risk of scandal." Sacheverell, who was by all accounts the

"Perfectly Delightful"

closer brother to Ladew, has been described in words that could have equally applied to the American: he possessed a unique "mixture of charm, wit, sensitivity, and imagination"; his friend James Lees-Milne has said that the "most fascinating" thing about Sitwell "was his conversation—he flitted from bough to bough, twig to twig so rapidly you couldn't keep pace with him. It was about exotic birds in the West Indies and then you'd find he was talking about architecture in Naples then about nunneries in the Balkans."[58]

The three men assuredly shared the ability to see the folly in the world and to laugh at it. Osbert, for instance, once visited China and spent some time at the ancient college of the imperial eunuchs, chatting at length with the eldest member. "'Tell me, young man,' the old castrato asked him, 'do you have a group of people like us where you come from?' Osbert thought carefully before replying, 'Indeed we do,' he said. 'We call it Bloomsbury.'"[59]

Also like Ladew, Sacheverell Sitwell enjoyed writing about his latest passions. And, like Ladew, Sacheverell's topics were "bewildering in their diversity." They included Angkor Wat, Spanish baroque art, English painting, gardening, Mozart, and travel. "As a cultural influence," one modern critic has written, "Sacheverell is considered to be an elitist and anachronistic amateur in a time of deeply researched, narrowly focused specialists and adversarial art critics who have rejected the idea of beauty as relevant to art." Yet as John Betjeman wrote of him in 1969, "What a relief you are after the fearful pedantry & dull art history which kills enjoyment & just gets scholarships for people & breeds more dullards." Finally, not believing in God, Sitwell made "the beauty and humour he found in life and art his religion"[60]—and that sounds like the Ladew who worried about having to spend eternity trying to make conversation "with a lot of dull saints."

Unlike Ladew, though, Sacheverell Sitwell actually completed and published his books, and they—all sixty-eight of them—remain landmarks in their fields. His *British Architects and Craftsmen* (1945), for instance, has been called historically significant for having "played an important part in the revival of public interest in the English country house after the Second World War," not that Harvey Ladew, who owned a first edition of the book, needed any encouragement to appreciate English country houses![61]

During Ladew's stays in Market Harborough he met Sir Harold and Lady Zia Wernher, devotees of the turf who became the closest of his English friends. After World War II, the Wernhers often spent the winter with him in Florida, and, after one visit, he wrote his sister in 1948, "The Ladew Girls [his nickname for his three female servants], who are very good judges, like the Wernhers better than any of my friends—and next to them the Airlies." He concluded this assessment by noting, "Zia was wonderful to me all those years I hunted in England. She is a charming person and I am devoted to her."

Zia Wernher (born 1893, née Anastasia Michailovna) was the elder daughter of Countess Torby and Grand Duke Michael of Russia; her father, a grandson of

A surprisingly disgruntled-looking Ladew while hosting his favorite English friends, Sir Harold and Lady Zia Wernher, at the races in Florida (note the palm trees) in 1947.

Czar Nicholas I, was exiled by his cousin Czar Nicholas II for making a morganatic marriage to Countess Torby. Lady Zia was, therefore, a great-great-granddaughter of Catherine the Great. (Her maternal great-grandfather was Pushkin.) In 1917 she married Harold Wernher, eldest son and heir of the South African diamond magnate Julius Wernher, who was created a baronet in 1905. In 1903, Julius Wernher purchased the estate Luton Hoo, in Bedfordshire, and hired the architects of London's Ritz Hotel to remodel the existing Adam-designed house. The results, wrote one scholar, certainly "reflect the profuse grandeur of the Edwardian period."[62]

Luton has been called "a museum first and a country house second." Indeed, it must have been, for its marvelous contents included "superb Beauvais tapes-

"Perfectly Delightful"

tries," furniture by Robert Adam, Lamerie silver, important works of Titian, Rubens, Reynolds, Lely, and Hoppner, as well as contemporary canvases by Sargent and Munnings. "But the real stars are the objects. The ivories, enamels, Renaissance bronzes and jewelry cannot be equalled by any other private collection."[63] Ladew's friends did nothing to lessen that effect when they took over, for Lady Zia filled it with one of the world's grandest collections of the works of Peter Carl Fabergé, which she inherited from her Romanov ancestors. The grounds, featuring a Capability Brown–designed park, equaled the house, and it both amused and depressed Harvey to tell his sister that while Julius Wernher had employed sixty gardeners at Luton Hoo, "Harold and Zia were down to 30"—but, he wailed, "I can't get ANYONE to help me in Maryland!"[64]

English servants held a special fascination for Ladew, who had never experienced anything quite like the strict hierarchy that existed "below stairs." When he spent one weekend at Mentmore, home of the huntswoman Baroness Burton, he asked his valet, the faithful Sherin, to make a full report on life among the servants. Accordingly, Sherin described the staff's two dining rooms, one decidedly inferior to the other. While Sherin was pleased to have been granted admission to the better one, Ladew's American chauffeur became "furious" when he found himself relegated to the less chic one. Ladew loved to learn odd bits of information about those who made up an English staff such as the duties of "tweenies" and how footmen were selected: he was told that since a footman wears knee britches, the "prime requirement for the job was well developed calves."

During one stay at Luton Hoo, the Wernhers took their American friend to a servants' ball. "Zia asked me to wear my pink coat as she wanted to make the occasion as festive as possible. . . . After we played a few rubbers we all went down to a large room which was used as a recreation and living room for her staff. Ordinarily it was furnished with comfortable chairs and sofas, a ping pong table and a radio, but that night the furniture had been removed and the whole room had been attractively decorated with bunting, potted plants, and flowers. Many servants from the surrounding country houses had arrived, the band was there and all was in readiness for the party to begin. The music started and Zia opened the dance with the butler while Harold partnered the housekeeper. I had the first dance with the Fernie Huntsman's wife, a most attractive young woman. I was very much impressed by the democratic spirit of this party. There was nothing condescending in the attitude of the hosts nor anything servile in their guests' behavior. I don't think that in our country such a party could be given and it made me admire the English even more."

One season his friends Charles and Olive Greville rented a "large and lovely" house in Oxfordshire. (The American-born Olive married the third Baron Greville in 1909.) They asked Ladew for a spring weekend, which climaxed in a dinner dance given by the duke of Marlborough at Blenheim Palace. Ladew felt a bit nervous about going to Blenheim because the duke's former wife (née Consuelo

Luton Hoo (c. 1950), seat of Lady Zia and Sir Harold Wernher at a time when Ladew knew it well. He wrote his sister that the Wernhers were "down to 30 gardeners"; they had their work cut out for them tending the estate's formal parterres and rose garden (foreground) and Capability Brown–designed park.

Vanderbilt) was a good friend of his. But, since he had "read so much about" the house and its gardens, newly laid out by the duke and Consuelo, curiosity overcame fear, and he went. When the Greville party arrived, they found "a moon and many lights," which gave them "a good view of this enchanting dwelling with its formal gardens" of parterres, reflecting ponds, and fountains: Ladew "could not have been more excited." The duke led them "through a succession of beautifully furnished rooms," finally reaching the ballroom, where a band was playing and people were dancing. When introduced to the new duchess, Ladew was a bit put off by her appearance and later learned that "she had been to a plastic surgeon to have her nose carved into a more Grecian shape. After carving her face, the surgeon had filled the excavation with wax. Unfortunately the wax had recently melted producing a large lump on one side of her nose."

He recalled another dinner at the Grevilles' "when the butler came into the dining room obviously drunk." Olive Greville, infuriated, found a pencil and wrote on one of the menus, "You are very intoxicated. Leave the dining room and do not return," and passed it to the servant. On reading the note, the butler "walked down to a duchess whom he had worked for and disliked and handed her the message. The duchess was very surprised on reading it, but fortunately the matter was soon explained to her."

Ladew recognized how "fortunate" he was "to be asked to stay in quite a number of the 'Stately Homes of England' during the 21 years" he hunted there. He wrote in his unpublished memoirs that he sometimes felt as though he were "wandering through the pages of endless numbers of *Country Life*." It is known, from his notes, that he was a guest of the earl and countess of Leicestershire at the vast, Palladian-style mansion Holkham in Norfolk ("how wonderful to be asked for Christmas"), of the earl and countess of Berkeley at Berkeley Castle in Gloucestershire, of the duke and duchess of Rutland at Belvoir in Northamptonshire, of Lord Sackville (cousin of the great gardener V. ["Vita"] Sackville-West) at Knole in Kent, and of the marquess and marchioness of Northampton at Compton Wynates in Oxfordshire.

Reveling in these weekends, Harvey discovered that he particularly "loved breakfasting" in an English country house. "It is full of surprise and almost like a treasure hunt. A great variety of food is hidden about under covered and heated dishes. . . . At the first of these breakfasts I attended I nearly starved. I did not know where to look for anything, especially the coffee, and was too embarrassed to ask and show my ignorance. But I soon learned. Starvation is a great leveler." But, like most Americans, the sheer size of these houses astonished him, as did their miles of corridors, the difficulties involved in navigating one's way through them, and the arcane and baffling routines their owners accepted apparently as a matter of course. Bathrooms particularly confounded him. He was once asked to Deene for the annual Hunt Ball. The evening proved particularly festive, and Ladew wrote, "[The] next morning, but not *very* early, I rang for my morning tea. Soon after this I put on my wrapper, gathered up my sponge bag, soap, and shaving things and started on a long walk—one might almost call it a constitutional—down a series of chilly corridors to the bathroom that had been assigned to me."

Of course, the important point about Ladew's English visits is that he took the time and trouble to look at what was around him and that he had the intelligence to understand—really understand—what he was seeing. This certainly stood him in good stead when he came to design his house and garden in Maryland. For

Ladew (far right) relaxing at the Drummond family house in Northamptonshire around 1930. Mrs. and Mrs. George Drummond and their daughters are on the left; other guests included the duke of York (later George VI) and his equerry (in hat).

example, in the gardens he admired the allées at Clumber, the terraces and topiary at Renishaw, and the superb use of water at Blenheim, and all found expression at Pleasant Valley; conversely, after those morning "constitutionals" to a shared water closet, he made certain that every guest room in Maryland had its own well-equipped bathroom.

For years Ladew maintained a small flat in London, which he used for a few weeks each year in the spring before returning to America. "I loved London," he wrote. "Paris is very beautiful, but in a totally different way and it has never had the same charm for me." He joined Boodle's and kept up membership in that ancient club the rest of his life. "I enjoyed going there in the late afternoon for a cup of tea or a few drinks and a chance to write a few letters." His favorite flat was a ground-floor one he found in the raffish neighborhood of Shepherd's Market. "In the early morning I could hear the street cries of men selling coal, flowers, or fruit. The flat was primitive but had a lot of old world charm—as well as old world inconveniences. Heat was obtained by dropping a shilling into a machine which burned for a certain time. There was a gas ring in the bathroom on which I could heat water for tea or coffee and boil eggs for my breakfast." He made his digs particularly homey by planting a few window boxes and by filling the rooms with a few real treasures mixed in with curiosities acquired in the Portobello Road

"Perfectly Delightful"

stalls: "[I] loved it all and felt so much more a part of London than if I had been staying more luxuriously at Claridge's."

His social life—while active in the country—positively exploded during his London stays. One undated period newspaper clipping described a particularly grand Twelfth Night party, organized by Lady Sligo, attended primarily "by young people," and decorated with "festoons of white leaves, silver ribbons, and a few cleverly-introduced red flowers arranged so that the foyer was transformed into the likeness of one giant chandelier." Lady Sligo asked Lord and Lady Carisbrook to judge the costumes, "helped by Mr. Harvey Ladew, who," the paper approvingly noted, "mounted the Prince of Wales during his stay on Long Island." Ladew particularly enjoyed attending debutante dances held "in the beautiful old homes" around Berkeley Square. "I never will forget how lovely they were. On warm spring nights the young people would come out to the balconies overlooking the square and its small park and couples would stroll about the street to the tunes from the dance orchestras."[65]

One of Ladew's more unorthodox London evenings—even he called it "most unusual"—came when Herman Oelrichs asked him to a dinner at the Embassy Club. When he and his fellow guests sat down, they discovered that Oelrichs had arranged for the dinner to be served and eaten backwards. Accordingly, waiters brought them demitasses and liqueurs; then came, in sequence, peach Melba, a savory (devils on horseback, Ladew recalled), partridge and vegetables, an endive salad, hot soup, and finally his "favorite food, the best possible caviar," all accompanied by "wonderful wine and champagne. The menu had not been written out so each dish was a surprise and much laughter accompanied its appearance." Interestingly, in one of his "Mapp and Lucia" novels, all the rage in the twenties and thirties, E. F. Benson had one of the characters, "Quaint" Irene Coles, treat herself to a "backwards dinner"; whether art influenced reality or reality influenced art remains unknown.

Amusing as that Embassy Club dinner seemed, without doubt Ladew's favorite London hostess was Laura Corrigan. Born Laura Whitlock in Waupaca, Wisconsin, in 1879, she married the Cleveland steel magnate James Corrigan in 1915. When he died in 1927, she inherited a fortune, moved to London, bought an enormous house, and set out on a career of entertaining in the grandest possible way. Elsa Maxwell, no stranger to parties, wrote that "the British have always looked with tolerant amusement" at ambitious hostesses such as Corrigan "if their dinners are lavish enough and their antics amusing." "Laura was definitely an amusing character. I remember that some of the London socialites, for a joke, started the rumor that Prince George would come to Laura's first party. Somehow the Prince heard of this and took a notion to show up the snobs. He actually came. Laura was so overwhelmed by this that she stood on her head in front of the assembled guests."[66] Ladew recalled that Corrigan's London parties featured tables overflowing with baskets of red roses, American performers entertaining, after-dinner prizes such as gold cigarette cases—the last "usually won by royalty."

When World War II broke out, Corrigan moved to Paris to work for the Allied cause. She lived in an apartment at the Ritz and, wrote Ladew, "devoted herself to doing as much as she could for American prisoners." Unable to get access to her money in America for her good works, Corrigan had to sell "some of her fabulous jewels, which included a very large square emerald." One day while riding the Ritz elevator, "she came face to face with Goering and saw he was wearing her emerald ring on his fat, chubby finger." She used some of the funds to start a soup kitchen for the poor, which she operated "rather incongruously at the back door of the Ritz." Since she worked on her own, not part of any organized group, Corrigan was free to devise her own uniform: "very snappy," Ladew judged it, "with a little gold medal on a chain and sheer silk stockings." After the war the French government awarded Corrigan the Legion of Honor. Evelyn Waugh's observation that Corrigan was "quite bald and wore a wig"[67] completes the picture of this extraordinary person.

Ladew's London life undoubtedly peaked in 1937, King George VI and Queen Elizabeth's coronation year, when the metropolis reverberated with festivities. Harvey found himself invited to a ball given by the duke and duchess of Sutherland, "the most glamorous occasion of the season," as one newspaper dubbed the soiree.[68] "Nothing like the display of jewelry is likely to be seen again." The Sutherlands created a ballroom by placing a huge tent next to their London mansion, Stafford House, and Ladew remembered that "priceless tapestries had been brought from several of the duke's many country houses and completely covered the walls of the marquee."[69] The receiving line included the new king and queen and Ladew's favorite royal, "Queen Mary, a regal and impressive figure in a lovely pale blue and silver brocaded gown." Once in the tent, he found "royalties from all parts of the world," including Prince Michael of Romania, the Princess Royal and her husband (the earl of Harewood), Princess Juliana of the Netherlands and Prince Bernhard, the duke and duchess of Kent, and "many maharajas, resplendent in their native dress and turbans and priceless jewels." When the music began, a gossip columnist spied Ladew "dancing with the former Princess Cecile of Greece, whose tiara of huge diamonds and emeralds [could] only be described as a complete and outsize crown. Later, Mr. Ladew partnered Lady Zia Wernher, whose lovely sapphires and diamonds were shown off by a silver dress."[70]

Typically, Ladew arranged to end his era of English hunting seasons spectacularly. In the summer of 1939, as most Americans focused on the New York World's Fair and with war clouds gathering in Europe, he decided to stage a transatlantic epic—"Hounds Across the Sea"—to see if he could hunt on two continents within two days. Also typically, he immortalized the experience for a magazine, in this case his favorite, *Country Life*. In discussing the idea with his Maryland neighbors,

"Perfectly Delightful"

the Edward McLeans, he "unguardedly remarked that it might be fun to fly over on a Clipper." The McLeans "jumped at the idea," and the project took on a life of its own. Ladew began to get cold feet about flying over the Atlantic, as he "had seen it in its angrier moods." "[I] tactfully suggested to the McLeans that, though I was, of course, terribly keen to fly, I really felt they owed a duty to their two innocent children. They are a very charming couple but I fear they are totally lacking in parental instincts, for they seemed unmoved."

So, in his usual way, he decided that as long as he had to go through with it, he "might as well get as much fun as possible out of the situation." He planned to hunt in Maryland on a Friday and then drive to New York and spend the night. The following day he could board the Clipper to England, arrive in Southampton on Sunday, and then hunt with some local group. But when he wrote to the British Library of Information to find a hunt near Southampton, he was told curtly, "There is no foxhunting this time of year in the British Isles. The season does not open until November 1." (One wonders if the excitement of the trip kept him from remembering this important point himself.) The McLeans suggested going to Scotland to shoot grouse, but he dismissed the idea because "it would be extremely unconventional to do it on a horse." After some thought, he hit upon a solution—the Devon and Somerset Stag Hounds, who just happened to

The dining room (!) in the Glenn L. Martin–built Clipper that Ladew flew to England as part of his 1939 epic, "Hounds Across the Sea."

"Happiness comes in absorption"

be meeting the day in question. Relieved, he proceeded apace. He spent Friday morning cubbing with the Elkridge-Harford Hunt, drove to New York with the McLeans, caught a few hours of sleep, and arose at six o'clock Saturday morning.

His qualms returned, however, when he spotted the airplane, which "looked disturbingly smaller" than he had imagined it. But once he was aboard, relief came when he discovered that there was "a very good bar on the Clipper." A great Baltimore friend, Fife Symington, met the trio when the plane touched down in Southampton. Symington came armed with Ladew's riding clothes and had rented a two-seater for the 150-mile drive to Devon. (The McLeans chose to skip the hunt.) After he checked into his picturesque inn, where "great clusters of purple clematis and roses clambered up" to his window, he took a crash course in stag hunting and then rode off to the meet. The landscape left him breathless: "I have never seen a more beautiful country. Hunting in Devon is like hunting through a great garden with a haze of purple heather dotted here and there with clumps of yellow gorse." Everything went as planned (except for a thunderstorm), and his adventure became a favorite item for the English and American press. He particularly relished the squib that appeared in the *Tatler*, which called the feat "heroic" and wondered, "Why didn't his English friends throw ticker tape and tear up telephone directories to give him a hero's welcome?"[71] He probably wondered why, too.

T. E. LAWRENCE: "THIS INTRODUCES LADEW, WHOM YOU WILL LIKE"

Hunting foxes in Leicestershire and Italy; hunting movie stars in Hollywood; even flying across the Atlantic to hunt on two continents in two days—all these activities might seem more or less mainstream. Yet not all of Ladew's ventures could be so called. Who today would consider a trek across the deserts of Arabia or into the mountains of Bolivia for a fun-filled holiday? But Ladew undertook both those journeys in the 1920s and did so with his customary élan.

The former trip grew out of his seemingly unlikely friendship with T. E. Lawrence—Lawrence of Arabia. The two men appear to have met in early 1921, while Ladew was in England hunting. Curiously, though, Ladew, usually so thorough a chronicler of his own comings and goings, is silent on when he met Lawrence, what they did together—even on his own reactions to the hero's tragic death in 1935. Some might construe this uncharacteristic self-censorship as important.

A recent biographer of Lawrence has opined that "every generation has its own heroes," adding that "Lawrence filled this role for the 1920s and 1930s." Lawrence fought the last holy war—as a freelance British soldier who won the confidence of the Arabs, led them into battle against the despotic Turks, risked his life on daring missions behind enemy lines, and masterminded the liberation of

"Perfectly Delightful"

Ladew, suffering no air-travel fatigue, with the Devon-Somerset Stag Hunt in 1939: "Hounds Across the Sea" triumphant!

Damascus. His was the exception to the usual stories about World War I—life in the filthy trenches, no clear objectives, week after week in the mud, hundreds of thousands of soldiers killed to gain a few acres of land only to lose the "gain" a couple of weeks later. Lawrence's war, on the other hand, "could be romanticised without any sense of guilt; it had been waged in the desert and had been one in which the individual could still dominate the battlefield. . . . [He] rode rather than ran or crawled across a battlefield. He was his own master, not another's pawn."[72] Simply put, Lawrence's war was the war as it should have been. Moreover, Lawrence, with his handsome features, blond hair, and piercing blue eyes, "looked the part of a hero,"[73] and that, of course, merely made his exploits all the more glamorous.

Immediately after the war, Lawrence participated in the Paris Peace Conference and worked with his wartime colleague King Feisal to help forge the first Arab-Zionist peace agreement. In 1919 he accepted a fellowship to All Souls College, Oxford (he had graduated from Oxford's Jesus College in 1910), in return for which he was expected to write a book. Life at Oxford did not suit him, however, for he always felt on display. So he accepted the loan of a flat in London (14 Barton Street) from the eminent architect Sir Henry Baker, where he spent most of his time in relative anonymity. Then in January 1921 (just about the time he met Ladew), Winston Churchill, secretary of state for the colonies, appointed him an advisor to the Colonial Office on Arabian affairs. The two formed a mutual admiration society of the highest order. Lawrence deemed Churchill the ideal public man—free of thought, bold of initiative; Churchill returned the compliment and called Lawrence "one of the greatest human beings alive in our time."

Yet however pleasant Lawrence's life might sound today, he hated every minute of it. First off, he despised governmental bureaucracy. "Lawrence was not an office man," a co-worker recalled. "Paperwork vexed him greatly and he avoided much of it by hurling files into his waste-paper basket."[74] In late 1921, he decided to resign his post in the Colonial Office, which he did in July 1922. Lawrence also detested his fame and grabbed every chance to escape into obscurity. This quest for anonymity came to a head in August 1922 when he enlisted in the Royal Air Force under the assumed name T. E. Ross.

The reason for this dissatisfaction, many now believe, lay deeper than simple impatience at bureaucratic ineptness. The real reason was that Lawrence didn't want to be known for his foreign office work or even for his battlefield wiles: he wanted to be known for his literary work. "Art was the one area where Lawrence still dared to dream," one biographer has noted.[75] He befriended and was befriended by the leading English literary lights of the day, including Ezra Pound, Robert Graves, George Bernard Shaw, E. M. Forster, John Buchanan, Christopher Isherwood, W. H. Auden, John Maynard Keynes, Thomas Hardy, and Siegfried Sassoon. He also grew close to the painter Augustus John, who drew two famous portraits of him. When John sold one to the duke of Westminster for one thousand pounds in 1920, Lawrence wrote the painter, "Really, I'm hotter than I thought." He jokingly added, "Of course I know you will naturally think the glory is yours—but I believe it's due to the exceeding beauty of my face."[76]

Through Siegfried Sassoon, Lawrence met Noël Coward, who first felt the war hero was "an inverted show-off" but later deemed him totally charming—"he was charming to me, anyhow." Coward let Lawrence attended a rehearsal of *Private Lives*; afterwards they went to dinner and, "at an obscure restaurant where Lawrence could be sure of anonymity," he "hardly took his eyes off Coward."[77] A correspondence developed between the two men, which led to one of the more lighthearted stories about Lawrence. In his quest for privacy, he had taken to using only his RAF enlistment number, 338171. Coward, bemused, began one letter to the war hero, "Dear 338171 (May I call you 338?)." Lawrence responded, "It is very good to laugh; and I laughed so much and made so many people laugh over your 'may I call you 338.'"[78]

Lawrence had developed an interest in the arts as a child, and in the 1920s

"Perfectly Delightful"

Augustus John's sketch of T. E. Lawrence, who commended the artist for capturing "the exceeding beauty" of his face. Ladew framed a copy of the sketch and several letters Lawrence wrote him to create a little shrine to their intriguing friendship.

this, and his general love of literature, gave him the idea of starting his own private art press. "What he wanted most," Ladew wrote of his friend, "was to have a little house in the country and his own printing press. He had apparently planned rather a Horace Walpole 'Strawberry Hill existence' without the luxuries and crowds of guests Horace would have insisted on." Harvey went on to say that Lawrence wanted to print the books he had written on special paper and to set the type with his own hands. Ladew said that Lawrence discussed having him invest in the press—"He wanted me to print his books"—but nothing seems to have come of it. Instead, Ladew, who "very much wanted to do something for T.E. Lawrence, who had been exceedingly kind" to him, decided to "scour the

London book shops for very old books on the art of printing and sent him some nice ones."[79]

Dissatisfied with the RAF, in 1923 Lawrence decided to become "an intermittent exile from the society of artists and writers"[80] and joined the Royal Tank Corps, this time under the name of Shaw. Stationed in Dorset, he found a dilapidated cottage, Cloud's Hill, near his base. He rented the cottage—after rejoining the RAF in 1925—then bought it in 1929; he fixed it up, and it became home for the rest of his life.

While at Cloud's Hill, Lawrence began his massive translation of the *Odyssey*. In 1928 Bruce Roger, a distinguished book designer, convinced him to undertake the project, and the book came out in a deluxe limited edition of 530 copies in 1932. In October of that year, Lawrence had to write E. M. Forster, "Sorry about this. I cannot send you a copy," explaining, "The thing costs twelve guineas, & I got only a handful of them."[81] Whether Lawrence gave one to Ladew is unknown—but the American did obtain a copy, and it still graces the bookshelf at Pleasant Valley Farm.

Lawrence led a Spartan existence at Cloud's Hill. "Alcohol was banned and the cuisine was minimalist, with guests being offered tins of preserved meat and can openers." That sounds a most un-Ladew sort of life. Yet for all their seeming incompatibility, the two men found they had much in common. First, they were virtual contemporaries, Lawrence having been born in 1888, Ladew in 1887. Second, both were, if nothing else, independent, free spirits. Both men also, in varying degrees, tried to shed off past encumbrances. Lawrence's generation of Englishmen placed themselves "on the side of youth" against "the fuddy-duddy boneheads who had mishandled the war." They, thus, favored "individualism and rejection of worn-out men and stale ideas."[82] Ladew's innovative nature took a different form from Lawrence's, of course, but innovator he nonetheless was, in gardening, in interior decoration, and in what is today called "lifestyle." And Ladew had certainly grown up in a family of unconventional people—simply recall his mother, the society woman who ran the leather factory.

Moreover, just as Ladew proudly noted his seemingly incompatibly diverse interests and characteristics—aesthete and sportsman, bon vivant and sometime scholar—Lawrence's life and personality embodied "contradictions and inconsistencies" one authority has called "extraordinary. His diverse selves did not merely bifurcate into recognizable opposites (commanding/meek, sociable/solitary, masculine/feminine) but fragmented into apparently disconnected characters."[83] Yet neither man was an anarchist. Lawrence became the very embodiment of the British Empire, and Ladew, for all his fondness for vaudevillians, never missed a chance to dance with a duchess.

And despite their wildly and widely varied interests, neither man cared much for politics, which actually hurt Lawrence's literary career: while he was "admired by the younger generation of writers," he chose to keep himself outside their circle because "the left held no attractions to him, nor did he give any attention to the social and economic problems of his own country, which increasingly occupied the thoughts of other contemporaries."[84] Much the same certainly could have been said of Ladew, who dealt with the depression by riding to hounds in Northamptonshire.

Finally, neither man married. Nor, despite rumors and speculations about romantic entanglements with this or that society woman, did either man apparently ever give the slightest indication of wanting to marry. One Lawrence scholar suggested that the war hero felt "extremely uneasy with all women but menopausal matrons."[85] Similarly, a late 1920s gossip columnist for one of the New York papers dubbed the "tall, dark, good looking nephew of the famous Berry Wall" the "despair of the ladies, withstanding their melting glances without a quiver."[86]

Lawrence, regarded as one of the century's great letter writers, penned "few" notes in the years 1921–22[87] and instead busied himself in completing his literary masterpiece, *The Seven Pillars of Wisdom*, in resolving various Middle East political crises, and in wrestling with his own personal demons. His friend and biographer Robert Graves has written that "in the winter of 1921–22 Lawrence was in a very nervous condition." The war hero "did not eat or sleep enough" and "came as near as anyone could do to a complete breakdown."[88] He had spent the fall in the Middle East working to arrange peace settlements among the Arabs and between the Arabs and the Jewish settlers in Palestine and only returned to England in December 1921.

But he did find time to write several notes to Ladew. The American framed many of them—including a print of the John portrait of Lawrence at his most beautiful—as if to create a sort of shrine to this friendship. And friendship it must have been. As has been noted, those months in 1921–22 were deeply emotionally trying for Lawrence, and it does not seem humanly possible that anyone, in the midst of a near breakdown, would take time off to pen letters of introduction on behalf of a mere acquaintance. The letters, however, only add to the mystery of their relationship. For instance, on January 10, 1922, Lawrence wrote to Ladew to arrange a meeting: "I'm afraid I live in London: Colonial Office from 10 AM till bedtime & then asleep in Barton Street behind Abbey. If you wish to be severely official, please call on me in this dismal place. If you want me to be human, lunchtime is my safest offer." He then suggested, "Oxford is possible: by pre-arrangement I can take a day off: and a night off, if it would amuse you to see how they live at All Souls . . . xiv century: there is no steam heat: & you have to walk across a court to bathe & a court and a cloister to dine." (Such caveats certainly suggest that Lawrence knew Ladew's fondness for domestic comfort!) "Would you like any night next week," the Englishman continued. "Vacations: nobody there probably but ourselves. Or if the night sounds too formidable would you like to lunch there with me, any day next week."[89]

Whether Lawrence actively encouraged Ladew to explore the vast, largely unchartered deserts, whether Ladew thought up the adventure as an expression of his friendship with Lawrence, or whether the innate romance of the trip simply struck his fancy will forever remain unclear. Preparing for his 1921–22 hunting season, Ladew bought a book about travel in Arabia for his shipboard reading. (The book is inscribed "Harvey S. Ladew / S.S. Aquatania / November 1921.") In England, he bought Doughty's *Arabia Deserta* and wrote in it, "HSL / London / Jan. 1922." That latter book was a particular favorite of Lawrence's: first published in 1888, it had been out of print for years, but through "Lawrence's persistent efforts" and "on condition that Lawrence would write an introduction" to it, a new edition came out in 1921; this is the edition Ladew bought, and one must assume he purchased it at Lawrence's urging. "Every student of Arabia wants a copy," Lawrence stated in his introduction. "There have been many well-endowed Englishmen travelling in Arabia," he continued, "and most of them have written books. None has brought away a prize as rich as Doughty."[90] Ladew's copy contains some sheets of paper filled with his penciled scribblings about Arabia. Recently, members of the T. E. Lawrence Society examined the papers and suggested that they look like notes taken in conversation between Lawrence and Ladew.[91]

On January 24, 1922, Lawrence wrote Ladew that some sort of trip might be worked out—a friend named Moore had just come "by road from Teheran to Tabriz and thence to Tiflis." "Says it is possible if you behave carefully & don't arouse suspicion." He added a philosophic postscript, "EVERYTHING EVERYWHERE IS CHANGING (Motto & Description of Middle East)." He also encouraged Ladew to contact Moore—a "nice fellow"—at home ("28 Ebury Street, S.W.") to discuss various routes.[92] Ladew apparently did so. He also asked a friend, Major Alexander Powell, to accompany him. Ladew had met Powell during World War I, and Powell's profession of travel writer doubtless rang sympathetic chords both in Ladew, who so much enjoyed traveling and writing himself, and in Lawrence, who had his own literary aspirations.

Lawrence also provided Ladew with letters of introduction to sheiks and to the resident English population, there to help colonize parts of the former Ottoman Empire. On March 7, 1922, he wrote "K.C." (Sir Kinahan Cornwallis, one-time director of the Arab Bureau), "Ladew may want to travel about Irak and with him is Powell, a writer. If they want to travel they will need help. If they need help, who so fit as to help them as the Advisor to the Interior? If they want to meet Kings and Queens [he knew his Ladew!] who so fit as the A to the I as before? Obviously it's all your job & the better you do it the more splendid will be your picture in my mind." On March 9, 1922, he wrote "Graves" (Philip Graves, Egyptologist and half brother of the writer Robert Graves), "This introduces Ladew, whom you will like. He & his friend Powell (in your line of business) are going somewhere in the East & will decide in Constantinople where it had better be. If you can help them in any way please do so." Lawrence sent copies of

"Perfectly Delightful"

these notes to Ladew, then busy chasing foxes in Leicestershire, with a penciled note, "Here's a bunch of letters. It doesn't include one from W. Churchill, because Thursday is his Middle East speech & Wednesday is Ireland and it isn't fair to talk to him privately till after that." With a P.S., "Send me word before you next come through & we'll meet."[93]

So, aided and abetted by Lawrence of Arabia himself, Harvey S. Ladew left his manicured English gardens for the uncharted deserts of Arabia. Powell captured their experiences in his book *By Camel and Car to the Peacock Throne*, published in 1923 and illustrated with snapshots taken by Ladew, "the most enthusiastic amateur photographer I have ever known." Powell begins the tale reminding readers that he and Ladew had indeed embarked on a true adventure, for men and women then had "less knowledge of [Arabia] than of . . . the polar regions." Indeed, "the Europeans who have penetrated its mysterious interior [could] be counted on the fingers of one's two hands." Moreover, their journey would be made at a camel's slow 2½-mile-an-hour pace through "oven-like heat, suffocating dust, and deadly monotony of hot blue sky and hot orange desert" and "with roving tribes of lawless Bedouin bandits an ever-present worry."[94]

Ladew ("as good-looking as Fredric March and as romantic as Gary Cooper")[95] suggested they "make the first stage of the journey, from Paris to Constantinople . . . in his car, which he kept in England." Powell was somewhat surprised when they "rendezvoused a fortnight later at the Crillon" to find that the car "was an open Rolls-Royce, as shiny black as a hearse and as long as a Pullman." They survived the 2,000-mile drive and arrived at the Turkish capital, where they apprised the British embassy staff of their plans. The official response proved less than encouraging: "Of course you *may* get across all right, but we can't guarantee your safety. All we can promise is that, if the Bedouins do capture you, we'll send some planes and jolly well bomb the beggars until they let you go."[96] This, Powell and Ladew deduced, was the bureaucrats' "way of dissuading [them] without actually forbidding [them]." "But it had precisely the opposite effect to that intended, for to us there was something distinctly romantic and attractive in the prospect of being carried off by desert raiders and of being rescued by British bombing-planes, like the hero and heroine in 'The Green Goddess.'" In fact, the two men were already envisioning "the gray planes booming down the sky, the chrysanthemums of smoke and flame as the bombs burst over the black tents," as well as "the [British] commander, a slender, sun-bronzed youth in khaki and leather flying-helmet," who would "scramble from his cock-pit and approach us."[97]

They recovered themselves from these reveries long enough to tell the official that his warning only heightened their desire, and they promptly boarded the steamer *Lamartine* and sailed to Palestine. Four men formed the party: Powell himself; DeWitt Hutchings, vice president of the Mission Inn in Riverside, California, former Princeton baseball hero, and "a collector of temple bells, old manuscripts, and Spanish pictures";[98] Ladew, who spent "his winters riding to hounds

Ladew began his 1922 Arabian trek by taking his Rolls Royce convertible from Paris to Constantinople. He flew the Stars and Stripes from the car's fender to celebrate his arrival.

with the Meadow Brook or the Pytchley"; and Ladew's aforementioned young Irish valet, Sherin, "who had been in the service of the Duke of Portland until the World War had caused him to discard the ducal uniform. . . . He had a joke or a pun for every occasion, he never lost his temper, and he was equally handy with a pressing-iron, a frying pan, or a gun."[99]

They docked in Beirut and hired a "young New Zealander, a former aviator," to guide them to Jerusalem. There the group found themselves stymied, since "professional guides and outfitters" were unknown. Frustrated and about to abandon the venture—Lawrence or no Lawrence—they treated themselves to a party, Hutchings having "discovered a row of square-faced bottles labeled 'Gordon's gin.'" "[We] borrowed a galvanized iron pail into which we squeezed the juice of two dozen Jaffa oranges and poured the contents of three bottles of gin. Adding sugar and a chunk of ice obtained from the local meat-market, we stirred the mixture with a cane. By the time we had emptied the bucket, nightfall was at hand." They sank into sleep.[100]

The following evening, they had all but resolved to abandon the project.

"Perfectly Delightful"

"While we were debating the matter over the coffee and cigars in the garden of our hotel, . . . Mr. Palmer, the energetic and efficient young Englishman who is his Britannic Majesty's consul in Damascus, dropped in upon us." Palmer told them of a camel merchant named Mohammed Bassum who had a caravan starting out for Baghdad the next day. They raced over to discuss the matter with the Arab, who, on learning that the group required "at least six baggage-camels," set the price at nine hundred dollars. "Exorbitant, of course, but, to put it inelegantly, Hadji Mohammed had us by the short hair and he knew it. Instead of Baghdad or bust, it would be Baghdad and busted." The Arab also agreed to pay any ransom, should the group be captured by Bedouins, except for "acts of Allah"—"if, for example, you should be shot or have your throats cut." That, Powell admitted, "had the effect of momentarily dampening our enthusiasm."[101] Still, in for a penny . . .

Powell took some pains to explain why they needed six baggage camels, for he helpfully included in his narrative—"for the guidance of those who contemplate a desert journey"—a list of necessities. The first essential, of course, would

While in Arabia, Ladew snapped this photo of his favorite valet, Wilfred Sherin, an Irish lad who had evidently decided to go native.

About 1925 Sherin and Ladew made a tour of Greece. As Ladew wrote beneath this photo-graph of the two of them, that trip was "not on Elsa Maxwell's yacht!"

be water, and the Powell-Ladew party equipped themselves with ten cases of Evian. Since each member of the group did "insist in sleeping on a bed," "folding canvas cots equipped with a U-shaped hood fitted with mosquito netting and Is-inglass windows" got packed. Also a folding metal table, one "comfortable chair" per person, an air pillow, two blankets, as much sheeting as possible ("as I have a constitutional aversion to sleeping in soiled bedding"); a gasoline stove and fuel; lanterns and "electric torches"; agate-ware cups and plates; straw mats ("which obviated the necessity of dressing while standing on bare ground"); a .45 Colt ser-vice automatic and four Mauser rifles along with sufficient ammunition; "a sup-ply of cold-cream for sunburn" and eau de Cologne ("wonderfully refreshing after a long day in the saddle"); medicines such as iodine, ammonia, boric acid, and quinine; field glasses; trinkets to give local chiefs ("jack-knives, mouth-organs . . . and silk handkerchiefs"); "a dozen tins of lime drops," tea, "two cases of light wines—Medoc and Sauterne," Champagne, coffee; "tinned tomatoes" and, for real food, pâtés de foie gras, tuna fish, anchovies, Camembert cheese, jars of jel-lies, and cans of artichokes, asparagus, and hearts of palm—such delicious vict-uals that they "might have been eating at Ciro's or Voisin's." As for clothing, Ladew (perennially on the international "10 best-dressed" lists) and Powell rec-ommended jackets with lots of pockets, jodhpurs ("which . . . can be made by an

"Perfectly Delightful"

Indian tailor"), short-sleeved shirts, silk handkerchiefs, a fleece-lined trench coat, tinted goggles, boots and shoes "large enough to allow for the swelling of feet from the heat," a pith helmet, "shorts, golf-stockings, and slippers" to change into at night ("nothing is more restful"), and "lounge-suits of light-weight flannel." "That pretty well covers the subject of equipment."[102]

On the morning of departure, they arose to discover that Bassum's caravan had already left, so they had to motor from Jerusalem to catch up with it in "three decrepit Fords, piloted by the most villainous-looking trio of town Arabs" Powell had "ever set eyes on." They missed their rendezvous point, had to spend the night in the desert, and decided that "Mr. Ford's ideas" of what constituted comfort were "radically different from the late Mr. Pullman."[103] That evening also gave rise to one of the most famous episodes in the entire Ladew saga. Powell recalled being awakened in the middle of the night by Ladew, who told him, through chattering teeth, that he was going through his bags looking for his dinner jacket, which he found and donned and thereby avoided freezing. The rest of his life Harvey liked to tell listeners that Uncle Berry had admonished him "never to go any where without [his] dinner jacket. He was right."[104]

Next day they finally did meet the caravan. Powell wrote that he had "never seen a more completely satisfying figure than Sheik Ghazi Mansour," the caravan leader: "almost too picturesque to be real—a tall, slender, hawk-nosed, black-bearded Arab" astride a "high red saddle, with its long tassels almost sweeping to the ground." In sum, "he looked for all the world like the Arabs of fiction and the motion-picture screen." The caravan consisted of sixty camels and about thirty servants. The sheik kindly provided a personal attendant for the American contingent, "the most faithful, cheerful, willing fellow" Powell had ever seen. Despite all those qualities, however, the young man got sacked one day "when Ladew caught him smoking the last of his treasured Jockey Club cigarettes."[105]

Once in the desert, Ladew and Powell quickly wearied of the "smell of sweat-stained leather; the shrill, plaintive voice of a camaleer raised in Arab song; the intolerable glare reflected from sun-baked earth in quivering mirage; and, high overhead, the sun, a ball of molten brass." "If you dared to look up at it, its brilliancy blinded you." Powell said he struggled to keep sane by thinking of "New England wells brimming with fresh, cool water; of porcelain tubs in shaded bathrooms; of ice tinkling in tall, thin, frosted glasses." Ladew, "who possessed a pleasant tenor voice," sang songs to "break the monotony," one of which had a refrain, "highly suggestive under the circumstances, which ran 'The Gipsy warned me; the Gipsy warned me.'" Nonetheless, they pressed on and, "begrimed with dirt, blistered by the sun, and weary to the point of exhaustion," finally reached their destination, the Tigris and Euphrates Valley. They enjoyed exploring ancient Babylon, Ladew snapping photographs all the way, before reaching Baghdad, where they checked into the wonderfully named Hotel Maude.[106]

They then drove to Damascus, where Ladew became smitten with the gardens he saw there. He was particularly impressed by the Arabs' use of fountains and pools. The contemporary garden writer Russell Page observed, "Water rules in Damascus. You have only to put your ear to any wall in the old town to hear the sound of running water. Brought from the rivers . . . by a series of little canals, the water is divided again and again into ever smaller rills to be carried into each house to make fountain jets in the enclosed patios."[107] In a few years, using what he had seen in the Middle East, Ladew would create his own water-ruled gardens in Maryland.

After a few amusing days touring and photographing gardens, the Powell-Ladew party set off by car for Persia and the Peacock Throne. On reaching Teheran, they learned that the treasure room was undergoing repairs and hence closed to tourists. This caused Ladew to explode—"But we simply can't leave without seeing it," he screamed to Powell, who joked that they might cable the shah, then in Paris. "I'll do that very thing," Ladew asserted. After all, *he* was a close friend of Lawrence of Arabia. Powell instead decided to have tea with the prime minister, who cut through the red tape and arranged for the Americans to visit the throne room the next afternoon.[108]

They had planned to meander from Teheran up to a port on the Caspian Sea, thence to sail to Baku and board a train back to Constantinople. But the states of Caucasia roiled with political turmoil caused by the relatively recent Russian Revolution; bandits prowled every road; and a typhus epidemic beset the entire region. "It struck us," wrote Powell, "that the combination of Bolshevists, brigands, and typhus-carrying lice should make for a very interesting journey, and we looked forward to it with keen satisfaction." But after due (re)consideration, they decided to call off that leg of the trip and retrace their path back to Beirut.[109]

While en route, they were semicaptured by a band of Bedouins who insisted the group share a meal. The Anglo-American-Irish party perforce agreed and entered a large tent. "Thirty minutes passed. The Bedouins had ceased talking and, save for the buzzing of flies, dead silence reigned." Soon, however, a procession of servants presented the Arabs' guests with loaves of flat bread, "a capacious bowl of soured camel's milk," and, "swimming in a pool of urine-colored gravy, an enormous pudding of mashed dates." ("Is it my imagination, sir," asked Sherin, "or is this camel's milk slightly flavored with manure?") After some silence, Ladew announced, "'I'm not hungry,' regarding the banquet with extreme disfavor." Powell replied that if they wanted to get out alive, they'd better eat, "and eat a lot." To continue the tale, Powell wrote, "In a long and diversified life I have never witnessed, much less participated in, so fantastic a performance. Picture us, if you please, seated cross-legged on a carpet in the suffocating heat of a goatshair tent, stuffing ourselves with coriaceous bread and mucilaginous date-duff which we sluiced down our gullets with copious drafts of fermented camel-juice." When they had choked down what politesse required, they were freed to leave.[110]

The men separated in Constantinople, each member resuming his "civilian"

"Water rules in Damascus," wrote the great twentieth-century garden designer Russell Page. Ladew sensed as much, for he knowingly photographed the pools and fountains he saw in the Syrian capital in 1922.

life. Hutchings flew to Paris to buy a Madonna by Murillo, which he later gave to the National Gallery of Art in Washington, D.C.; Powell sat down to write his book; and Ladew, "accompanied by Sherin, of course," sailed to Dublin "to pick up a couple of Irish hunters" and then went off to join a shooting party in Scotland.[111]

One of Ladew's few specific goals while on the trip had been to capture and bring back a Persian wild ass for Childs Frick, father of his future Baltimore friend Martha Frick Symington. Searching for the ass, purportedly one of the world's rarer quadrupeds, added a sense of purpose to the otherwise vaguely conceived journey, and "whenever [the group] discerned a cloud of dust rising from the dreary plane, [they] would seize the field-glasses and examine it eagerly." But there were no wild asses to be seen, only "those discouraged-looking domestic asses." Much later, Ladew wrote Martha Symington that he had to tell her father, "The only wild asses I had seen were the two-legged ones in the streets of Baghdad."[112]

Ladew's career as a big-game trapper, however, rose to great heights, literally, four years later, when he joined a party and scaled the Andes to search for specimens for the American Museum of Natural History in New York. Actually, he underwrote the expedition ("defrayed the greater part of the expenses," is how the museum phrased it), which set out from New York for La Paz on January 7, 1926. Once again, Ladew was accompanied by Sherin. Heading the group was another close friend, George Tate, assistant curator of the museum's Department of Mammals. It was not until the journey was well under way, though, that Ladew fully realized that Tate's "one passion" in life was collecting mice and rats. "Not having known of his great interest in these small mammals, I was amazed to find that our equipment included some 300 mouse traps which we baited and set along mountain and jungle trails in Bolivia."

The routine of baiting and rebaiting mousetraps palled after a while. Ladew discussed the matter with Tate, and the two decided that whenever the bon vivant had had enough mouse catching, he and Sherin would be allowed to go off to seek their own amusements, activities, Tate diplomatically wrote, "that had little biological interest." After a while they would join up again, then part and rejoin, and so on. Notwithstanding (or perhaps thanks to) Ladew's lengthy absences from the main party, after four months, Tate and his crew had managed to acquire 625 mammals, 246 birds, and more than 1,500 plants, all "from regions not hitherto represented."

Once, when they were all together at 16,000 feet in the Andes, they captured a mouse. On returning to New York, Tate discovered that it was of "a species new to science" and saw to it that it was named "Thomasomys Ladewi," partial thanks to Harvey for subsidizing the trip. Years later, Ladew, somewhat pitifully and thoroughly uncharacteristically, called that "small contribution to science . . . the only worthwhile thing" he had ever done in his life. Few today would agree with that assessment.

"A foxhunter's earthly heaven"

As Long Island became more and more suburbanized in the 1920s, it became less and less agreeable to sportsmen like Harvey Ladew. Hunting requires thousands of contiguous, open acres, free from the wire fences that can cut deep into horse flesh. Consequently, by the mid-twenties Ladew began to look around for a place more congenial to his way of life. He found that in the My Lady's Manor section of Maryland, a land of rolling hills and prosperous farms roughly 20 miles north of Baltimore, centered on the quiet village of Monkton. There he discovered and purchased the venerable Pleasant Valley Farm, which he and his team of architects and decorators made over so it exactly fit his particular personality. They created a house and grounds where everything is in harmony, and the beautifully proportioned spaces for living express all that Ladew held dear: beauty, comfort, horses, whimsy, and the fine arts.

Naturally, horses and hunting brought Ladew to Maryland. Shown here, Harvey's photo of Bob Six, who worked as Ladew's groom in the Free State from 1930 to 1939.

He also set about to fit in with the entrenched, civilized society he found on "the Manor": he joined the ancient Maryland Club in 1933, became a subscriber to the Bachelors Cotillon,[1] and made Pleasant Valley an integral cog in the equestrian machinery that propelled, and to a degree still propels, life in that rural part of Maryland. Yet while he respected what the Free State had to offer, he also gently injected his own brand of urbane, cosmopolitan artistic life into the sleepy countryside. He welcomed the cream of international society—and meritocracy— to the somewhat provincial Manor, and he joyously shared these old friends with his new Monkton neighbors, thus bringing an extreme amount of pleasure to those locals whose talents or personalities appealed to him. No wonder his Maryland friend and neighbor Elizabeth Constable recently commented, "The social life immediately moved up a bit when he came to the county."[2]

"Where I have been happy ever since"

Naturally, hunting lured Harvey Ladew to Maryland. He first visited the Free State in the early 1920s with his bosom friends Joe and Molly Davis, with whom he had hunted on Long Island and in England. "Joe said he had heard great tales of the wonderful hunting country in Harford County and thought it would be fun to try it," Ladew reminisced. "There was at that time no organized hunt there, but Mr. John Valentine, MFH of the Radnor Hunt, brought his hounds there every season and stayed at Mr. Rush Streett's big, ramshackle farmhouse."

Ladew and the Davises arrived by car. "After leaving the well-paved streets of Baltimore," Harvey recalled, "we started out on a very bumpy country road. There were little white farm houses and near them roomy red barns." The trio finally arrived at the Streett house, where conditions bordered on the primitive. Ladew, though, called his stay there "the greatest fun" he had ever had. "It was like living in a big boarding school, with laughter and parties going on all the time." He recalled, "One evening I was in a lovely hot bath, but the fellow in the tub opposite me had come in too late for this luxury," Ladew having taken all the hot water. "One of the local Marylanders whose name it is just as well not to mention, asked my neighbor how he was enjoying his bath and the answer was, 'Not at all. It is very cold.' 'Oh,' said our friend, who had warmed himself very thoroughly with a lot of Scotch, 'I'll fix that for you.' He reached up and took a lamp off one of the brackets and tossed it into his friend's bath. There was of course an explosion. The unfortunate fellow was unhurt, just very frightened. I was out of my tub in an instant as I feared I might share the same fate."

On another night "a lot of the younger fox hunters went to a Hunt Ball." On returning, Ladew's great friend Florence Loew expressed her desire for a glass of milk. There was none to be had in the icebox, but, since "everyone was in good spirits and a lot of good spirit was in them," of course someone "suggested that

"Perfectly Delightful"

Farmington, c. 1920, the "big, ramshackle farmhouse" that served as the first headquarters of the Harford Hunt Club.

they go out to the nearest pasture and drive a cow" into the house. "This idea was accepted with enthusiasm." They found a cow, herded her inside, and then, "roaring with laughter," determined to milk her "by the light of matches. This proved impossible and the cow added her moos to the general racket." The party then "decided to shove the animal into Childs Frick's cubicle." Frick, the man who had asked Ladew to bring back a Persian wild ass from Arabia in 1922, grew "furious" at the disturbance and "with great difficulty pushed the poor animal backwards out of the room." Finally, "the roaring, dishevelled and rather drunken boys retired for a few hours sleep" before the morning hunt. "We were all very young in those days and, I suppose, very foolish."

Despite—or perhaps because of—such carryings on, Ladew spent more and more of his hunting time in Maryland and less and less in New York. The changing face of Long Island certainly played a part in this incremental relocation, for he wrote that even back in the twenties the country around Brookville and Westbury "was beginning to be very built up."[3] In fact, a 1933 issue of *Polo* magazine dismissed the Meadow Brook country as "restricted in size, overburdened with houses, intersected by highways."[4] In addition, Ladew, by now used to galloping over the hills and through the valleys of England, began to find Long Island "very flat." By way of contrast, a contemporary *Sunpapers* article noted that Harford's rolling terrain "might be set down in the famed English country and nothing would seem amiss." "What a natural wonderful country I found in Harford," Ladew wrote. "Cattle grazed contentedly in lush green pasture land. There were still many snake fences to be seen. There was not a strand of wire anywhere. . . . It was a foxhunter's earthly heaven."

And there was the Harford Hunt Club, organized in 1912 and incorporated in 1915 through the efforts of John Rush Streett, his brother-in-law Frank Bonsal, Eugene Levering Jr., and John R. Valentine. As Ladew noted, hounds and horses were kept at Farmington, the Streett farm, which covered some 400 acres along Pocock Road and Jarrettsville Pike. In 1915, Bonsal, who lived nearby at Verdant Valley Farm, and Valentine agreed to serve as joint masters and accepted a present of fifteen pairs of hounds, given to the new club by the more venerable Green Spring Valley Hunt Club.[5]

The Harford Hunt gradually attracted a cosmopolitan collection of chasers of the fox from New York, Pennsylvania, and New Jersey. This infusion of "outside" wealth enriched the club, enabling it to purchase the farm and farmhouse outright for forty thousand dollars in 1927. Members thereupon embarked on a massive building program: they added an annex to the old dwelling, erected new stables, a bank barn, a mess hall, grooms' quarters, huntsman's cottage, two tenant houses, and spacious kennels. Several members, perhaps weary of the carryings-on in the clubhouse, erected private bungalows of their own on the club grounds. Among this number one finds Long Islanders Ambrose Clark, Harry Nicholas, and Harvey S. Ladew, who designed and built himself a one-story, hipped-roof cottage he named the Cloister. Complete with gently columned entrance, graceful south-facing bow window, picket fences, hound-and-fox weather vane, and a long arcaded service wing, Harvey's bungalow synthesizes 1920s equine charm.

Increasingly enamored of the Maryland countryside, on November 29, 1929, Ladew took title to a little more than 200 acres of Harford County farmland.[6] The bulk of the property, known as the "Scarff Farm," conveniently bordered the Hunt Club's holdings. The *New York World*, in a column called "This and That about Society," breathlessly (if erroneously) told its readers that "Harvey Ladew, well known sportsman, ha[d] purchased a plantation on the Eastern Shore of Maryland." Continuing, the paper opined, "Hardly a more delightful spot could be found in the country than this graceful, picturesque countryside that has so far been undisturbed by progress." Warming to its subject, the paper gushed, "Food is plentiful and of the best, the climate is temperate [and] a ride to the hounds on the Eastern Shore is full of good, exciting chases through woods where the holly and mistletoe grow and sometimes even along the shoreline of the Chesapeake, with the air filled with the tang of the sea." At the risk of injecting a note of pedantry, one must point out that although that description of the Eastern Shore rings true, the only problem is that My Lady's Manor is nowhere near the Eastern Shore: one would have to ride some distance from Ladew's farm to get a whiff of "the tang of the sea"!

Ladew enjoyed the region's association with the British peerage—but in his own, witty way. He told of meeting one visiting woman rider on a hunt: "We hacked home together. As we neared my house she stopped to read one of the roadside signs put up by the historical society. It gave the very attractive name of the part of the country in which I live, 'My Lady's Manor,' and told that some ten thousand acres here had been given to Lady Baltimore by her husband in 1700. After reading this, my new acquaintance remarked, 'Oh. I suppose Lord Baltimore wanted to save the taxes!'"

Harvey was not the only non–Free Stater to find Maryland attractive. In the 1920s, the *Sunpapers* reported that Harford County might soon "boast a tax list resembling a page from the *New York Social Register*," since sportsmen had "accumulated thousands of acres" and were "remodeling ancient farmhouses and building stables." "Metropolitan society is settling down in a quiet Maryland countryside." His fellow New Yorker Bryce Wing (at whose wedding he served as an usher) purchased 162 acres across Pocock Road from the hunt club in 1928 and erected a beautiful brick five-part dwelling in the best neo-Georgian tradition. Chalmers Wood, Thomas Eastman, and Laddie Stanford, all New York friends, also began riding with the Harford Hunt, joining such indigenous sportsmen as Alexander Griswold, Edna Parlett, and the Lurman Stewarts.

Edward S. Voss, another Long Islander, purchased the Atlanta Hall farm, whose hundreds of acres lay just south of Ladew's holdings. Voss, a watercolorist of some note, made his particular contribution to the club. Determined to improve the quality of hounds, he imported bitches "from some of the finest English packs," observed *Sports Illustrated*.[7] The club's legendary huntsman Dallas Leith recalled, "Mr. Voss liked English hounds and he brought over quite a few. The Duke of Beaufort gave him some [including] a real good bitch, Dauntless. We bred Dauntless to Middleburg Red River and her pups turned out pretty good, 'specially one we called Daring." Voss then sent Daring back to England via the liner *Queen Mary* as a thank-you gift to the duke (he "had a little argument with the dockmaster about the 'special permission'"), and the duke "thought Darin' was *outstandin'*. He was so proud of her he wrote a letter about her to the head of the MFH Association of America."[8]

On buying the farm, Ladew sold his place in Long Island. He then sold his hunt club bungalow to Chalmers Wood, moved from the bungalow to a cottage on the Pleasant Valley farm, and started to work on his new house—"where I have been happy ever since," he wrote in the 1960s.[9]

Ladew liked to decry the primitive condition of his new house. "It was in shambles," he told his friend Susan Sage in a 1970 interview, "and the only garden consisted of a couple of old lilac bushes."[10] But whether he knew it or not, while the house may have been a ruin in 1929, in its day it was a showplace. For he had bought the Scarff Farm; he had bought a piece of history.

He purchased the property from the heirs of Joshua H. Scarff, who had died there in 1885. Tracing the history of the Scarffs takes one back to the mists of colonial Maryland, for generations of the family had prospered on farms that covered the fertile hills and valleys of north central Maryland. In 1814 the federal government taxed Joshua's ancestor Henry Scarff III on "one Dwelling House of Wood, one story 20 feet x 15," as well as "one Shed Room 14 x 9," "one Kitchen of Wood 10 x 15," "one barn of wood 24 x 16," a frame stable and corn house, and two stone structures, a meat house (12′ x 19′), a springhouse (12′ x 10′), and 178 acres. In all, land and buildings were valued at $1,044. The "dwelling house" and "kitchen" almost certainly refer to the present office and dining room; the existing stone springhouse could well be the one mentioned in 1814; and it is possible that the frame shed, standing in 1814, became Ladew's card room in the 1930s. In addition, Scarff owned "two male slaves between the ages of 12 and 50" valued together at $600. Since there was no mention of a quarter, one assumes they lived in the house or in the "shed room."

Scarff had inherited his holdings from his farming father, Henry Scarff II, who had inherited the land and buildings from *his* farming father, Henry I. Henry III, however, not satisfied with profits derived from the plow, would earn himself at least a footnote or two in the state's economic and industrial history. He saw a crying need to bring the upper county up to date financially and convinced his neighbors to establish a bank, which he and they did in 1869. That bank, now named the Jarrettsville Federal Savings and Loan, was the first in Harford County. Scarff, who served as the bank's first president, said he wanted an institution where local people could "entrust their savings" and one that would "encourage home ownership." The bank, which made its first loan (to James Nelson for $400) in January 1870, has been quietly meeting that need for more than a century.[11]

The prosperous Scarff also helped pioneer the nascent American iron industry. In the early 1800s, he recognized that his lands contained valuable mineral deposits, and he arranged to sell iron ore to the La Grange Iron Works, an enterprise on Deer Creek just north of the present Rocks State Park. Scarff and a few others also started an iron industry of their own, the Sarah Furnace, located on the west bank of Winters Run near Scarff's farm. According to Alva Mary Amoss and Alice Harlan Remsburg, in their delightful booklet *The Gateway*, "Harford had the natural resources for the iron industry: red clay containing iron; quantities of wood for charcoal; waterpower; and labor." Since the new Republic had a great need for domestically produced iron, small furnaces such as Scarff's opened throughout the East. Amoss and Remsburg note that "Sarah Furnace was a self-sufficient community" with its own general store, post office, blacksmith shop, cobbler shop, schoolhouse, and residences. At the furnace's peak, Scarff's workers annually transformed 3,000 tons of iron ore valued at $5,250 into 1,100 tons of pig iron worth $28,600.[12]

In the mid-nineteenth century, entrepreneurs discovered large iron deposits in the Midwest, thus rendering small East Coast furnaces such as Sarah obsolete and inefficient. Accordingly, in the 1840s, Scarff and his partners sold their interest in the operation. But, note Amoss and Remsburg, in its day Sarah Furnace "played a role in the early iron industry in the United States and was a step toward the highly scientific furnaces established near the Great Lakes." The furnace closed for good shortly after the Civil War, and the land was divided into the 100- and 200-acre farms that still characterize the area today.

Scarff used some of his iron-forged wealth to enlarge the frame farmhouse of his ancestors by building a large stair hall/double-parlor addition along the north wall of the old dwelling. In massing and detail, this addition bears close resemblance to double-parlor residences put up in Harford and Baltimore Counties in the 1820s and 1830s such as Woodside, built for Dr. Joshua Wilson in 1823, and the Reverend William Finney's Oak Farm of 1821.

When Henry Scarff III died in 1844, he bequeathed three thousand dollars in cash to his daughter, Julia Ann Jarrett, and left the rest of his holdings to his sons, James K. and Joshua H. Scarff, to "share and share alike." Joshua eventually bought out his brother and lived at Pleasant Valley in some style. For instance, he probably made some additions to his inherited dwelling, for the distinctive attic windows, with their Chinese Chippendale paning, bear close similarity to attic windows found in Hidden Valley Farm, a brick house built in 1855 by Joshua Green. The 1897 *Portrait and Biographical Record of Cecil and Harford Counties* describes Green as a man whose "success in the farming and dairy business [made him] one of the richest farmers in the district,"[13] and it seems likely that he and Scarff, then rolling in industrial wealth, could have hired the same artisan to embellish their residences with similar stylish attic windows.

Scarff continued the agricultural traditions of his ancestors, and his estate inventory, made on his death in September 1885, shows ox carts, "dairy fixtures," wagons, "miscellaneous farm tools," "potatoes in the ground, estimated value $25," four mules, a yoke of oxen, twenty-three hogs and pigs, nineteen sheep, one bull, sixteen cows, four hives of bees ($2), and "Hay in two Hay Houses, $250." His inventory also includes a room-by-room breakdown of the house, and the spaces match up precisely with the spaces in the dwelling Ladew bought: parlor, hall, dining room, and kitchen (all on the ground floor), as well as four bedrooms, a garret room, a "hall leading to the garret," and a full cellar.

Joshua Scarff evidently possessed a certain noblesse oblige, fitting to one whose family had enjoyed local prominence for generations, and graciously gave some land to the local Methodists, on which they built the present Ebenezer Church. Continuing this magnanimity in his will, Joshua instructed his sons to take care of "the colored woman who [lived with him], Ann Williams, and her son Benjamin Williams" should they become "disabled from age or disease." He also freed his son Charles from a five-hundred-dollar note, left two hundred dollars to another son, Dr. John Scarff, six hundred dollars to one daughter ("Sally E. Wiley, wife of Dr. Wiley"), and parcels of land to other children.

"THE DISTINCT PERSONAL EXPRESSION OF ITS OWNER'S TASTE WAS NEVER DILUTED"

Although Harvey Ladew described the Scarffs as "a nice old farm family," he wrote that when he bought their admittedly "handsome" residence in 1929, it looked a little tired: "there was no plumbing, no electricity, no heat."[14] Finding an architect who could bring new life to the old house didn't prove difficult, since he had the perfect person at hand, James W. O'Connor. The two had already enjoyed one immensely successful collaboration, when O'Connor assisted in remodeling the Box in Brookville for Ladew a decade earlier. And, not to be overlooked, O'Connor had also worked for Ladew's Grace in-laws and, in fact, through marriage had Grace associations of his own.

Although the bulk of O'Connor's practice lay in commissions from the Roman Catholic Church, including scores of buildings for the Archdiocese of New York and an elaborate assemblage for Manhattan College at 242nd Street,[15] he found special pleasure in designing a series of Long Island country houses. He viewed these jobs "as a treat," according to his daughter-in-law, and he earned a certain respect in the field, too, for a book titled *The Mansions of Long Island* describes these estates as the work of "top architects, James O'Connor, in particular."[16]

The best American country house designers in the 1920s and 1930s—including Lawrence Hall Fowler in Baltimore, William Lawrence Bottomley in New York and Virginia, Mellor & Meigs in Philadelphia, Julia Morgan in California, and of course that "top" architect O'Connor—caused something of a revolution in taste. Whereas the previous generation borrowed styles in a freewheeling way—building a Loire Valley château here, a Tuscan villa there—O'Connor and his contemporaries deplored the nineteenth-century mansions that were "Italian, French, Japanese, anything!" He and his peers welcomed "the return to a simpler tradition."[17] They felt, as Bottomley said in a 1929 interview—the very year Harvey Ladew bought his Harford County farm—that a new (or remodeled) country house "should fit its setting" and "its character should reflect the best cultural traditions of the locality." Accordingly, they studied indigenous building styles and created new houses within those idioms. As Fiske Kimball, Thomas Jefferson scholar and director of the Philadelphia Museum of Art, wrote in his 1919 pioneering work on the subject, "modern" country house architects favored "the conscious revival or perpetuation of local traditions of style, materials, and workmanship." This is especially true, wrote Bottomley, in the American South, where country house architecture is "among the finest things we have" because "it is still vital."[18]

Even a cursory examination of O'Connor's work shows that he wholeheartedly embraced this new way of thinking. He himself stated his thoughts on the subject in print: "There was no doubt in my mind as to the style of the house," he wrote of one commission. "[Thus while] houses of French and Spanish type may look well in certain localities, for this Long Island landscape, to my mind at least, Georgian architecture is entirely suitable and appropriate."[19] The houses he designed underscore his words and range from a sprawling yet symmetrical neo-Georgian mansion for J. P. Grace near Great Neck (with eight bedrooms and an eleven-room servants' wing) to a series of relatively small frame cottages in the towns of Syosset, Locust Valley, and Brookville.[20]

Actually, even though O'Connor created the spaces and shells at Ladew's Pleasant Valley house, the project might best be viewed as a group effort, since decorators Billy Baldwin, Jean Levy, and Ruby Ross Wood (wife of Harvey's hunting companion Chalmers Wood) offered advice for the interiors, and Harvey S. Ladew, éminence grise, loomed over it all. For it is important to bear in mind, notwithstanding the international renown of those decorators and architect, that the rooms really were, in fact, essentially the creation of Ladew himself. Billy Baldwin has written that when Ladew asked Jean Levy to join the team, Harvey told him he hoped he would not be insulted. Baldwin replied that this did not insult him at all and expected that he "could probably learn a lot from Jean Levy." "Yes," said Ladew, "and me, too. You can learn a lot from me as well." Baldwin added that "this was no idle jest because Harvey was constantly traveling, honestly remembering, and never forgetting anything he saw which made an impression. Consequently, the decoration of what had begun as an old unpretentious farmhouse turned into quite a remarkable performance."[21]

Ladew and his co-workers created a house whose interior "atmosphere came from England, principally the 18th century," but they did not copy any single structure. Instead they fashioned their own interpretation of the style, thereby creating an original work of art which is forever stamped with Ladew's own unique personality and reflects his—and only his—interests. For instance, Harvey insisted that they "keep the signature of the fox everywhere," which explains the fox heads in the Chippendale mirrors in the parlor as well as the ubiquitous stirrup cups, boot racks, and hunting horns. In sum, "no matter how large it [the house] got the distinct personal expression of its owner's taste was never diluted."

One old friend has noted, "Everywhere there appears his love of a mixture of all times and nationalities, quite like 18th century England—an empire of findings

To the original Scarff farmhouse Ladew and his architect, James O'Connor, first added a service wing and garage, which appear to the right in this 1930s hunting scene. Interestingly, a few years later Ladew placed his topiary hounds about where the hounds in the foreground are panting.

gathered from all over the world. And that house had the rarest of all elements—and that was *wit*. I do not mean that he was 'winking' at you, but I do mean that there was humor, especially in the pictures and objects. This quality is rampant in the gardens as well."

The Ladew/O'Connor/Baldwin/Wood/Levy group moved quickly, and Augusta Owen Patterson, house and garden editor for *Town & Country*, gave a progress report on their work in the magazine's May 1936 issue. Ladew, with O'Connor, "spent a summer," she noted, "subtracting what was wrong and adding what is right with a tact which would reconcile the most querulous antiquarian to the changes." During those months, "Mr. O'Connor added a consistent American-Greek Revival portico on the driveway front and a columned porch of the Mount Vernon type on the side which overlooks the private steeplechase course" Ladew had just constructed. O'Connor also built a lower and smaller-scale service wing at right angles to the old house and connected it to an old smokehouse (transformed into Ladew's pressing room) by means of a small colonnade. In this new wing, O'Connor killed several design birds with one architectural stone: the small scale of the addition instantly distinguishes it from the original structure and emphasizes its inferior status, while its placement serves to act as "a division between the house lawn and stable yard." A photograph taken to accompany Patterson's article shows that Ladew originally placed a round pigeon house in one of the ancient locust trees that until 1997 dominated the "racetrack" side of the house, and Patterson deemed the bird cote "as picturesque in Maryland as in Provincial France."[22] Ladew and O'Connor also built a four-bay garage (with chauffeur's quarters above) at the end of—and perpendicular to—the service wing.

Moving into the dining room (the Scarffs' kitchen), Patterson noted that "when a boarded fireplace [was] opened up, the room began to show possibilities." She particularly liked the fact that it had "not been kept self-consciously early-maplewood-and-cherry-American" but instead suggested "that reasonable contrast found in numerous old houses in this country." She singled out for spe-

White doves ruffling their feathers at one of Ladew's bird cotes, 1935: "as picturesque," wrote Town & Country, *"in Maryland as in Provincial France."*

cial praise the "hunting panel from an old gouache screen which exactly fitted the space between the two windows." (Plate 15.) As for the furniture, she likened Ladew to George Washington, who "had his best furniture sent over from the mother country," and she particularly admired Ladew's "set of six arm chairs": "almost as hard to find as a genuine Clouet."[23]

When Patterson guided her readers' attention to the original farmhouse dining room, she, yielding to the romance of the place, observed "a hutch" between kitchen and dining room, "through which they passed the fried chicken and cider on feast days" in the eighteenth century. Ladew and O'Connor decided to turn the old dining room into an office. Dissatisfied with the original walls because they weren't "folksy" enough, the two demolished an old "cow barn," carefully saving the pine planks, which they "waxed to a mellow tone,"[24] and then used the boards to panel the room. Poking around an antique shop during one of his English hunting seasons, Ladew found three painted-glass windows, became instantly smitten with their horses-and-hounds motifs, and bought them. He then had to carry them "practically under his arm to the ship" for the voyage home and then store them in New York until the day came when he could build "a bay to do them honor." That day came after he bought his Maryland farm, and the windows immediately found a place of honor in his new office.

To the north of that oldest part of the house lay Henry Scarff III's Federal-era addition of stair hall and double parlor. The New Yorkers liked the stair but fused the small double parlors into one great space. O'Connor gave unity to the expanded room by means of a new cornice and mantle (based on originals in Annapolis's famed Hammond-Harwood House) and pedimented door surrounds, based on nothing but the client's imagination and good taste. The cornice and fireplace certainly show that architect and client played the game well. Scarff built his addition a half century after the Hammond-Harwood House was completed. Thus, these details, if they had been original to the house, would at best be called "*retarditaire*," and Ladew and O'Connor knew that it would have taken a generation or so (i.e., to the years when Henry Scarff went abuilding) for such fashionably designed woodwork to filter out from the colonial capital to the hinterland. How correct Billy Baldwin was when he observed that his friend Harvey "never could resist a little fantasy."

When it came time to paint the drawing room, Baldwin recalled that Ladew chose "a beautiful lemon color with a heavy glazing, and for the dado between the chairrail and the baseboard Miss Levy had worked out an extraordinary, almost chocolate-colored paint with a very soft glaze." The wall opposite the fireplace was dominated, then as now, by a massive mahogany breakfront, home to Ladew's ever expanding collection of Staffordshire, Chelsea, and Meissen foxes. Much of the floor space east of the fireplace was given over to a grand piano. Leith Griswold, whose parents, Jack and Arabella Symington, visited Ladew's house virtually from the moment he purchased it, said that "Harvey really didn't play the piano all that well. He kept it so friends could use it when they stayed with him." Friends? "Oh, friends like Cole Porter."[25]

As if anticipating the importance horticulture would play in Pleasant Valley's future history, Ladew and his decorators selected other furnishings and fabrics to make the living room, as *Town & Country* put it, "as full of color as a July garden." Augusta Owen Patterson particularly admired "all the delphinium blues" of the rug as well as the chintzes, which displayed "the best grade of red and white hollyhocks on a well-covered background." Baldwin wrote that "once, when in England, Harvey's eyes feasted upon a miracle of material that he innocently bought for curtains" for the new drawing room. This "miracle" material was a heavy dark serge; to set it off, Ladew crafted valances of "four pieces of eighteenth-century dark blue heavy needlepoint in the design of festoons with multicolored flowers, quite bold in color and in scale, with tiebacks of large wool tassels in the same colors as the valances."[26]

Ladew and his crew had progressed that far when the depression hit him hard. Baldwin accurately recalled that "there was no limit to the amount of money he spent on the things to eat. There was caviar all the time [and] champagne flowed like water,"[27] but the bad news from Wall Street began to unravel the seams in

Ladew and O'Connor fused two poky parlors to create this majestic space. The cornice and mantel were adapted from those in the Hammond-Harwood House, Annapolis. Town & Country *praised the room's fabrics for being "as full of color as a July garden."*

even Ladew's deep pockets and he had to put further plans for the house on hold. "Ultimately," *Town & Country* told its readers in 1936, "another wing will be thrown out, with the little summer house serving as a terminal."[28] Or as Ladew explained, "I had just finished restoring the main house and had excavated for an addition to it when the dark days of the depression arrived. I remember that I planted a privet hedge around the gaping hole and I used to tell friends, 'This isn't a sunken garden. It's a depressed garden.'"[29]

After about a year, his finances had bounced back enough for work to resume. Now—elated at having beaten the depression—Ladew gave full vent to his love of England and to his sense of fantasy. "Harvey's taste was really more European than American," one friend observed. "He used lots of white which was Syrie Maugham's influence, and he loved the idea of lacquered walls, which he borrowed from the great English country houses."[30] Ladew had met Syrie Maugham in England and kept himself well versed in her theories and ideas.

As if to memorialize the sixteenth-century country houses he knew so well from his English hunting seasons, Ladew decided to build an "Elizabethan Room" onto his new dwelling. He found wood paneling for the room in a shop on London's Dover Street and often proudly stated that he had the only Elizabethan Room he'd ever seen that wasn't dark oak. Instead, it was pine; not only that, it was a pine that didn't even grow in England: "We think it came in the 15th century from Scandinavia," the dealer told him. Ladew found a pattern for the room's plaster ceiling in an old book, had it made in New York, and then shipped it down to Maryland in sheets. Harford County artisans fashioned the windows and stone sills.[31] Baldwin wrote that of all the spaces in Ladew's Maryland house, he himself especially "liked the small Elizabethan room where we very often had breakfast."[32]

On yet another of his hunting trips, Ladew bought a rare oval Chippendale-style partners' desk. (The only one like it in the world, according to Harvey, belongs to the Knightsbridge barracks of the Royal Horse Guards.) When he brought this treasure back to America, he found it was too big and unusually shaped for the drawing room or the tiny office and moaned that he didn't know where to put it. According to legend, Bryce Wing said, "Well, Harvey, I suggest you build a room around it," which is precisely what he did. The room, north of the Elizabethan Room, has always been known as the Oval Library, in deference to the splendid desk that caused and determined the space's very existence.

Ladew purchased a deeply carved pine door for the library on yet another of his English hunting holidays. (Plate 16.) He and a friend, Arthur Vernay, who ran a fashionable antique shop in New York, found a pair of doors that came from West Haley Hall, a country house in Norfolk. The doors were "attributed to William Kent," according to an article Ladew clipped from a magazine. Each man bought one of the pair for about one hundred pounds; Ladew installed his in his new library; Vernay resold his for twenty-five hundred dollars, a sum Ladew liked to quote.

Ladew designed his Oval Library, one of the "100 Most Beautiful Rooms in America," around an oval partners' desk.

Opposite the pine entrance door, Ladew placed an extremely rare green-and-white marble fireplace, made in Ireland and elaborately carved with motifs near to Harvey's heart, including fox heads at each end and a hunting scene in the center. Ladew said he bought the mantel "from old man Crowther" at Syon Lodge; he purchased the wonderful mantel clock, which plays four hunting tunes on the hour, at a shop in Shepard's Market, near his favorite London flat.[33] In 1958, Helen Comstock included the library, generally regarded as the triumph of the house, in her book *One Hundred Most Beautiful Rooms in America*. The magazine *Town & Country* agreed and called the library "the best room in the house . . . , designed and built by James O'Connor in the style of the Adam brothers."[34]

Upstairs, Ladew and his decorating team continued the themes they began on the ground floor: stick to the idea of regionalism (if at all convenient), give in to whimsy (if at all possible), and, when stylistically stymied, keep English country house eclecticism as a guiding light. At the head of the main stair, they combined two tiny chambers to create a spacious suite of bedroom, bathroom, and sitting room for the Squire of Pleasant Valley. They also concocted a made-to-order aubergine-colored lacquer paint for the new little sitting room, and that may have been the first time this hue had been seen on American walls. Baldwin wrote that "Harvey's rooms never looked 'new' or 'decorated' even the day they were finished—and they took years to finish! . . . These rooms grew like gardens

In the 1930s Ladew greatly expanded the old Scarff farmhouse (the three-story section and the low wing to its right). *He kept the original mid-nineteenth-century attic windows with their distinctive Chippendale-style paning and added a service wing (out of picture to* right) *by 1936 and a wing for his Elizabethan Room and Oval Library (*left) *the following year. Here he greets Mrs. Joseph Cooper, c. 1960.*

and often became like unweeded gardens, especially his own rooms which were a mass of chaos and confusion, evidences of his catholic taste and insatiable intelligent curiosity."[35]

Patricia Corey recently recalled that Uncle Harvey kept the guest room above the office (across the hall and down three steps from his suite) for her special use. She remembered that he had been keenly following the restoration of Monticello, and, as a gesture to the multifaceted Jefferson, the multifaceted Ladew designed an alcove bed for the room, aware that such beds were favorites of the Virginian's.[36]

When it came time to decorate the bedroom suite over the Oval Library, rooms he created for his sister's more or less exclusive use, he called in his decorator friend Marian Hall for help. Yet here, too, the client refused to be bossed by professionals and made real contributions of his own. He painted a whimsical "morning glory" wallpaper on the north (fireplace) wall, for example, and he installed a fanciful trompe l'oeil panel in the suite's dressing room. He had discovered the panel at Park Bernet and bought it ("I think it's so beautiful"), but he

"Perfectly Delightful"

didn't know what to do with it. He tried it in his studio for a while but then "found it would just fit on the wall" of the dressing room and moved it there. Actually, "just" stretches the point, for it proved smaller than the allocated space, and he "had to paint the gap." He did give Hall free rein in the adjacent bathroom, and she made it an outstanding example of art deco design, complete with beveled mirrors, shiny exposed chromium fittings, and hard-edged colored glass details. Harvey did, however, manage to equip the otherwise stylish space—Astaire and Rogers would have loved it—with his signature bathroom touch, a dull metal box for his beloved English toilet paper.

Ladew and his team had completed the new/old house by early 1937, just in time for him to leave it and fly to England for another season of hunting. An issue of the *Tatler* from that year noted that the Squire of Pleasant Valley was arriving in London at the end of the month. "Like many of his countrymen he has taken a flat on the Coronation route." The magazine went on to describe "Harvey's delightful farmhouse thirty miles from Baltimore" and its "elegant oval library for fifteen hundred books."

While working on his own residence, Ladew also spruced up the farm's aging barns to make them suitable for his prized Thoroughbreds and revamped the

Ladew and Billy Baldwin painted the walls of the MFH's upstairs sitting room aubergine, possibly the first time the color appeared in an American house.

grounds to make them suitable to his idiosyncratic needs, adding, for instance, a private race track in the valley east of the house. (His adventures in the garden are discussed in Chapter 4.) Keenly sensitive to the pleasures of the palate, he laid out an herb garden near the house and, beyond the new garage, a garden, where he grew his favorite French vegetables. Finally, he turned the eastern third of one barn into "an enormous studio with a couple of guestrooms. Harvey used to give small dinner dances in the studio, which were wonderful because of the great scale of the room."[37]

The house—indeed, the entire property—also provided him with a superb set. He himself then filled the set with "actors"—his many, varied friends—and everyone saw to it that the drama ran continuously, as Pleasant Valley Farm rollicked in virtually nonstop entertaining. All sorts of people "would come and stay with him in Maryland," Billy Baldwin recalled, "so there was a constant house party going on, engineered by the 'Ladew Girls.'" Baldwin explained that the term "Ladew Girls" referred to "three very old women who worked for Harvey and adored him. Margaret [Narborough] was the chef. She was Scotch, almost completely deaf, and a perfect tyrant. Mary [McKenzie] was the butler and Harvey's valet as well. Katie [Kelleher] was a wizened little woman of indeterminate age" who served the meals. "All three of those women adored Harvey and they, in turn, were adored by his friends."[38]

Ladew also obviously adored his "girls" and typically refused to think of them as being anything but flawless. He often told his sister that though the world around him was wracked by depressions, wars, and riots, fortunately, he "never worried," a blissful state of mind that required him to overlook—or to just not see—weaknesses or imperfections in those near him. For example, Billy Baldwin remembered one particular day around 1950 when he, Ladew, Horst, and Valentine Lawford were eating lunch: "We heard the most unearthly crash from the next room which sounded like what we thought was another Hiroshima, but not at all. It was simply that poor Katie had dropped an entire tray of a complete set of Waterford glass which she had just removed from the dining-room table." The decorator then made the important point that "Harvey was a naive person and he refused to believe anything he didn't want to. The sad part about Katie and the Waterford was that she had been imbibing much too generously of the juleps before lunch. Harvey said, 'Poor old Katie, she is just getting too old.' He never for a minute allowed himself to think of her as having been drunk."[39]

BECOMING "A MARYLANDER IN FACT"

A 1929 *Sunpapers* article about Ladew's purchase of Pleasant Valley Farm noted that the grantee wished "to become a Marylander in fact." Of course, while it could be argued that Harvey was far too cosmopolitan to become *anything* "in fact," he did throw himself into the Free State way of life with his usual energy and verve.

In November 1932 he hosted the first of the Harford Hunt Races at his private track, "one of the most fashionable events of the Maryland hunting and racing season," reported the *Sunday Sun*.[40] He enjoyed the experience enough to hold races again in 1933, 1934, 1937, and 1938. The outings usually featured four or five separate events including brush, hurdle, timber, and flat races. "So it is assured," wrote Baltimore society columnist "Billy Bachelor," in the *Sun*, "that Pleasant Valley Farm, the estate of Mr. Ladew, will be the mecca . . . for a great number of those whose principal interest is in equine affairs, as well as for the still greater number who like to go places and do things."

Ladew usually gave a luncheon party on racing days "at his colonial residence" (as the *Sun* called it) for the judges and a number of out-of-town friends who attended the horse show. "Tables were set on the terrace, and made a gala appearance. Bowls of scarlet sage on each long white table carried out the colors of the Harford Hunt." Sometimes these guests included friends one does not normally associate with horses, such as Edna Ferber and Moss Hart. Both, though, like their host did their best to fit in, and the *Sun* approvingly found Ferber "quite versatile at her choice of sports." But, then, as the paper observed, "When one is in the cream of America's hunting country, one must not only be 'horsey' but 'houndsy' and 'foxy' in order to enjoy every minute of the old homestead. Everyone decided Miss Ferber got a 'kick' out of her brief visit." Hart, too, endearingly draped himself in local color—literally—for a photograph taken shortly after Ladew bought the Maryland farm shows the playwright standing beside his bemused host, both in flawless pink coats and jodhpurs and equipped with horn and stuffed fox.

In 1933, Harvey accepted the demanding job of MFH for the Harford Hunt. He did so at an important point in the club's history. Partially as a depression-era economy move, on October 8, 1934, Chalmers Wood, president of the hunt, wrote to the Elkridge Hounds to propose a merger. Officers of the Elkridge, a venerable institution dating from 1878, accepted, thus forming the Elkridge-Harford Hunt. Headquartered in the Pocock Road complex, members of the new club elected Wood the first president, Charles Reeves vice president, Dean Bedford secretary, Alexander Griswold treasurer, and Harvey Ladew MFH.[41]

Ladew took his role as master seriously and even shortened his English hunting seasons in order to devote the necessary time and energy to his Elkridge-Harford duties. Dallas Leith, who served as huntsman for the club from 1938 until retiring in 1978 with the title huntsman emeritus, recalled, "[Ladew] had some of the best huntin' horses you *ever* saw. We always had good horses to ride when he was master. You couldn't beat 'em. He was a great sportsman." Asked if he found the master independent, Leith barked, "Independent! One day a friend of his got feisty when Mr. Ladew jumped all over him . . . [and] Mr. Ladew said, 'I'll send you home. I'm right even when I'm wrong.'" Leith recalled that if the master thought the horses and hounds had had enough (and "he ought to know, he hunted every day"), he would simply announce, "'Dallas, take the hounds in.' Didn't ask *anybody*. They'd had a good day and that was enough."

Ladew's work with the hunt club attracted notice from the English press,

The Mount Vernon portico as seen from the south; from it, one viewed Ladew's private steeple-chase track, which, in 1934, drew quite a crowd.

"Perfectly Delightful"

Moss Hart stayed with Ladew at Pleasant Valley Farm in the early 1930s, when a revival of Show Boat *previewed in Baltimore on its way to Broadway. Ladew wrote under this photo of Hart and him, "A Hunting We Will Go."*

which must have pleased him no end. The society columnist for the *London Daily Sketch* of February 12, 1937, for instance, noted, "Like any horsey community, Harford County is sufficient unto itself. A gracious old clubhouse, white wood with green shutters—a style you must have noticed in the movies—is surrounded by bungalows where the rich live simply, plus plenty of hot water and chicken Maryland twice a day. The state was English in the days of Lord Baltimore and it remains so." The writer deemed the Harford Hunt "as famous as the Quorn back home." "The Master, Harvey Ladew, a former Pytchley regular, owns a delightful farmhouse thirty miles from Baltimore filled with antique furniture, sporting prints, and models of stage coaches. It is far more English than anything in England."[42] One can sense the master beaming with delight at that!

The master faced his greatest challenge on April 15, 1938, when a fire ripped through the clubhouse, destroying the main part of the building as well as most of the paintings, furniture, and trophies. But members' morale remained high, and they immediately decided to rebuild. Ladew, no doubt thrilled by the thought of a new project, formed a committee consisting of himself and his friend Edna Parlett to go about the business of rebuilding. He also called in O'Connor, fresh from triumph at the Pleasant Valley library, for advice and then polled members for suggestions. (One suspects this was at most a courtesy.) Moving quickly, the threesome devised a splendid Georgian revival replacement for the old, ramshackle structure. The building proved an immediate success, and Elizabeth Ober, who covered the equestrian world for the *Sunpapers*, credited the "united efforts, good taste, and hard work" of the team for producing a "clubhouse with great charm combined with luxurious comfort."[43] Indeed, the Ladew-Parlett-O'Connor clubhouse remains, in the words of club historian, J. Rieman McIntosh, "a great asset."[44]

Having given the club a new headquarters, Ladew retired as MFH in 1939.[45] That year he also decided to discontinue racing at his farm. The club picked up the slack, though, and held a point-to-point of its own in 1940, the forerunner of the point-to-points still held annually on the first Saturday of April.[46]

Not one to limit himself in any endeavor, Harvey Ladew did not restrict his hunting to the Harford. As he wrote, he found it "always fun to have an amusing day or so with another hunt," and once he and several Harford friends vanned their horses 20 miles to William du Pont's Fair Hill estate, which sprawled over several thousand acres of Maryland, Delaware, and Pennsylvania. (Much of the property is now Fair Hill State Park.) Their host, Ladew recalled, greeted them cordially: "[He] said he hoped we would have a good day with his hounds. The hounds themselves were rather unusual. They were small and of a reddish tan but, as I knew that everything Willie did was carefully studied and perfectly arranged, I was sure this hunt would be good fun. It certainly was. Over a number of fields and a number of fences we went when suddenly we reached a field that was high above a wide main highway far below us, a highway leading to New York, filled with motor cars and trucks. Suddenly I had proof of Willie's efficiency. To my amazement he had built a bridge over the wide road and when the fox reached the bridge he turned and ran over it, the hounds and the hunt following. I think it is the most unusual thing I ever experienced hunting."

Ladew soon gave his new interest in Maryland hunting literary form, just as he had with earlier enthusiasms and as he would again—and again. He plunged into the task of writing a definitive history of hunting in the Free State, part of which appeared in *Town & Country*. In the article, he notes that although the sport dates from colonial times in Maryland, the first organized institution, the Elkridge, wasn't founded until 1878. Even so, he proudly reported that it was the second oldest in America. If the Elkridge didn't get the prize for being the oldest, it did for shaping the fashions of American hunting. For example, Ladew credited Elkridge members General George Brown and his son Alexander with introducing the now common hunting pink coat to this country.[47]

Shortly after V-J Day, Ladew penned a cheerful piece for the *Sunpapers* to celebrate the fact that the war was "over at last," and with the return of members who had been in the armed services, "normal hunting" could resume. "There is a very youthful element in our present field which is good to see and promising for the future," he wrote. "But," he added, "it does make me feel like the 'Oldest Inhabitant.' They all seem to have perfect hunting manners in deference to my great age." He also found another fact "rather depressing": "[I] realize that one of our best riders, Mrs. Ben Griswold, is now a young matron and the mother of two eligible sons (aged three and five) for I can remember her as little Leith Symington."

Late in life he planned to write a magazine article on the Maryland Hunt Cup. He got as far as the title ("Maryland's Big Day") but never completed the

Ladew (right) *attends the 1949 Preakness with* (from left) *Mrs. Spalding Lowe Jenkins and Senator and Mrs. Millard E. Tydings of Maryland.*

piece. The few roughed notes that remain make one wish he had: "The Maryland Cup—how it started" "A gay weekend in Md. House parties—luncheons and cocktail parties the day of the race. Then the Hunt Ball. A dinner dance in Baltimore. Hundreds of men in pink coats making a sight that I have hardly seen surpassed at any English Hunt Ball. The ballroom beautifully decorated and they managed to get a picture of the winning horse and rider in the owners' colours done at the last minute and hanging at the end of the ballroom." "Photos of race—the crowd on the hill—the picnic grounds. Only one race which starts at 4 o'clock. Then a rush to several big cocktail parties before rushing home to dress and motor to Baltimore. The riders are amateurs which adds to the social part of the scene as they have many friends to wish them luck and many of the horses are well known to the spectators who have hunted alongside of them in their various hunts." "Photo of Sen. Brewster's cart bringing friends to the race course. The whole countryside turns out for the race—farmers, local shopkeepers, etc." "Photo of person standing next to the biggest jump to show its height."

He thoroughly enjoyed his literary projects, even though he was fully aware of his shortcomings: "Having read a great deal of classical and modern French literature, several Spanish books, and am now stumbling halfway through Dante's Hell in the original Italian text," he confided to his sister in 1968, "I realize I am not much of a writer. I just dash along as things cross my mind."[48] In Maryland he began (but never completed) his autobiography, "Around the World in Eighty Years," and started a series of what he called "Thumb Nail Sketches," also left incomplete. One called "Gaston," though, shows promise: "Gaston is the Maitre d'Hotel at a popular New York Night Club. Fairly tall and well built, his handsome features, distinguished manners and bearing, and perfectly cut clothes give him the appearance of a foreign diplomat rather than of a waiter. In reality he *is* a diplomat, if ever there was one, for his job calls incessantly for the most delicate tact. He must know which clients should be given the choicest tables, show them to their places with just the proper degree of servility, flatter their vanity by remembering the special wines and dishes they prefer, and let them sense"—and the manuscript abruptly ends.

He even tried his hand at doggerel, and one wonders what on earth he had seen that caused him to jot down,

If asked to a Kennedy ball
To be held by Bob's pool in the fall
Among other things
You should bring water wings
And a very chic drip dry Dior.

In 1936 *Town & Country*'s Augusta Owen Patterson had the acuity to observe, "There is another side to Harvey Ladew that is redolent of anything but the stable. Of the library and studio rather. For he is as well read in French and English as a professor of either, plays the piano with considerable distinction, and . . . wields a brush or a chisel with equal dexterity. Both the house on Long Island and the new place in Monkton, Maryland, are filled with the choicest objects picked up in the course of never-ceasing travels."[49]

Thus one should not be surprised to learn that even as he immersed himself in the Maryland equestrian scene, he did not ignore his many other interests. Indeed, two of his closest Baltimore friends, Alice Garrett and Mary Wright, had no interest at all in the equine world. "Alice did not hunt and she did not ride," wrote one intimate. "I don't think she even knew what a horse looked like."[50] Ladew himself commented that Mrs. Wright and he "became friends although she did not hunt." He added, "We had a bond in common. We both loved to read and especially French books," and he faithfully lent her "the least naughty ones" from his shelves. W. H. DeCourcy Wright, the Franco-bibliophile's husband, on the other hand, "so enjoy[ed] country life and hunting that he [spent] practically all day in the saddle."[51] All this, of course, simply parallels Harvey's English experiences, for, as noted, he grew close to Osbert and Sacheverell Sitwell even though the two brothers detested the hunting set. It is all further proof of Ladew's many interests: one can almost see his mind at work, thinking as he meets someone he'd like to know better, all right, if you don't like hunting, perhaps you like music . . . or painting . . . or the theater—or travel in Arabia!

Harvey wrote that Mary Wright's family "had known Uncle B. when he was a young man," adding, "it was not difficult to figure out that she belonged to the FFBs," presumably First Families of Baltimore, his play on First Families of Virginia. Giving rein to his always ready romantic streak, he continued that he had seen and admired "her family's beautiful silver that the faithful old black slaves had saved by burying in the orchard before the D.d Yankees invaded their plantation on the Eastern Shore and also the many beautiful family portraits that had been miraculously preserved by the faithful slaves who hid them in faroff mountain caves while the War raged." Thus, he "knew that Mr. and Mrs. W. were the real thing as far as Maryland families go."

Mrs. Wright looked askance at many of Ladew's local hunting friends and once told him flat out, "You don't know the right people in Baltimore." He feebly replied that most of his fellow hunters seemed "full of Southern courtliness." Wright sniffed, "A few of them are among our oldest families but not all of them by any means," and told him, in tones that brooked no objection, "I want to give a reception for you to meet them." Ladew wrote that "she did give the reception at her lovely country place where the walls were crowded with portraits of her

"There is another side to Harvey Ladew," who is shown in his studio, c. 1950, with a statue of his favorite royal, Queen Mary, complete with one of her signature hats.

ancestors painted by Peale." Bemused, he said, "[I] felt like a debutante minus the little Victorian bouquet I should have been holding."

"Alice Garrett was a friend I always loved to see and it was great fun to go to her dinner parties," Ladew wrote. "In Baltimore one usually met the same attractive people and was apt to know just whom one would be seated by and what food we would have, for depending on the season it surely would be delicious soft crabs, wild duck, quail, or terrapin. There was nothing wrong with that, but at Alice's one never knew whom one was to sit next to—perhaps Rubenstein's lovely wife, or not impossibly Gertrude Stein." Others, such as Billy Baldwin, agreed: "Alice's house was the one place in Baltimore that I loved to go to for one never knew whom one was going to meet there. Artists, musicians, scientists, actors and actresses, ballerinas and possibly champion boxers. She cared not a

"Perfectly Delightful"

thing for what people call society and was totally bohemian. She was only interested in people who had done something or who had given the world something from their work."[52]

Alice Warder had married John Garrett, an heir to one of Baltimore's larger industrial and banking fortunes. Garrett, a career diplomat, was posted to embassies throughout the world including the Hague, Berlin, Rome, and Paris; in that last city, Alice Garrett, a fierce and intelligent patron of the arts, championed and befriended such innovative geniuses as Sergei Diaghilev of the Ballets Russes and the writer Jean Cocteau. In the 1920s, John Garrett inherited the mansion Evergreen, in Baltimore, and the couple returned there to infuse vitality into the city's sometimes moribund intellectual and artistic life. Ladew doubtless met

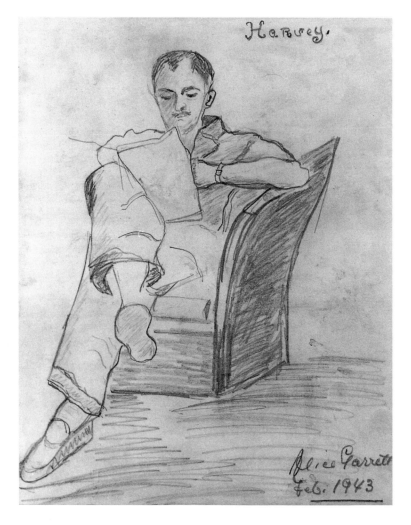

While visiting Ladew at his Florida house in February 1943, Alice Garrett made this pencil sketch of him.

the Garretts through Jack and Arabella Symington. Among the Garretts' closest friends (Arabella Symington taught Alice Garrett how to make a martini),[53] the Symingtons also figure prominently in the very first photos taken of and by Ladew at Pleasant Valley. One particularly evocative image shows host with the Symingtons, Margaret Cottman, and Colonel Powell—of Arabian trip fame—sitting on the front steps with Ladew's Scottish terrier, "Judy," curled up in front.

Harvey wrote that "Alice had a lovely little theater she had made out of a bowling alley on her grounds. It had been decorated, believe it or not, by Bakst. In the spring, Alice gave a series of concerts. A celebrated quartet would come to her place, Evergreen House, and rehearse for their coming tour for about a month." This was the Musical Arts Quartet, who stayed at Evergreen annually in the spring and fall, each time for six weeks.

Curiously, despite their scorn for the conventional and eager embrace of the experimental, neither Ladew nor Garrett had any interest in most contemporary painting. Or, rather, they had an interest in it; they simply detested it. For example, Ladew wrote that while he "greatly admired Picasso's early work, especially the artist's beautiful drawings," he felt that "his latest works were done merely to astonish the public and to make money." Around 1960 he wrote to his sister that Picasso "admitted in an interview to a reporter in *Le Figaro* that he had only painted these absurd figures with several eyes and noses because several people in the Art World who affected to understand them took them seriously and that they sold for enormous prices." (The purported interview, in fact, was a hoax, dreamed up by the futurist Giovanni Papini and published in a book of mocking falsities, called *Il libro nero*.)[54] Ladew continued to belittle cubism, and when his Maryland neighbor Elsa Voss painted a portrait of the Elkridge-Harford MFH in a decidedly neo-Picasso manner, as if to show that anyone could do it, Harvey gleefully gave it a place of prominence at Pleasant Valley and hung it right above his framed letter from the Prince of Wales.

Ladew also loved to tell of the time Garrett staged "a little art show in the Mount Vernon Club. Alice exhibited a painting in the manner of Pollock, though the color was her own, and with it there was a sign which read, 'Mrs. Garrett will do these paintings at $5.00 a yard.' She had a good sense of humor!" Richard Howland, former professor of art history at the Johns Hopkins University, tells a similar story. Howland recalled that he helped Alice Garrett create a fake Pollock, which she took with her to her suite at New York's Pierre Hotel, "where she held court in the spring of 1948." Alfred Barr, director of the Museum of Modern Art, came to pay a call on Garrett, saw the canvas, and exclaimed, "Why Alice, I didn't know you collected Pollock." Garrett responded, "I don't collect Pollocks. I make them."[55]

In addition to their mutual disdain of nonrepresentational art, Alice Garrett and Harvey Ladew shared a love of languages. He wrote that "Alice spoke French very well and read a great deal of it. She also had a limited knowledge of German."

Picasso held no charms for Ladew, and he was delighted when Elsa Voss painted this spoof "cubist" portrait of the MFH.

Then, "when Mr. Garrett became Ambassador to Italy, she made a serious study of Italian. Alice felt that her Italian was pretty good and she decided to give a lecture at the Embassy on Picasso. Unfortunately her Italian was anything but perfect and at one point she came out by mistake with a very pornographic word which, of course, convulsed her distinguished audience, though they were too polite to roar with laughter. However the story was at once repeated to the King and he begged Alice to repeat the lecture for his benefit. She again came out with the four letter word, and the King was hardly able to conceal his amusement." (In a similar vein, Ladew loved to tell of the time one purported balletomane told George Balanchine how much she enjoyed his staging of *Les Syphillis*.)

He wrote that Alice Garrett also "went in" for dancing: "But that was before my Baltimore days so I never saw her perform." On one memorable evening, "Alice and Billy [Baldwin] were doing a wild flamenco and making a lot of noise stamping in time to the music and clicking castanets when Alice tripped and pulled Billy down with her. She was quite a large woman, and she landed on his leg and broke it so the dance ended and he was carried off to the Hopkins Hospital. In later years he would sometimes pull up his trouser legs and exhibit two scars saying, 'This one is where Alice Garrett broke my leg and this one is where Harvey Ladew's dog bit me.'"

However briefly Garrett and Ladew were able to enjoy each other's company (she died in 1952), they did so intensely. They even managed to contribute something of their own to the art scene of their adopted city, for they organized what *Town & Country* called "the first exhibition of hunting and racing art ever brought together in America."[56] The duo prepared a catalog for the show, to which Ladew, who served as chairman (Garrett as vice chair), contributed a foreword. The exhibition, on view at the Baltimore Museum of Art from April 21 through May 10, 1939, consisted of 136 paintings, prints, and sculptures. Ladew lent his own fine Munnings (*The Afternoon Ride*) and coaxed others from his family, including his niece Patricia Grace's Landseer, *Hunter and Dog*. He acquired the bulk from his hunting friends in Maryland and New York: Ambrose Clark, the E. F. Huttons, the S. Lurman Stewarts, Edward S. Voss, C. V. Whitney, and Bryce Wing all lent canvases. Victor Emanuel, who had purchased the Ghost back in the 1920s, contributed four watercolors by Lionel Edwards which must have filled Harvey with nostalgia: *The Quorn at Quenby*, *Meet of the Pytchley at Rockingham Castle*, *The Pytchley near Oxendon Church*, and *The Cottesmore away from Ranksboro Gorge*.

Although Ladew, in the role of gentleman amateur, pretended not to take his painting seriously, he did enter one landscape, *5602 Charles Street Avenue*, in the Peale Museum's 1948 "Life in Baltimore" exhibition. He felt confident enough to price it at three hundred dollars, making it the show's second-costliest item. (Only the distinguished painter Herman Maril asked a higher price, five hundred dollars; most artists suggested one hundred dollars for their works.) The judges awarded Ladew Honorable Mention, commenting, "Although he has been painting for many years, this is his first public showing." Another local critic commented that the canvas "would make a good cover for the *New Yorker*."[57]

Harvey's artistic creativity led him to explore many media. Rather late in his life he developed an interest in papier-mâché and enjoyed creating shadow boxes, one of which he placed prominently on the second-floor landing of his Maryland house. He also enjoyed making shadow-box portraits of friends including Consuelo Balsan and Ambrose Clark. He once proudly told an interviewer that the owner of a shop in Palm Beach, the Incurable Collector, liked his portrait of Clark and put it in his shop window for a week. "He wanted me to make twelve of them because he said a lot of people wanted to buy them." Flattered, he considered it until his friend Susan Sage wisely counseled against it, telling him, "You can't do twelve pieces—you'd be bored to death."[58]

He also maintained the interest in illustration he had developed as a boy. For decades he drew his own deliciously ironic Christmas cards and whimsical cocktail invitations. His love of costume parties has been noted, and he found his true artistic heaven when he could not only organize a fancy dress party but design the

In 1939 Alice Garrett and Ladew curated the first exhibition of sporting art held in America at the Baltimore Museum of Art. Museum staff staged this publicity photo of Harvey.

invitations for it as well. This he did for the "Beard and Bustle Ball" and, perhaps most memorably, for a revel called "The Last Night of Pompeii, a Roman Orgy." The "Roman" invitation noted that "Supper and Bachanalian [*sic*] Refreshments" would be served and requested guests to "wear suitable costumes of the Roman Era—B.C. 287–525 A.D." (Elizabeth ["Bibber"] Dow recalls that he asked her and a few other Maryland matrons "to dress as Vestal Virgins.")[59] He went all out for the Roman Orgy and spent days constructing a papier-mâché volcano, complete with orange tissue-paper lava that was pushed into the air by small fans and illuminated by red spotlights.[60] No wonder Elizabeth Constable recently commented, "He had great ideas for parties. Wonderful parties." She also recalled that the diva Rosa Ponselle often sang at these gatherings: "Harvey just wanted his friends to have a good time."[61]

A keen follower of fashion, possibly in emulation of his Uncle Berry, "The King of the Dudes," Harvey was delighted to be included among the list of Baltimore's ten best-dressed men for 1949. Mary H. Cadwalader, who met Ladew on the hunting field in the late thirties, recalled him as "so very stylish and terribly concerned about his fawn britches."[62] His papers contain several lists of clothes to bring to Florida; on one he wrote, "Look over old shirts—get possible new ones—try Billy's shirt maker," Billy Baldwin not surprisingly having a tailor who earned the discriminating Ladew's respect. "People always said that a little bit of extra color was applied to the skin tone of his face," one friend reminisced, "and I think it's likely true."[63]

5602 Charles Street Avenue. *This Ladew painting won honorable mention at the Peale Museum's "Life in Baltimore" exhibition of 1948.*

"Harvey was terribly bright," wrote one intimate, "and I think he found that there were not too many Baltimoreans up to his level of cleverness and awareness."[64] Ladew himself recognized the somewhat conservative nature of most of his Maryland neighbors. He described one luncheon at which he arrived with particularly "shocking" guests. The story went back to a weekend he had spent with Alice Astor, "then married to von Hofmannsthal, whose father had written the libretto for *Der Rosenkavalier*," at the Astor place on the Hudson, "a very large grim-looking mansion." There he met Iris Tree, "a very attractive and witty and unusual person" who "designed her own clothes and looked exactly like the lovely DuMaurier illustrations for Trilby." He also met Count Friedrich Ledebur, "a handsome Viennese about seven feet tall with flowing brown hair," who, according to Ladew's friends Horst and Valentine Lawford, "was in charge of part of the Austrian government's herd of Lippizaner horses,"[65] which must have pleased the foxhunting Marylander.

Tree and Ledebur eventually married and, en route to Mexico for their honeymoon, spent a few days with Harvey at Pleasant Valley. Their host had been asked by some neighbors for Sunday brunch; he inquired if he could bring his newlywed houseguests and was assured they would be welcome. But then he "began to wonder how the Ledeburs would dress for this party as they often wore the most extraordinary clothes." "However it didn't worry me too much as I knew that the Baltimoreans, though they might be startled, would be amused." When the three assembled to drive to the party, Ladew breathed a sigh, for while "their costumes that day were certainly a bit unusual—they might have been even more so." The *graf* had chosen a traditional green Austrian loden jacket and lederhosen, and the *graffin* appeared "covered in American Indian jewelry—big hunks of turquoise set in silver—bracelets, buckles and a necklace." Ladew added, "We made, I thought, quite an imposing entrance and for a moment all conversation in the room ceased." "We just thought he was great fun," said Leith Griswold. "He had the most marvelous sense of humor. You'd even call it a sense of the ridiculous,"

Ladew loved to draw up party invitations and fill them with subjects as disparate as a somewhat bibulous rope jumper, an unhappy Vesuvius, and topiary martinis.

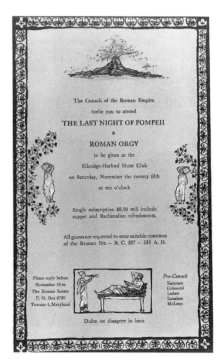

The only thing Ladew enjoyed more than designing invitations for parties was attending the parties themselves. Here he appears with Leith Symington Griswold (Mrs. Benjamin III) at the "Night in Siam" gala held to honor Alexander Brown Griswold—an expert on Asian art, Ladew's friend and neighbor, and Leith Griswold's brother-in-law.

and added that one "never came away" from a visit to Pleasant Valley "without having something to remember, to laugh about."[66]

Ladew's friends Gilbert and Kitty Miller certainly left many memories. He was one of the leading Broadway producers of the time and also owned a theater in London's West End. In these projects, he benefited enormously from his wife's wealth, which she inherited from her father, banker Jules Bache. In many ways, Kitty Miller, as iconoclastic as Ladew himself, eclipsed her husband in the field of "being a character." Billy Baldwin, who met the Millers in 1945, wrote, "She represented all the reasons I wanted to be in New York. I admired her taste enormously." He added that Kitty Miller kept extremely high standards and "there were very few people that passed her judgement." But Harvey did, and the Millers often visited him. While they were probably more visually acceptable to Ladew's Maryland neighbors than the Ledeburs had been—"Kitty never did anything but dress to the teeth. It would never have occurred to her, not even once in her life,

"Perfectly Delightful"

to think of being seen without being perfectly and beautifully dressed"—one can't quite picture her in the de rigueur rural costume of muddy tweeds.[67]

Nor can one so picture another of Harvey's closest intimates, the renowned photographer Horst. Born in Germany in 1906, Horst moved to Paris in 1930 to study architecture and design with Le Corbusier.[68] Soon after, he met the internationally known photographer Hoyningen-Huene, who made him his favorite model and protégé. Taking up the camera himself, Horst became one of the most respected and famous fashion photographers of the century. Ladew and Horst and Baldwin met in the 1930s when Baldwin was beginning his career as a decorator and Horst had just started as a photographer for *Vogue*. (Baldwin wrote that he often admired Horst "playing tennis outside my apartment windows, which looked upon the Sutton Place tennis courts.")[69] Horst, who had become an American citizen, served with the army in World War II. Discharged in 1945, the photographer bought 7 acres of land of the old Tiffany estate in Oyster Bay, Long Island—very near Ladew's former haunts. He then designed a house for himself, "with the help of an American architect, Ed Tauch—Cole Porter's great friend." He also laid out extensive gardens for the property: "Early in 1947, standing at his garden door, Horst envisaged three *allées*, fanning out from the house like the radii of a semicircle"; each allée would "be lined with evergreen trees and shrubs of varying shape and foliage and contrasting shades of green." The garden immediately took shape, for "friends of all kinds pitched in with gifts of trees, shrubs, and plants."[70]

One wonders if Ladew was among these friends. Horst frequently stayed at Ladew's houses, as guest books attest. Did he admire the allées at Pleasant Valley Farm? Did he listen to Ladew when he proclaimed his love for them?[71] The photographer also kept flocks of "cooing fantail pigeons," as well as "four miniature dachshunds, perpetually asking to be taken hunting rabbits."[72] Interestingly, Ladew raised fantail pigeons at his Maryland farm and, in his later years, became absolutely besotted with a dachshund bitch of his own, as discussed in Chapter 6.

"AMERICAN EQUERRY TO HIS ROYAL HIGHNESS"

While based at Pleasant Valley, Ladew renewed his acquaintanceship with the Prince of Wales, an acquaintanceship that grew into a true friendship, especially after the prince's marriage to Wallis Warfield Simpson. Of course, Ladew, like most people in the Western world, had closely followed the courtship between the prince and Mrs. Simpson. But, unlike most people, Ladew did so through friends who knew the principal players. One of these was Myrtle Farquharson, head of the Scots clan Farquar. "I was very fond of Myrtle and always enjoyed seeing her when I was in London," he wrote. "She had many friends, all interesting or amusing—artists, actors, musicians, writers. Her parties were the greatest fun."

Because Queen Victoria had purchased the Balmoral estate from the Farquars, the head of the family was always supposed to be on tap to welcome the royal family when they migrated to their Highland retreat. Once in 1936 the prince invited Wallis Simpson to visit Balmoral, and she accepted. Only later did an equerry point out that His Royal Highness had previously agreed to open a hospital in Aberdeen on the day Simpson was due. The prince decided to skip the hospital, infuriating most of Scotland. Ladew wrote, "The day before Wallis was to arrive [area residents] painted very insulting things on many of the walls she and the prince would pass on the way to Balmoral. I will not say the kind of things they plastered

Harvey loved this photograph of his friend Myrtle Farquharson, head of the Clan Farquar, dressed as Little Bo-Peep at a party given by Cecil Beaton.

on the walls but will leave it to the reader's imagination. Myrtle told me that she and the mayor had to paint out the remarks the evening before Edward drove down to the station to meet his future wife."

After Edward's abdication, most of his English society "friends" dropped him and began to curry favor with the new King George VI. Osbert Sitwell observed this. While the intellectual Sitwell had viewed the former Prince of Wales's decidedly middlebrow life with contempt, the hypocrisy he witnessed in 1936–37 truly appalled him, and "in a fit of bad temper, he took to his bed and wrote what proved to be the most effective poetic satire of his life," a diatribe in verse called "Rat Week." Because the poem "was so libellous," Sitwell knew "it could not possibly be published until long after his death." But a few privately typed copies "made the rounds of Society and soon everybody who mattered seems to have seen it." Ladew, whose open, easygoing nature left no room for hypocrisy of any sort, was of course among the select few to receive a copy. He kept his and carefully pasted it into a scrapbook. (Harvey's social-climbing nemesis Chips Channon, on the other hand, dismissed it in his diary: "Osbert Sitwell has written a poem, not a very good one, called 'Rat Week' in which he lampoons many deserving people.")[73] Transcribed, with the mistakes in punctuation one would expect in something amateurishly produced, the verses read, in part:

Where are the friends of yesterday
   That fawned on Him,
     That flattered Her;
Where are the friends of yesterday,
   Submitting to His every whim,
     Offering praise of Her as myrrh
To Him?
 . . . That nameless, faceless raucous gang,
   Who graced Balmoral's Coburg towers,
Danced to the gramaphone, and sang
   Within the battlemented bowers
     Of dear Fort Belvedere;
     Oh, do they never shed a tear?

 . . . Oh, do they never shed a tear
   Remembering the King, their martyr,
     And how they led him to the brink
   In rodent eagerness to barter
     All English history for a drink?

What do they say, that jolly crew?
Oh . . . Her they hardly know,

They never found her really *nice*
(And here the sickened cock crew thrice):
Him they had never thought quite sane,
But weak, and obstinate, and vain;
Think of the pipe; that yachting trip!
    They'd said so then ("Say when, Say when")—
The rats sneak from the sinking ship.
What do they say that jolly crew,
    So new and brave and free and easy,
What do they say that jolly crew,
    Who must make even Judas queasy?

Questions regarding a role for the former king, newly created duke of Windsor, puzzled the British government for years. Rumors ran rampant (and still do). Some even speculated that the Windsors "would establish a part-time residence in Maryland and that David had appealed to Harvey to find him a dovecote in the Maryland hunting country, with stabling." Many "were already picturing 'Handsome Harvey' as American Equerry to His Royal Highness."[74]

In October 1941, shortly before the Windsors made their first visit to Baltimore after their marriage, Myrtle Farquharson happened to be spending a weekend at Pleasant Valley. Ladew, capable of seeing humor in virtually any situation, wrote that he "suddenly thought she might be amused to see the little house in Biddle Street where [Wallis Warfield] had lived with her mother." They drove into town and were surprised to see that the house had been turned into a museum. "As we reached the door we saw flags flying and on either side large plaster figures of the British lion and unicorn. A big sign hung above all this. On it was written 'Home of the Former Wallis Warfield. Admission Fifty Cents.' This was so unexpected that our laughter started even before we entered the museum."

The curator greeted them and took them into a double parlor, where they viewed "a portrait of the duke which had probably been painted by a second rate sign painter" over one fireplace and "a portrait of Wallis (by the same sign painter)" over the other fireplace. The lady guide pointed out various objects, including some glass purported to be "the Black Prince's celebrated diamond." The visitors started to giggle, only to receive the reprimand, "Please don't laugh. This is a shrine." They composed themselves and went upstairs. When they reached the bathroom, their guide asked Myrtle "if she would care to step into Wallis's bathtub as it was supposed to be lucky to make a wish in it. Myrtle declined with thanks." Then Harvey, in a burst of inspiration, asked their guide to bring the replica crown and scepter from downstairs. "As I had brought a camera along, I suggested that Myrtle put on the crown and sit on the 'throne' and that I would take her photo. She was delighted with the idea and said she could hardly wait to send it to the Duke of Kent and Marina." The guide cooperated, but, wrote Ladew,

"The bathroom was so small I had to climb into the tub to take the picture—but I did not make a wish."

When the royal couple arrived in Baltimore for their official visit, they found a town turned on its head. Ladew, of course, relished every detail. (He loved to tell of one dinner party when "Wallis astonished the party by wearing a short evening gown—Baltimoreans were very displeased!") Baltimore's Mayor Jackson decided to throw two receptions, a massive one on October 10 at City Hall and a somewhat smaller one on the 13th at the Baltimore Country Club. On the 10th the *Sun* published the page-long list of, as the paper captioned it, "the 'lucky eight hundred'" invited to meet the distinguished duo at City Hall. Ladew wrote that he was "one of the 'lucky ones.'" He recalled, "There were so many present that we were not all privileged to shake hands with the Royal Pair, but we passed them in a long line, bowing and smiling. Our famous opera star, Rosa Ponselle, sang 'The Star-Spangled Banner,' but not 'God Save the King,' as of course he had abdicated."

A few days before the couple arrived, Ladew got a phone call from a cousin of the duchess, Dorothea Deford, inviting him to a small party she and her husband, Robert, were having on October 12. ("She was only able to ask three of her friends . . . and had been given a list of the others to invite.") He accepted and was told, "I will send you the instructions tomorrow." Ladew "found this rather odd," as he had "been around quite a lot and thought [he] knew how to behave on most occasions." Anyway, these "instructions" arrived in the next day's mail:

Be here promptly at 7:45 P.M. Sunday Oct 12th.
After you are presented to His Highness he is addressed as Sir.
The Duchess as Duchess.
No one may be seated unless His Highness requests it.
Gentlemen to wear dinner coat and black tie.
No discussion of war or politics unless His Highness opens the subject.
Gentlemen follow the ladies after dinner to the drawing room—then retire.
Later when they return no one may be seated unless His Highness requests it.
Do not address His Highness unless he addresses you.
His Highness requests that no risqué stories be told.

One can only imagine Harvey's eyebrows rising as he read the list. Naturally, he decided to have some fun. The day of the party he sent a box of flowers to his hostess and telephoned to regret that he could not attend. Whatever was the matter? Was he deathly ill? No, came the reply. "But I have been thinking over the 'Instructions' and I realize that I could not sit through a dinner party without telling one dirty story." After a terrible pause, Deford "had a laugh," and the tension was broken.

He arrived at the Defords—at 7:45 as ordered—and found that the other

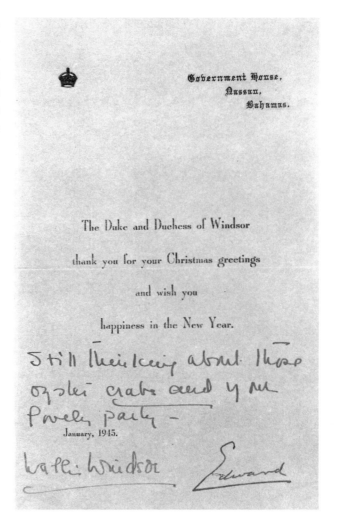

Government House,
Nassau,
Bahamas.

The Duke and Duchess of Windsor

thank you for your Christmas greetings

and wish you

happiness in the New Year.

Still thinking about those
oysters crabs and your
lovely party –

January, 1945.

Wallis Windsor   Edward

guests consisted of "quite elderly prominent dowagers and before long their legs
gave way and they wanted to sit down." Eventually a door was flung open, and
Edward and Wallis entered. "The duke was very polite and charming but he knew
no one in the room until he reached me. He at once asked me about many of his
American hunting friends." While the two men chatted away, "the whole procession was held up so long that it began to be quite embarrassing." Harvey continued, "Wallis, whom I had never met, came along next with Mr. Deford and at
length, I feel sure, gave Edward a push in the derriere."

Ladew and the Windsors visited each other frequently in the 1940s and 1950s,
sometimes in Baltimore, sometimes in Florida, sometimes in the Bahamas, where
the duke served as governor (Ladew wrote that "Wallis compared Nassau to Elba"),
and sometimes, as is discussed in Chapter 5, in France. Once the couple stayed
with Harvey at Pleasant Valley. During that visit, he decided to treat his guests to
a real country dinner of quail. But then he realized that his cook didn't know how

to deal with gamebirds. Panic set in until he recalled that his neighbors Benjamin and Leith Griswold employed a woman who was wonderful with quail, so he phoned to ask if he could borrow the great cook. "He didn't want us," Mrs. Griswold still remarks. "He only wanted our cook!"

Like most who met her, the duchess left Ladew enchanted. "Wallis could tell the most wonderful entertaining stories and had beautiful manners," one admirer wrote, adding that there were two particular fields "in which she excelled and in which she had no peer: those were her clothes and her knowledge of food," the latter being "fit for the gods."[75] Perhaps that explains why one of Harvey's favorite possessions was his copy of *The Duchess of Windsor's Cookbook*, which the duchess had inscribed to him. Ladew loved the book and annotated it with check marks to indicate favorite recipes. He wondered, though, if it ought to have been called the *duchess's* cookbook after she had told him, "I only gave them one recipe. It was how to cook one of those giant 300-pound turtles." "Well," Ladew grinned to his new friend, "that will be very useful to the American housewife."

4

"The art of personality"

In her survey of contemporary horticulture, historian Jane Brown stated that the overarching theme of her book "is that the 20th century garden is the expression of a very personal art, the art of personality."[1] How true that is for the Maryland garden of Harvey Ladew, a man who dedicated his life to "the art of personality." Decades of absorption in the fine arts had so developed his sense of aesthetics that he approached his landscapes not only with a knowledge of plants and soil but with an artist's eye for the refinements of color of flower and form of foliage. Nothing in his garden is there by accident. He chose each plant, each "room," each vista, for a reason, and when he chose—and rejected—he drew from a wealth of personal knowledge and a well-developed aesthetic sensibility.

Moreover, although he always lamented his lack of formal education—"I was taken out of school every year and dragged abroad," he wrote more than once—he brought to life a keen intellect, bouncy sense of humor, and an eagerness to see, read, and experience as much of the world and its pleasures as he could. In 1929 not many people in America had seen as much of the world as he had—living as a houseguest of a maharajah, taking a camel caravan across Arabia, weekending in the stateliest of Britain's stately homes, hosting a Belgian prince, matching wits with the witty. He had lived a life as no one else had, distilled these experiences, and gave them vegetable form in his Maryland garden: of course his garden, like his house, would be as wonderful, as unique, and as *civilized* as he was. "The visitor leaves with a bounce in her step," a writer for the Garden Club of America gushed after a visit to Ladew's green—and white and yellow and pink—wonderland in 1966.[2] One hopes that readers will leave this account of his garden making with a bounce in their hearts and will agree with him that life indeed can be "perfectly delightful."

Even admitting that gardening is a deeply personal art—and that Harvey Ladew's garden is truly *sui generis*—garden historians should not treat horticultural works as isolated creations. Instead, one can and should make connections and trace influences. Just as Gertrude Jekyll "learnt much from the little gardens" that helped make English waysides the "prettiest in the temperate world"—"One can scarcely go into the smallest cottage garden without learning or observing something new"[3]—so should one today acknowledge Harvey Ladew's debt to Jekyll, to other great early-twentieth-century English gardeners and publications, and to the verdant masterpieces of the Italian Renaissance. These debts will, of necessity, be general in nature since it is usually impossible—and rarely useful—to look for exact "quotations," for similar individual features. Rather, one may reasonably look for similar sensibilities.

ARTS AND CRAFTS INSPIRATION

Ladew often said that he inherited his love of gardening from his parents. If so, he must have meant a *general* love of gardening and plants and out-of-doors life. He emphatically did not inherit—that is to say, copy—the manner of gardening he knew as a boy on Long Island. He grew up when fashionable gardens in America and England were characterized by formal bedding out and by great masses of tender plants clumped together for summer effect, a lavish process family greenhouses made possible. But in his Maryland garden, Ladew embraced a totally different approach to horticulture. And the history of what and how he planted in Maryland crystallizes, in effect, a massive change that took place in gardening first in England, then in America, and then throughout the world.

Unprecedented wealth coupled with undreamed-of technological advances allowed those who grew rich in the nineteenth century to create gardens that truly showed off, and to an extent mirrored, their vast fortunes. Carpet bedding, vividly hued parterres, grandiose French-inspired landscaping, exotic plants brought back from distant lands and wintered over in hothouses constructed as flamboyant skeletons of intricately cast iron, all evinced the power and wealth of England during Victoria's reign and in the first full generation of post–Civil War America.

But as the century drew to its sooty close, a few sensitive souls began to rebel. This sort of gardening, they felt, may have been fine for municipal parks, but it lacked hominess. Thus a new generation of English gardeners, headed by Gertrude Jekyll, William Robinson, and Reginald Blomfield, turned for inspiration to the all-but-forgotten cottage gardens of preindustrial England. Their training, taste, education, and (it must be said) own private fortunes resulted in gardens more sophisticated and varied than any cottager would have made, but their inspiration was clear and acknowledged.

William Robinson led the attack on Victorian planting plans with his many best-selling books, such as *The English Flower Garden* (1883), "perhaps the most influential gardening book ever published in England."[4] In his highly important tomes, Robinson thundered against bedding out and rigid axes and suggested they be replaced with vines clambering up walls and with folksy mixings of native

The gardens at Harvey Ladew's parents' Long Island estate, Elsinore. After growing up among such plantings, Ladew spent the rest of his life in stylistic rebellion against them.

plants, old roses, hardy shrubs, bulbs, and herbaceous perennials.[5] Many felt this reaction a bit extreme, and in 1892 Reginald Blomfield published *The Formal Garden in England* to counter Robinson's polemic. Blomfield, a disciple of William Morris, Richard Norman Shaw, and other leaders of the arts and crafts movement, rebelled against the excesses of high Victoriana but had an equal distaste for the overly romantic "naturalness" Robinson advocated. A trained architect, Blomfield stressed the importance of structure in a garden[6] and had little patience for blindly scientific botanists. "To plan out a garden the knowledge necessary is that of design," he stated, "not the best method of growing a giant gooseberry."[7] He and other arts and crafts adherents looked back for inspiration to Tudor and Stuart gardens with their walled enclosures, sculpture, summerhouses, terraces, water, and allées. Topiary became another integral part of arts and crafts gardens (one authority has called the movement "topiary's saviour")[8] because of its associations with gardens of the past.

TOPIA, TOPIARIUS, AND TOPIARY

Harvey Ladew may not have been "topiary's saviour," but he certainly became topiary's New World champion. "I was surprised to find that the majority of Americans have never even heard of the word 'topiary,'" Ladew wrote, and he set

"Perfectly Delightful"

about to right that wrong. He created, as the Garden Club of America phrased it in 1971, "the finest topiary garden in America made without professional help," and its fame spread throughout the nation.[9] He related, "Once when I was motoring to Florida, I stopped off in Charleston. A charming young woman I met there said to me, 'I saw your lovely garden in Maryland. Those wonderful hedges and all that beautiful Tipperary.' It was hard to keep from laughing and I thought I would never again hear anything as funny about my garden but when I reached Palm Beach a man said to me, 'Mr. Ladew, your name came up the other night at a dinner party. I understand you are the authority on Utopia.'" And as so frequently happened with his interests, Ladew put down his gardening thoughts on paper; the urge within him to create was so strong that he not only created individual objects in various disciplines but also felt compelled to create a verbal history of the disciplines themselves. Thus he roughed out (and unfortunately never completed) an analysis of his own work with clipped shrubs. He called it "An American Topiary Garden," and in it he also presented some how-to tips for those who wished to make their own yew peacocks.

He began by defining topiary as "the cutting and trimming of shrubs such as

In the early twentieth century, gardeners in England used clipped yew hedges to form room gardens, such as these at Rous Lench Court in Worcestershire. In 1922 Christopher Hussey praised Rous Lench in Ladew's favorite magazine, Country Life *(where this photograph first appeared), for "its green allées" and "clean-cut lines," which "fill us with expectation as to what lies around the next corner."*

Harvey Ladew's undated pencil-sketch portrait of himself in his "American Topiary Garden."

cypress, box, or yew into regular and ornamental shapes." He explained, "It is usually applied to the cutting of trees into urns, vases, birds, and other fantastic shapes which were common at the end of the 17th century and through the 18th, but it also embraces the more restrained art necessary for the laying out of a formal garden. Yew and holly trees cut into fantastic shapes may still be seen in old fashioned cottage or farmhouse gardens in England. The Latin *topiarius* meant an ornamental or landscape gardener, and was formed from *topia*, a term specifically employed for landscape painting used as a mural decoration in Roman houses."

To illustrate his subject's ancient origins, he pointed out "traces of it" in Egyptian temples and tomb paintings: "But they seem to be only of low hedges bordering walks and flower gardens. Pliny's garden in Tuscany was famous for the great amount of 'living sculpture' it contained and, in a letter to his friend Apollinaris, he gives a very detailed description of it. His garden was full of topiary pieces—wonderfully designed and beautifully clipped birds, animals, a fleet of ships, and many other things."

Ladew then skipped several hundred years to point out that

in the 17th century in France and Holland topiary had become a highly developed art. Nurserymen produced well designed complicated pieces such as ships in full sail, battling warriors, and other amusing subjects. Wealthy young Englishmen on the "Grand Tour," armed with letters of introduction and often accompanied by a tutor qualified to lecture them on art, architecture, and the customs of the countries they visited, were enthusiastic over the so-called "French Gardens" they saw which were so much brighter and gayer than the gardens of their own country. The gardens contained turf or brick paths edged with boxwood, fountains, sundials, stone or marble benches shaded by flowering trees, and flower beds in which amusing and interesting topiary pieces were placed. The travellers began to ship quantities of topiary statuary back for the gardens of their dwellings and could hardly wait to get home and start the gardens that would be such a novelty and so diverting to their friends. So, before long Topiary and French Gardens became the fashion in England. English nursery gardeners soon began to produce equally amusing ones and some of their lists still exist or can be found in old books on topiary gardening.

Artistic styles change, and Ladew told his readers that by the eighteenth century topiary had become unfashionable. "A crusade against formal gardening and the art of topiary in particular was led by many prominent men such as Addison, Pope, and Horace Walpole[, who] began to write against these foreign introductions which they referred to as 'Tortured Trees.' They felt that nature was more beautiful when it was left alone and that shrubs should never be sheared into shapes for which they were not intended. Whole gardens were plowed up and one looked out on a more rural scene."

Harvey S. Ladew then modestly entered the fray on behalf of the topiarists. He couldn't resist taking a few shots at the "absurd and ludicrous" acts of the "so-called Landscape Gardener" extremists, who "transplanted large trees to give the effect of the edge of a forest and even planted dead trees among them to give it a more realistic look." He had great fun ridiculing "several of the more enterprising noblemen" of the eighteenth century who built sham caves in their gardens and populated the caves with hired "hermits," usually villagers or farmers paid to sit at the entrance to the caves "in a sack-cloth garment tied with a rope." "When darkness came the hermit would rush back to his family in the village, stopping at the local pub for a few beers with his amused friends. One hermit who had a large family in the village was not as saintly as he looked. He was having an affair with one of the dairy maids and when it was discovered he was promptly defrocked and discharged."

GERTRUDE JEKYLL AND THE "MATURE PERSON'S ART"

Squabbles over matters of garden taste weren't restricted to the eighteenth century, however. When Blomfield published his book, for instance, he set Robinson's blood boiling—precisely as he had hoped. To retaliate, Robinson wrote a scathing attack on Blomfield's work, dismissing it as "nonsense." He also sneered,

"There is plenty for the architect to do without spoiling our gardens."[10] All-out war loomed. But then entered the eminently sensible peacemaker, Gertrude Jekyll. Writing in the *Edinburgh Review* of 1896, she despaired that things had "taken on a somewhat bitter and personal tone" and added that as far as Robinson and Blomfield go, "both are right and both are wrong."[11]

In words that might be used to describe Ladew, Jekyll has been described as one who embraced "gardening as a mature person's art": "For it to become such an art it has to demonstrate a distillation of personal knowledge and experience as well as an awareness of aspects of history beyond the personal span. Miss Jekyll allowed all her tastes and knowledge to flow freely into her gardening." Moreover, and just like Ladew, Jekyll "was one of those people who never stopped learning, for whom enthusiasm over some new project or interest became an essential part of her life."[12]

She was also, by training and inclination, a follower of the arts and crafts movement; in fact, "her arts and crafts connections continue[d] right through her gardening career."[13] Jekyll expressed her ideas in writing and produced a dozen best-selling and still useful books, including *Wood and Garden* (1899), *Home and Garden* (1900), *Water and Wall Gardens* (1901), *Some English Flower Gardens* (1904), and *Colour in the Flower Garden* (1908). A talented watercolorist, Jekyll explored the possibilities inherent in single-color gardens, that is, "a garden for blue plants, or a white garden." Intrigued, she wrote, "I have in mind a whole series of gardens of restricted colouring."[14]

All the favored arts and crafts features would probably have become visually muddled had it not been for one of the movement's more important revivals, namely, "room gardens" composed of a series of adjoining discreet spaces formed by hedges and walls. As Penelope Hobhouse pointed out, "Renaissance garden rooms became the inspiration for Edwardian garden designers, and provided the English gardener with the greatest and most inspired opportunities for planting."[15] The very phrase "room gardens" implies architectural origins. "The garden is seen as a continuation of the rooms of the house, almost a series of separate out-door rooms, each of which is self-contained and performs a separate function," wrote Hermann Muthesius in his three-volume study *The English House* of 1904–5.[16]

Plant specialists liked garden rooms because the style allowed them to create separate spaces for water gardens, alpine gardens, rose gardens, and (another arts and crafts creation) herbaceous borders. Within each "room," plants could be given their proper soil and microclimate without threatening the unity of the whole.[17] Room gardens had another advantage, too, namely, that of allowing their owners to derive utmost enjoyment from a particular plant's period of bloom: they could gaze rapturously at the early spring wildflower "room," say, during its brief peak and then forget about it until the next year and move on to the iris "room" or the rose "room." (As Jekyll put it in *Colour Schemes for the Flower Garden*, a successful garden is one that "devotes certain borders for certain times of the year," each "region [to] be bright from one to three months.")[18] In addition to their practical use of dividing up spaces, room gardens and "their seclusion," writes Clive Aslet, held special appeal to romantic arts and crafts devotees, who easily succumbed to the charms of these "places of quiet and retirement, sheltered from the outside world by a yew hedge or a tapestry of roses and jasmine against the garden wall."[19]

Such gardens, for all their seeming spontaneity, required careful thought and planning. Or, as Blomfield phrased it, "Our art does not allow us to leave our conception sketched out. The idea must be thought out to the uttermost."[20] The noted poet and gardener V. Sackville-West agreed and described the typical arts and crafts garden as possessing "a kind of haphazard luxuriance, which of course comes neither by hap nor hazard at all."[21] Harvey Ladew, too, believed in careful planning: before a single spade of earth was turned over at Pleasant Valley, he had made a detailed plasticine model of how the finished 22 acres of gardens would look.

Sir Herbert Baker, in whose London flat T. E. Lawrence lived when Ladew met him in the early 1920s, said that Jekyll's "outstanding possession was her power to see, as a poet, the best simple English country life of her day."[22] Jekyll's *Gardens for Small Country Houses* of 1912, jointly written with Sir Lawrence Weaver, depicts a countryside "covered with gardens of a uniform charm and order, all with straight lines and convenient enclosures, with fine brick and stonework and lush planting, all speaking the good sense and propriety that she regarded as English virtues."[23] How this impression must have appealed to Ladew, with his love of Old World order and charm! In 1947, while hunting in Ireland, he wrote his sister, "I really do love being here. I am not happy unless I can be in some part of the 'old world' part of the year. I love everything about this little village—the jingling carts, the donkeys, flocks of goats wandering through the main street."[24]

Jekyll began her own epochal garden, Munstead Wood, in the early 1880s. While the word "epochal" may sound extreme, Jane Brown has stated flat out that "twentieth century English gardening begins at Gertrude Jekyll's Munstead Wood," a 15-acre, triangular-shaped plot in Surrey. Brown has written that Jekyll "was well equipped for the making of her undoubted masterpiece. She had been learning about plants all her life, she had made careful notes about all the flowers and gardens she had seen all over Europe and England, and through her painting . . . she had developed her taste and understanding of colour and design." To ensure that "every part of the garden was capable of giving a virtuoso performance at distinct times of the year," Jekyll planned Munstead as "a series of garden rooms . . . disposed according to soil, shelter, and purpose": there was a spring garden, a hidden garden, a June garden, a summer-peaking herbaceous border, and a primrose garden.[25] She also designed a gold garden and wrote in the *Jour-*

Gertrude Jekyll's Munstead Wood, photographed for Country Life *in 1897 and used in her* Gardens for Small Country Houses.

nal of the Royal Horticultural Society that she hoped entering it "even on the dullest day, [would] be like coming into sunshine."[26]

In 1885 the forty-five-year-old Jekyll met the twenty-year-old architect Edwin Lutyens when she asked him to design a new house for her at Munstead Wood. He agreed immediately. "Here was a garden awaiting its house," he wrote, "a setting where already the innermost integrities of arts and craft held sway."[27] The seemingly odd couple then embarked on one of the most felicitous partnerships in the history of English art, wherein he designed superb country houses and she devised perfectly complementary planting plans for them. Their houses and gardens, even when new, seemed to glow with the patina of age partly because both members of the team believed in thoroughly integrating brick and mortar with

"Perfectly Delightful"

leaf and bloom and felt, in Lutyens's famous phrase, that "the house should spring out of the briar bush." They gained their first commission in 1893, and the pair eventually worked together on more than a hundred different projects, so many that the words "a Lutyens house in a Jekyll garden" became a catchphrase to denote the very best Edwardian England could offer. Even today, scholars recognize that Lutyens houses and Jekyll gardens represent "the art of living elegantly, but not opulently, in the country—merely with everything of the best."[28]

Great Dixter in Sussex certainly ranks among the finest of these creations. Laid out in 1911 for Nathaniel Lloyd, "an authority of topiary,"[29] the 6-acre garden consists of a series of compartments. Near the medieval timbered house (with its Lutyens additions), they take the form of small, formal rooms punctuated by topiary birds and abstract shapes and linked by terraces, walls, paths, and yew

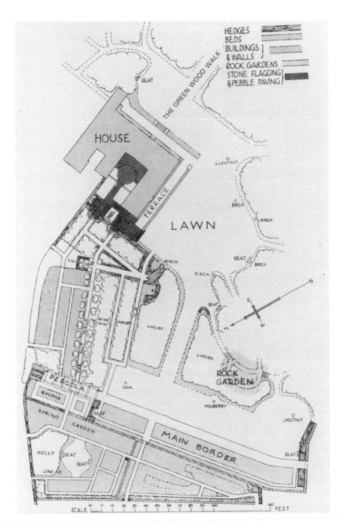

Munstead Wood plan as it appeared in Gardens for Small Country Houses.

hedges. Then come spaces given over to the garden's famous herbaceous borders, now planted by Dixter's current owner, Lloyd's son, Christopher, in his intentionally shocking experimental color schemes.[30]

For decades, Christopher Lloyd has used his regular column in the magazine *Country Life* to describe his gardening efforts at Dixter. Founded in 1897 by the romantic, country-loving businessman Edward Hudson, *Country Life* devotes its pages to celebrating "a strong love of England and all things English." It also "supported the Arts and Crafts lifestyle in every aspect and brought the Arts and Crafts garden to life."[31] It certainly brought the creations of Jekyll and Lutyens to life, for Hudson deeply admired their work. He commissioned three large houses from Lutyens and one garden from Jekyll, saw to it that his magazine carried dozens of lavishly illustrated articles praising their latest successes,[32] and published her wonderful *Gardens for Small Country Houses*. (The book was republished in 1997 with the title *Arts and Crafts Gardens*.)

"A KIND OF CULT"

The revolution sparked by Jekyll and Lutyens—whose flames *Country Life* fanned each week—changed garden design throughout England. Russell Page, one of the preeminent post–World War II gardeners, observed that "a kind of cult developed around these gardens and there are hundreds of charming small gardens made by keen amateurs who derive their inspiration from these . . . models."[33] Indeed, the pair's influence crossed the Channel (and ocean) and can be traced to France and America.

For example, it is a certainty that Harvey Ladew knew of Lutyens and Jekyll: he was a virtual lifelong subscriber to *Country Life*, he dutifully clipped many of Christopher Lloyd's columns, and his much used copy of *Gardens for Small Country Houses* (6th ed., 1927) still graces the shelves at Pleasant Valley Farm. Moreover, during his prolonged hunting stays in England, he made careful examination of British houses and their arts and crafts gardens, with their rooms, topiary, and single-color flower beds. "We used to hunt right through those estates in England," Leith Griswold recalled. "There was topiary all over them. We had to dodge trees and jump hedges." She particularly noted that she, her parents, and Ladew hunted over the grounds of Compton Wynates, a seat of Ladew's friend the marquess of Northampton and a place famous for its ancient topiaries.[34]

Country Life's current editor, Clive Aslet, called Rodmarton Manor in Gloucestershire "the best" of these Jekyll-Lutyens–influenced gardens in England.[35] As designed by Ernest Barnsley for the Hon. Claude Biddulph, the stone house, perhaps "the purest symbol of the arts and crafts movement," gives the impression of a group of cottages around a green, while the garden (also by Barnsley) functions as "a series of rooms and walks around the house." To Jane Brown, the composition reads as "a marvelous unwinding of a reel of images, with memories of William Morris, of *The Formal Garden in England*, of Lutyens and Miss Jekyll . . . all brought to life."[36] Rodmarton's present owners, Mary and Anthony Biddulph,[37] have recently restored this superb creation, trimming up the topiary yew peacocks and re-creating garden rooms (a white and gray border, a winter garden, a garden given over to sweet-scented plants) all framed by high stone walls and yew hedges.

Brown notes that "in response to Miss Jekyll's writings, one-colour gardens had a fling" in early-twentieth-century England.[38] The more notable of these include the double borders of blues, grays, and purples Norah Lindsay designed to flank Sir Philip Sassoon's swimming pool at Trent Park in Middlesex and the gardens Ladew's nemesis Chips Channon planned at Kelvedon Hall in Essex: "one of the earliest in England to be planted in a series of outdoor rooms, each enclosed in a hedge or wall, and each planted in its own subtly devised colour scheme."[39] They also include the blue borders and gold borders Lord and Lady Iveagh laid out at Pyrford Court in Surrey. The Iveaghs, who knew Jekyll personally, designed their own house and laid out their own gardens, which they completed in 1927 — just in time for their American friend and houseguest Harvey Ladew to study and photograph them during his 1930 English hunting season, just months after he'd purchased Pleasant Valley Farm.

Early-twentieth-century planting schemes didn't always revolve around the color spectrum. Sometimes they were designed to reflect certain interests of the gardener. Ladew's own topiary fox hunt, of course, comes immediately to mind. Knightshayes Court in Devon, the county that played so large a role in Harvey's "hounds across the sea" epic of 1939, also features a "60-year-old fox and hounds topiary,"[40] created about a decade after Ladew began his. The hounds and fox at Knightshayes enact their perpetual chase atop a hedge, just as Ladew's did originally (as is discussed below).[41] The countess of Warwick—one of the period's great hostesses—also favored gardening by theme and created a Border of Sentiment, a Garden of Friendship (which contained plants given by friends each identified by a heart-shaped label), and a Shakespeare Border, where she planted "the flowers and herbs the immortal bard loved so well"—an odd selection indeed, consisting of roses, primroses, and violets as well as leeks, garlic, cabbages, carrots, and mustard. Another theme garden may be seen at Sedgewick Park in Sussex, whose owner, a former navy man, created a topiary man-of-war, complete with quarterdecks, masthead, and portholes.

Aslet cites Friar Park in Oxfordshire, made by and for the barrister Sir Frank Crisp, as "the supreme example of 'the eclectic approach'" to gardening.[42] Crisp filled his grounds with jokes and "dreadful mottos," just as Ladew would. Crisp also wrote a guidebook for "I.V.s," his abbreviation for "Ignorant Visitors," warning them not to view his Japanese garden and topiary garden "as indubitably pleasing objects in themselves" but as "specimens in a museum to illustrate the

Ladew photographed Lady Iveagh's newly made room gardens (many devoted to plants that flower in a single color) when he stayed with her in 1930.

taste of the period." Should any I.V. be so impertinent as to criticize Crisp's taste, he requested him or her to do so "not in the presence of any of the gardeners." Crisp advantageously used the compartment garden approach to lay out a separate water garden, iris garden, herbaceous garden, "Garden of Sweet Smells," alpine garden (including a scale model—"of very faithful appearance"—of the Matterhorn), and a "Skeleton Cave," featuring "the upper part of a Friar who had instantaneously passed from life to death, after the manner of an American 'electrocution.'"

Hidcote Manor in Gloucestershire, a county that became the center of the arts and crafts movement, has been called "one of the most beautiful, interesting, haunting gardens in existence" by the great garden scholar (and maker) Alvilde Lees-Milne.[43] Its creator, Lawrence Johnston, like Ladew, was born an American citizen with a British heart. In fact, the parallels between the two men—and their gardens—make it impossible to believe that they never met. But they didn't.[44] Instead, each, gardening within the same ethos and unaware of the other, produced fascinating, complementary creations.

Lawrence Johnston was actually born in Paris in 1871, the son of "well-to-do Americans who felt drawn to Europe." He enjoyed a childhood filled with "walks in the streets of Paris, visits to museums, visits to *châteaux* and *manoirs* with exquisite gardens," all of which "made a lasting impression upon the small boy."[45] He became a British subject in 1900 and bought a farm in Northumberland in

"Perfectly Delightful"

1902. He liked farming but not Northumberland, so in 1907 his mother purchased the 280-acre Hidcote Bartrim farm in Gloucestershire, on the same hill as the noted garden Kiftsgate, created by the Muir family, and just a few miles from the Biddulphs' Rodmarton. Johnston altered and enlarged the existing small stone farmhouse on the property and set out to make a garden. Working easily within arts and crafts dicta, Johnston created a series of twenty-two garden rooms around a T-shaped axis. "For seven quiet years the garden grew, and Lawrence Johnston worked alongside his gardeners. For he was no onlooker. He dug, and planted, and pruned as much as they did."[46] The result was a masterpiece of "the highest magic."[47]

Russell Page credits Hidcote's success to its designer's ability to relate the

Hidcote Manor, Gloucestershire—a garden "of the highest magic"—created by Lawrence Johnston in 1907 and photographed for Country Life *in 1921.*

<hr />

"The art of personality"

small garden rooms to the modest house, to link and separate each garden enclosure "by long axial lines," and to avoid any sense of "appearing confused" by his skillful use of "grass walks or lawns hedged with yew, beech, or hornbeam as quiet interludes"[48]—just as Jekyll advocated. Yet Johnston did not slavishly copy Lutyens's and Jekyll's designs. Rather, he took their general principles and used them, modifying them when he felt it necessary, to create a unique work of art. Blessed with a deep and wide knowledge of the arts, and a great friend of the "the blatantly fashionable Lady Colefax,"[49] of the interior design team Colefax and Fowler, Johnston had so finely developed his own tastes as to be able to know when to ignore "the rules" altogether. For example, in planning his herbaceous border—130 yards long and 18 feet wide backed by a high hornbeam hedge—Johnston "broke most of [Gertrude Jekyll's] color rules" and followed his own intuitive aesthetic.

Many now theorize that Johnston found it relatively easy to go off and follow his own aesthetic because he himself was an outsider. He was arguably a citizen of no country—not entirely American or French or English. He was also a practicing Roman Catholic in a country where the established church was Protestant, and he was homosexual at a time when British public opinion had driven Oscar Wilde into exile. Some feel that all these facts "account for the uniqueness of Hidcote."[50] Could this be said of Ladew, himself a product of a curious life between worlds—a New York native who spent half a lifetime trying to become a southern colonel, an aesthete enriched by industrialist money, and a half stay-at-home dilettante, half adventurer?

In 1920, Johnston, seeking a relief from Cotswold winter chills, bought a hillside on the Riviera. He then set out, with the help of Russell Page, to create a "Mediterranean paradise" within an arts and crafts sensibility. The hillside lent itself beautifully to terraced room gardens, and Johnston made twenty-two of them, all exhibiting "the same kind of confident dash that he had demonstrated . . . at Hidcote."[51] One terrace featured climbing plants on pergolas; he gave one over to succulents, another to red roses, another to tree peonies, another to blue-flowering perennials.[52] Although he generally favored indigenous plants such as olives and oranges, he traveled far for others and in 1927 and 1931 "undertook two enthralling expeditions."[53] The first trip, a four-month tramp from Cape Town to the Victoria Falls and back, resulted in a vast collection of plants unknown in England or France. On the second, to China, he discovered the wonderfully scented vine *Jasminum polyanthum*, which has become the delight of greenhouse gardens throughout the cooler stretches of Europe and North America, and the shrub *Mahonia lomariifolia*, a plant whose whorls of golden flowers now brighten many winter gardens. (Johnston liked his creature comforts—something else he shared with Ladew—and brought his chauffeur/valet and Italian cook along on his travels, just as Ladew included his valet, Sherin, on his 1920s treks through Arabia and the Andes.)

While in the south of France, Johnston surrounded himself with some of the leading gardeners, writers, and intellectuals of the day, including his fellow expatriate Edith Wharton. Johnston and Wharton frequently visited each other and toured nurseries together. They even collaborated to design a garden for Wharton's villa near the allées and parterres of Versailles, thus bravely bringing the arts and crafts movement to the heart of garden design formality. Johnston gave Wharton "an inspired scheme" of room gardens, including one of a single color—the noted blue garden, a small space surrounded by blue-flowering hibiscus clipped to 6 feet.

Others worked with Johnston and Wharton in the 1920s "to break free from the severe traditions of formality" which characterized French gardening. Prominent among these "liberators" were a couple of "daring and commitment," the vicomte Charles de Noailles and his wife, Marie-Laure. These great friends of Pleasant Valley (see Chapter 5) also befriended the creator of Hidcote. The vicomte and Johnston planned a plant-hunting trip to Burma in 1938 (but gave it up because of gathering war clouds), and Johnston, an avid sportsman, spent many happy hours playing squash on the French couple's court.[54]

Unlike Johnston and Ladew, both firm traditionalists, the Noailles ardently supported modernism in all the arts. In 1925, inspired by the landmark Exposition des Arts Décoratifs (which gave the world the style—and name—art deco), they hired the Armenian designer Gabriel Guevrekian to create a cubist garden for a modernist villa they built on their own Riviera hillside. "Probably the only Cubist garden ever created," it featured square beds filled, alternately, with ceramic tiles of red, blue, yellow and gray; orange trees rising from a groundwork of black stone; a mobile; and "twin rising beds of intersecting triangles." The garden truly "owed nothing to any established horticultural influences and stood alone as one of the most original works" in landscape history.[55] After World War II, the vicomte and vicomtesse created another garden on the Riviera. Perhaps more conventional—certainly more conventionally arts and crafts—the couple's second stab at landscaping consisted of a series of flat terraces, once exclusively given over to olive trees, but rehedged to create private, concealed garden rooms planted in different themes including "topiary box, cut into strange, mounded shapes."[56]

Harvey Ladew did not know Hidcote firsthand, although he certainly had seen and read about it in *Country Life*. He probably did, however, know the Noailles gardens, as he had frequently visited the couple in France during the 1940s. Did he ever visit Haseley Court in Oxfordshire? That remains a mystery, but his great friend Horst certainly did. Horst also knew well Haseley's American-born owner, Nancy Lancaster (née Langhorne), a niece of Lady Astor. Langhorne had married Ronald Tree in 1929. The couple left England and returned to her native Albemarle County, Virginia, where they acquired the Langhorne seat, Mirador, and hired the New York architectural firm Delano and Aldrich to spruce up the house on the property. They also asked Delano to plan the grounds. Soon, "a network of gardens stretched northward behind the house, webbing the little dependencies in hedges and enclosed gardens. The pattern was English—the arts and crafts enclosure garden . . . popularized by Lutyens and Jekyll which Nancy Tree must have seen hundreds of times in England."[57]

The Trees moved back to England a few years later and bought the great eighteenth-century mansion Ditchley Park in Oxfordshire. Horst's English-born companion, Valentine Lawford, met Nancy Tree in wartime Britain: "I remember how she sold her American family's beloved estate of Mirador at considerable personal loss when England was more than usually in need of dollars," Lawford wrote, "and how she chose to become a British subject when the war was at its height."[58] Eventually the widowed, remarried, and widowed-again Nancy Lancaster sold Ditchley and bought Haseley Court. In the 1950s, Horst and Lawford, frequent guests at Haseley, photographed and wrote up the house and garden for *Vogue*. Although they deemed the "thirty-two clipped boxwood chessmen" placed "in an intricate pattern of lavender and santolina" "the first of Haseley's glories," they also praised the "laburnum hedges, beech hedges, alleys of hornbeam flanked by apple trees," and "topiary parlour"—in all, Lawford later wrote, "a beautiful sequence of interlocking gardens, as surprisingly harmonious as a maze of rooms in an ancient, rambling house." Even though Lancaster credited many of the gardens' features to "suggestions of Charles de Noailles" (how intertwined the international gardening community was in the mid-twentieth century!), she was being modest. Her own artistic eye had been developed over the years working as a colleague of decorator John Fowler in the firm Colefax and Fowler, and many agree with Lawford that the "the Fowler-Lancaster collaboration" ranked as "one of the most lively and fruitful in the flourishing postwar English decorating world."[59]

One may infer that Johnston and Ladew believed, as most of their American contemporaries did, in the influence of "good taste" and further believed that "good taste" implied a patina, a knowledge of the world, especially of Britain, France, and the Italian Renaissance. Nor were they alone in feeling as comfortable on one side of the Atlantic as on the other. Ladew's friend Consuelo Vanderbilt (later the duchess of Marlborough and still later Mme. Jacques Balsan) made homes in the United States, England, and France; and Edith Wharton, who chronicled societal goings-on in her native New York, happily spent the last years of her long life in France. Other great transatlantic friendships developed among Gertrude Jekyll and Louisa King, who helped organize the Garden Club of America, and Beatrix Farrand, a niece of Edith Wharton, one of the leading garden makers of the century, and a cofounder of the American Society of Landscape Architects. Farrand amply demonstrated what she had learned on her visits to Jekyll at Munstead when she created her own masterpiece, Dumbarton Oaks, laid out for Mr. and Mrs. Robert Woods Bliss, in Georgetown, Washington, D.C. Before she began work on the 40-acre Dumbarton Oaks site in 1921, she "closely

"Perfectly Delightful"

1. Portrait of Harvey Ladew on the Ghost, painted by James Earl, c. 1922

2. "Can easily handle fifty naked ladies but please be sure they are free from all diseases," Ladew cabled his bulb seller; they appear healthy here. In the background, his signature topiary hounds and rider race across the grass in perpetual pursuit of a yew fox. The hunt scene, amusing in itself, also serves as something of a teaser: one passes through it before reaching the main garden and thereby gets a hint of the whimsies ahead.

14. *Gertrude Jekyll suggested that gardeners train roses and other flowering vines to create living "umbrellas"; this is one of Ladew's two wisteria and rose bumbershoots.*

13. *"I never attempted to shut out the Maryland countryside, which I love," wrote Harvey Ladew.*

12. The Great Bowl (with its oval swimming pool), terraces, and some of the clipped hemlocks that formed the garden's main axis. Photo 1992.

11. Ladew's topiary Chinese junk floats in a lotus-filled pool at the base of the Iris Garden.

10. "*Harvey had the most beautiful collection of iris,*" *one friend recalled.* "*There were three sweeps of color.*" *Photo taken c. 1955.*

9. The Sculpture Garden features clipped-in-yew versions of Churchill's "V for Victory" sign and top hat, seahorses (to remind Ladew of his beloved Florida), teacups, a pierced heart, and a butterfly alighting on a mushroom.

8. *The Laburnum Arch, a device frequently seen in English gardens, leads from the Yellow Garden to the main allée and the favorite* Man Walking a Dog *à la Henry Moore topiary.*

7. The Yellow Garden features this futuristic teahouse.

6. *Ladew designed flowering "hallways" to connect the "rooms" in his horticultural master-piece. The White Garden, shown here, leads from the Water Lily Garden to the Tivoli Teahouse.*

5. A receipt shows that Ladew bought the lead "Swan Boy" fountain, the centerpiece of his Water Lily Garden, from T. Crowther & Son, the noted gardening furnishings supplier at Syon Lodge near London, on August 31, 1939. The price was ninety pounds.

4. *The Rose Garden*

3A. *Ladew designed the main section of his Maryland garden around two axes: in this aerial photograph, taken c. 1985, one can discern the principal spine leading from the house (top), across the Great Bowl (with its fountain-fed swimming pool), and through the hemlock-lined "hallway" that separates "rooms" such as the Sculpture Garden (left) and the White, Water Lily, and Yellow Gardens (right).*

3B. *The garden's less obvious (from the ground) cross axis begins in the brick-walled, circular Rose Garden, traverses the Great Bowl, and follows the meandering stream of the Iris Garden to end in a topiary junk.*

15. *Ladew's intimate, low-ceilinged dining room features eighteenth-century French painted panels of hunting scenes; some of his favorite Worcester china fills shelves by the fireplace.*

16. *View from Ladew's Oval Library into the Elizabethan Room; he purchased the beautiful eighteenth-century doorway in the 1930s on one of his English hunting trips.*

17. *In the summer of 1947, Harvey Ladew spent ten days at Cap d'Antibes with the duke and duchess of Windsor; during his stay, the baron de Cabrol painted this charming beach scene featuring the duchess (in blue), the duke (standing), and other guests. Photo courtesy of Sotheby's.*

18. *Billy Baldwin as painted by Harvey Ladew, c. 1944. "In one of those moments when everything works," wrote Baldwin, "Harvey had caught me: the line of my shoulder, the line of the thigh, my head shape, hair, the whole thing."*

examined Jekyll's plans" and then designed a series of interlocking room gardens, "each 'room' having a particular function, such as the display of a particular type of plant or object. The limits of the rooms were clearly delineated by clipped hedges or walls of stone, brick, or some combination of materials."[60]

"Italian magic"

The American garden historians Mac Griswold and Eleanor Weller recently suggested that the success of Delano's garden at Mirador for Nancy Langhorne Tree was "perhaps due to joint classical and Italian inspiration."[61] In fact, the best of these "arts and crafts" gardens—Rodmarton, Hidcote, Haseley, and Dumbarton Oaks—aren't "pure" arts and crafts at all. A "pure" arts and crafts garden, a tract of, say, flat land divided up into rooms by high yew hedges, could easily run the risk of making a visitor feel claustrophobic, as if one were trapped in a maze. To avoid this unpleasant sensation, Johnston, Farrand, and other skillful designers varied the small rooms with dramatic vistas. And they found the inspiration for these vistas in one of the other principal influences on Harvey Ladew, the great *giardini* of the Italian Renaissance, which he had read about in books and had seen on his numerous trips to Rome, Florence, and the Veneto.

While Clive Aslet may write that "the cult of Italy, which gave rise to the Italian garden, was an American rather than English phenomenon"[62] and cite such popular American books as Edith Wharton's *Italian Villas and Their Gardens* (1904), with its exquisite watercolor illustrations by Maxfield Parrish,[63] in actual fact, England did not suffer from a shortage of books extolling the beauties of Italian gardening. For instance, J. D. Sedding, an architect whose work was much admired by the arts and crafts leader Sir Edward Coley Burne-Jones, wrote in his highly influential book *Garden Craft Old and New* (1892), "Of the gardens of Italy, who shall dare to speak critically? Child of tradition; heir by unspoken descent; inheritor of the garden-craft of the whole civilised world. It stands on a pinnacle high above the others, peerless and alone, splendidly adorned with straight terraces, marble statues, clipped ilex and box."[64] Other important English books on the subject include Sir George Sitwell's *On the Making of Gardens* (1909), H. Ingo Trigg's *The Art of Garden Design in Italy* (1906), and J. C. Shepherd and G. A. Jellicoe's *Italian Gardens of the Renaissance* (1925). All these had probable influence on Ladew's Harford County creation: he owned copies of Wharton's and Shepherd and Jellicoe's books, was a friend of Sitwell's sons, Sacheverell and Osbert (and visited the family's seat, Renishaw Hall), and knew that the great Jekyll herself had praised Trigg's work, smiling at his Italianate garden at Steep, with its terrace near the house, yew hedges, and varied levels, and noting "how admirably the slope [had] been employed to give a succession of interesting garden incidents."[65]

Wharton loved what she called "Italian magic." Still, she was commonsensical enough to write that garden designers in England or America should not try to reproduce an Italian garden literally but should instead strive for "what is far better, a garden as well adapted to its surroundings as were the models which inspired it." Moreover, she felt that since gardens were meant to be "lived in," they should be planned with broad terraces and with yew- (or holly-) lined paths laid out to make the terraces "easily accessible from the house" and to make "transitions from the dark wooded alleys to open flowery spaces or to the level sward of the bowling green." She further felt that the three primary elements of Italian gardens—water, marble, and "perennial verdure"—should blend harmoniously with each other and with the architecture of the main house. "None of these details was negligible to the landscape architect of the Renaissance," she lectured her readers. "He considered the distribution of shade, sunlight, of straight lines of masonry and rippled lines of foliage, as carefully as he weighed the relation of his whole composition to the scene about it." She also felt that the success of Italian gardens partially lay in their subdivision "into 'rooms' according to their purposes": these defined spaces, she wrote, "can range from secluded areas with enclosing foliage to a wide expanse of lawn or flower beds, to paths studded with marble statues or overhung with vines, to walled cloisters with soothing fountains."[66]

Sir George Reresby Sitwell's small book—an essay written during a long convalescence in Italy—has been called "the culmination of twenty years spent drifting through the morals, motives, scents, sounds, and dreams of two hundred generations."[67] Sitwell gave living form to his love of Italy when he transformed the gardens at Renishaw Hall in Derbyshire. Sitwell's younger son, Sacheverell, who with his wife, Georgia, frequently stayed with Ladew in Florida and Maryland (as guestbooks attest), wrote that when his father had finished his work at Renishaw, he left "a masterpiece that encapsulated both his own enthusiasm for Italian Renaissance gardens and the Edwardian enjoyment of such ornamented formality."[68] Sitwell created a series of terraces off the house's south facade and made them of different shapes and sizes to relieve monotony. Beyond the terraces, he also laid out a sloping lawn lined with axial yew hedges clipped so they terminate in obelisks and planted to divide the space into a series of squares and rectangles. He also arranged the obelisks to frame the openings from one area to the next and carefully placed statues of Roman gods and goddesses at strategic points—in all, a composition similar to, but different from, the axial hedges, topiary obelisks, and antique statues of Ladew's Maryland garden.

Harold Acton formed another Italianate link between Ladew and the Sitwells. He was born in 1904, a son of Arthur Acton, a cultured Englishman who had studied art in Paris, and Hortense Mitchell, an American whose father founded the Illinois Trust and Savings Bank and whose money enabled her husband to buy and furnish the sixty-room villa La Pietra near Florence. The "furnishing" went

Renishaw Hall, Derbyshire, seat of the Sitwell family, as painted by Richard Wyndham around 1930. Ladew got to know Renishaw well in the 1920s, thanks to stays there with his friends Osbert and Sacheverell Sitwell. Renishaw's classical statuary and topiary yew obelisks certainly suggest some of the garden devices Ladew would soon use at Pleasant Valley.

beyond the expected Renaissance tapestries and furniture; they included the most celebrated artists of the time, all of whom greatly influenced young Harold. Sergei Diaghilev and Leon Bakst of Ballets Russes fame, for instance, visited La Pietra when Acton was a boy, and meeting them convinced him he could—and should—devote his life to the pleasures of ballet and poetry and the serious study of rococo art. Interestingly, at about the same time, Ladew decided to devote *his* life to the pleasures of hunting, gardening, and dabbling in all the arts.

After Eton and Oxford, Acton lived in London with the other bright young things of the 1920s: he frequented fancy-dress balls and parties, befriended jazz singers, drank cocktails, and determined to become a writer. Although never as successful in the literary world as his friend Evelyn Waugh (who dedicated books to him), Acton remained an important fixture in the international art scene. After World War II, he lived for extended periods in Paris, mingling with Jean Cocteau, Gertrude Stein, Lady Diana Cooper, Marie-Laure de Noailles—and Harvey Smith Ladew, whose address book (still at Pleasant Valley) has addresses and telephone numbers for both Harold Acton and his mother. On the deaths of his parents (his father in 1953, his mother in 1962) Acton inherited La Pietra, returned to Florence, and spent most of his time there until he died in 1994. During those decades, he "held perhaps the best salon of his time, almost as if all the grand European hostesses ended in him."[69] He also devoted himself to the history of the villa and its garden. Writing of the latter, which his father had restored in 1904, Acton observed that the main plan consisted of "a series of broad terraces, each like a separate garden, levelled from the slope descending behind the house," with balustrades and "clipped hedges with niches for statues, ancient fountains with circular basins, and geometrical plots of grass surrounded by clipped hedges of box." The garden also contained an open-air theater with wings of yew and "globed footlights of box."[70]

"I suppose I was influenced by many things"

Sir George Sitwell had observed that "to make a great garden, one must have a great idea or a great opportunity."[71] When Harvey Ladew began his gardens in Harford County, he had both.

He arrived at Pleasant Valley Farm in November 1929 all ready to go, once stating that he "started the garden pretty soon after [he] got the house." Indeed, one of the more remarkable things about his work is the speed at which his plans reached maturity. Great gardens usually evolve over decades, even generations. Yet as photographs reveal, Ladew's Pleasant Valley was conceived and planted and achieved flowering maturity in breathtaking speed—no doubt because he brought the garden, at least conceptually, with him. He arrived in Maryland with a modest but telling horticultural library including Jekyll and Weaver's *Gardens for Small Country Houses*, Weaver's two-volume *Small Country Houses of Today*, *The Home Garden Handbook on Iris* (author unknown), H. Purefoy Fitzgerald's *Concise Handbook of Climbers, Twiners, and Wall Shrubs*, several anonymous "how-to" pamphlets on the culture of delphiniums and roses, J. C. Shepherd and G. A. Jellicoe's *Italian Gardens of the Renaissance*, Edith Wharton's *Italian Villas and Their Gardens*, and Muriel Cabot Sedgewick's *The Garden Month by Month*; of these, all but the last two, which came from New York publishers, were of English origin. He also arrived with the collected memories of forty years spent knocking about the world; most important, of a dozen lengthy stays in England. "Having travelled abroad a great deal for many years," he wrote, "I suppose I was influenced by many things I saw and attempted to reproduce some of them in a modest way." He even brought the physical beginnings of a garden with him to Harford County, for, as will be discussed, he had his favorite topiaries dug up from his garden in Brookville, Long Island, burlapped, hauled to Maryland, and replanted at his new residence.

All this—the books, the accumulated memories, the transplanted topiary— accurately implies that he knew what sort of garden he had in mind. "No one gave me any advice in gardening," he told a reporter for the *Sunday Sun*, "but I had read a lot and knew what I wanted."[72] What he wanted—what he created—might be thought of as a horticultural cross-pollination, a grafting of arts and crafts and Italianate sensibilities, 22 acres of enclosed, brightly hued planting areas set among dramatic sweeping vistas.

He envisioned two intersecting axes forming a Latin cross plan. The main one (1,100 feet in length) would lead from the house to a neoclassical domed structure he named the Temple of Venus. (Plate 3A.) The other would lead from a brick-walled Rose Garden to his Iris Garden, with its serene topiary Buddha and a topiary Chinese junk "sailing" in a lotus-filled pool. (Plate 3B.) At the axes' intersection, he planned a 2-acre Great Bowl, the rotunda (if you will) of his garden mansion, a place of almost baroque counterpoint, with a fountain-fed swimming pool in its center and its eastern "wall" formed by billowing topiary waves on which glide a dozen serenely swimming yew swans. A set of terraces—also of baroque drama—would lead from the Great Bowl up to the house. Recognizing the importance of "punctuation marks" in a formal garden, Ladew clipped large topiary obelisks at the spot where the walls of the main allée meet the Great Bowl. He also planned to crown the allée walls near the house (along the sides of the terraces) with smaller obelisks and to create a series of domes, birds, and other traditional topiary forms to accentuate and add excitement to each of the terraces near the house. (Plate 12.) How reminiscent it all sounds not only of Sitwell's Renishaw but also of the Villa Dona Dalle Rose at Valzanzibio, near Venice, visited by Ladew and described by Shepherd and Jellicoe as "an amphitheater of the hills, the ends linked by a great avenue flung across the valley, and in this arrangement of lesser avenues furnished with all the delights of an Italian garden, box hedges, sculpture, pools, and fountains."[73]

Finally, within that dramatic framework, Ladew saw a series of fifteen discreet garden rooms, each featuring a different theme or color scheme, the whole anticipating Lawford's comments on Haseley, "a beautiful sequence of interlocking gardens, as surprisingly harmonious as a maze or rooms in an ancient, rambling house." Although Harvey constantly tinkered with the plants in those rooms— tempted, like all gardeners, into trying one year's prize rose and another's prize tulip—he kept the framework, envisioned from the beginning, intact.

In his own unpublished garden history,[74] Ladew wrote of how Americans visiting England (such as himself) become "charmed by the lovely countryside they motor through" and by the villages with "cottages ablaze with colourful flowers from early Spring till late Autumn." That certainly suggests he had succumbed to the charms of the cottage garden. One needs only to skim the pages of *Gardens for Small Country Houses* to see some of the sources that inspired Ladew to create his Harford County masterpiece.

But since he based his new garden around that highly formal pair of axes which he thrust out into the Harford County countryside, one knows that he, like so many of his contemporaries, had also been bitten by the Italian Renaissance bug. In the 1920s, he had taken a day off from hunting with the conte di Frasso

Topiary allée and statues at the Villa Dona Dalle Rose at Valzanzibio, near Venice. Ladew visited the garden and owned a copy of J. C. Shepherd and G. A. Jellicoe's Italian Gardens of the Renaissance *(1925), from which this image was taken.*

to visit the gardens of Raphael's famous Villa Madama near Rome, a tamed, formal landscape "spreading from a central court to theater and loggias, and beyond to terrace on terrace of gardens." Moving up the Italian boot, one reaches the villas and gardens of the Venetian plain. There Edith Wharton fell in love with the gardens at the Villa Valmarana near Vicenza, calling them "a composition of exceptional picturesqueness" thanks to "the beautiful loggia attributed to Palladio, the old beech alleys, the charming frescoed fountain, and the garden wall crowned with Venetian grotesques." She told her readers, including Ladew, that "the beautiful countryside between Vicenza and Venice is strewn with old villas, many of which would doubtless repay study."[75] Harvey Ladew didn't need to be told to study the villas, though, for his letters to his sister, written from Venice, are filled with ebullient phrases describing his tours of those neoclassical villas and their axial, vista-filled gardens.

Ladew's longtime friend Elizabeth Constable noted that "Harvey loved vistas."[76] In 1968 he himself bragged to his sister, "One thing I have got that even Mr. du Pont has not are *several long vistas*—the sort you see in European gardens." Even into his eighth decade, when plagued by failing health and fears of going broke, he sought to escape those unpleasant realities by planning, recalled Constable, two more allées, one stretching up off the main axis near the Temple of Venus and another, "a pink allée, that was to go to the right of the iris garden all the way up to the horizon, to the Ebenezer Road," "a big pink halo around the

Buddha," he dreamily explained in a 1970 interview, with a wooden silhouette of a pagoda ("just the outline so you see it distinctly over in the trees"), and then "ALL pink horse chestnuts, dogwood, wigelias, cherry blossoms." "I don't think anyone has ever done it," he mused, "but I might just try."

In good classical fashion, Ladew carefully saw to it that the views at the end of his axes terminated in some definite point or object. Leith Griswold noted that "he liked a focal point at the end of a vista." In this, he found himself in good company. V. Sackville-West, for one, insisted that "the line of the hedge should spring from some definite point . . . and that, having sprung, it should continue to another definite point." Jekyll, too, demanded that vistas and axes "should always lead from one definite point to another; one at least being some kind of full-stop," or "something of definite value in the garden design."[77]

Jekyll deeply believed in the usefulness and beauty of summerhouses and pavilions placed in the garden, likening them to "an outpost where the amenities of the house and its more gentle employments can be enjoyed in a garden atmosphere." She felt that "a pavilion should not stand alone, but be tied to the rest of the scheme by orderly design" and thereby giving "dignity and scale to the main building." If close to the house, a pavilion should echo its style, as Ladew's Card Room and Pressing Room, extensions of the dwelling, do. But, Jekyll notes, "when a summer-house is placed in a remote corner of a garden and bears no definite relation to the main house, some latitude [in style] is possible." Ladew jumped at this stylistic loophole and used "some latitude" (indeed) when he designed his futuristic Yellow Garden pavilion: when building pavilions far away from the house, Jekyll said, "it is far safer to accept modernity as the governing factor and to build a garden-house that frankly expresses the age to which it belongs." Does any garden contain a better or "franker" expression of the atomic era than Ladew's Yellow Garden pavilion, whose steep roof and flaring eves caused one visitor to exclaim, "Why, it's George Jetson's teahouse!"[78] (Plate 7.)

Although Ladew did not share Jekyll's fondness for massive pergolas ("The pergola has become so popular," she wrote, "that there is scarcely an example of modern garden design in which it does not find a place"),[79] he did make a small-scale pergola of sorts when he lined up a series of 10-foot-tall metal hoops on which he trained laburnum. This, the Laburnum Arch, acts as a "hallway" to connect various of his garden rooms. (Plate 8.) And, mindful of his chromatic and stylistic manners, he placed a vivid, flame-colored Exbury azalea as the arch's focal point in the Yellow Garden.

In sum, Ladew created a triumphant combination of sweeping vistas and small enclosed spaces which stands unique in the gardening world, a testament to the sophisticated sensibilities of its maker. He himself typically dismissed his work ("Of course the whole place is crazy"), but then he was known for his gentlemanly modesty: "He never showed off," recalls Bob Six, who worked as Ladew's groom in the 1930s. "He never talked of his accomplishments."[80]

Ladew's near obsession with topiary began just as one would imagine; his Hollywood friends could not have scripted a more satisfactory scenario. Harvey wrote that during his English hunting winters he "saw a great deal of topiary, though none of it particularly interested" him. "There were usually very large pieces in geometrical shapes in the gardens surrounding large, ancient houses, but none of them would have suited a modern American garden. Many small cottages had pieces of topiary, but most of them were about the same design and very crudely made. I was amused at them when I first saw them, but I was seldom interested in any I saw."[81]

That changed, though, one morning about 1920 when he "was hunting in the Duke of Beaufort's country." "Hacking to an early meet, I rode along beside a very tall yew hedge bordering a large estate. As I looked up, I saw an astonishing sight that made me rein my horse abruptly and continue to gaze in amazement. On the top of the hedge about 100 feet above me I saw a whole Topiary fox hunt, beautifully modelled and trimmed, the fox running for his life closely pursued by a marvelously sculpted pack of a dozen hounds." He added—and one can see the twinkle in his eyes—that "though this hunt had been going on for fifty years, the hounds had never gained an inch on him." (His enthusiasm and excitement led him to overstate a bit: the hedge rose not 100 feet but 10; and the hounds number three, not a dozen.) He wrote that he "had to hurry on so as not to be late" but he knew he would never be happy if he "could not reproduce this marvelous piece of living sculpture in [his] garden on Long Island."

Harvey gained an introduction to the hedge's owner, Lady Blanche Scott-Douglas, sister of the duke of Beaufort. Ladew would have known the duke, master of the Beaufort Hunt and lord of Badminton House, by his nickname, "Master," a moniker alluding to that aristocrat's great interest in hunting. Indeed, that entire generation of Somersets (the duke's and Lady Blanche's family name) grew up with "foxhunting set in their blood ahead of speech. 'We are not allowed to hunt more than three times a week till we are five years old,' said one of them."[82] Curiously, although the duke was well known for his dislike of Americans, he numbered many of Ladew's Maryland hunting chums among his own inner circle. He wrote Ladew that he regarded Frank Voss, whose Atlanta Hall Farm lay about a mile from Ladew's Pleasant Valley, "a great friend," adding, "I have many of his paintings in this house."[83]

Ladew asked Lady Blanche "if she thought it would be possible to duplicate the topiary fox and hounds in not too many years." He recalled, "She was most encouraging and explained that as yew is very fast growing I could easily grow a topiary hunt such as hers in only two or three years. Of course my hedge would not reach the height of hers. She then explained how the animals had been shaped—they were grown in wonderfully made wire frames made by a man whose

Ladew's Maryland gardens, aerial (southeasterly) view (top) and vista from the north-north-east (bottom). Ladew's combination of Italian and English gardening sensibilities produced a landscape that may truly be called sui generis. *Note the clipped topiary yew obelisks, the axis suggested by the lined-up flights of steps, the "room gardens," and, on the middle terrace and in the small rounded "room" just off the main allée, his two "rose umbrellas," a device he lifted straight from the writings of the great Gertrude Jekyll.*

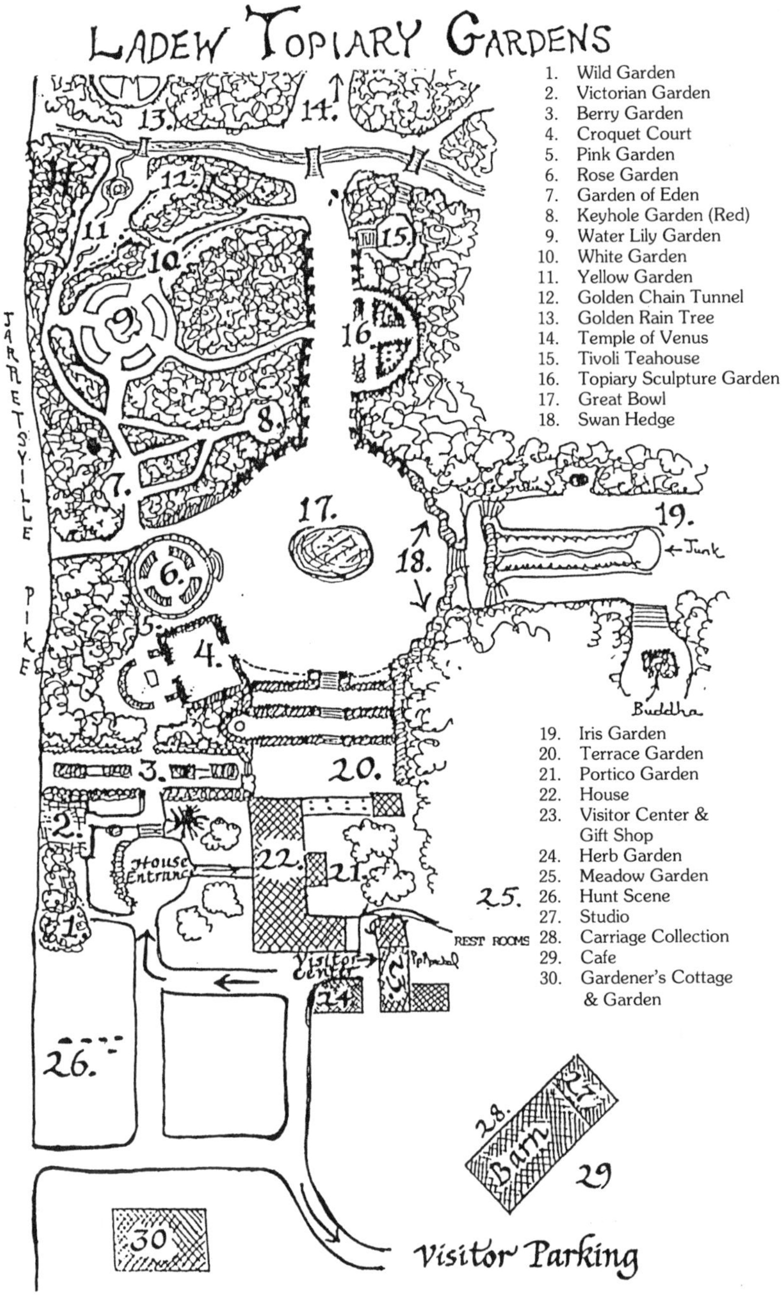

LADEW TOPIARY GARDENS

1. Wild Garden
2. Victorian Garden
3. Berry Garden
4. Croquet Court
5. Pink Garden
6. Rose Garden
7. Garden of Eden
8. Keyhole Garden (Red)
9. Water Lily Garden
10. White Garden
11. Yellow Garden
12. Golden Chain Tunnel
13. Golden Rain Tree
14. Temple of Venus
15. Tivoli Teahouse
16. Topiary Sculpture Garden
17. Great Bowl
18. Swan Hedge

19. Iris Garden
20. Terrace Garden
21. Portico Garden
22. House
23. Visitor Center & Gift Shop
24. Herb Garden
25. Meadow Garden
26. Hunt Scene
27. Studio
28. Carriage Collection
29. Cafe
30. Gardener's Cottage & Garden

JARRETSVILLE PIKE

←Junk

Buddha

House Entrance

REST ROOMS

Visitor Center

Barn

Visitor Parking

Layout of Ladew's Maryland garden, showing its highlights and variety.

address she gave me. It was easy to bend the yew into these frames and clip it. The cottage topiary I had seen had a very primitive look in comparison as it had not been grown in this way. I lost no time in ordering a fox and six hounds from this man who is (or was) a veritable artist and sculptor in wire and my hunt was started in America."

Eager for instant effects, on returning to Long Island, Ladew found "rather tall plants [of Japanese yew] for the animals." The imported frames "were welded to lead pipes which were driven into the ground" in his stable yard. With his yew fox and six hounds thus under way, he planted quick-growing privet for the hedge itself, hoping to achieve his version of the English hedge in the shortest possible time. It worked, and a photograph (c. 1925) of the stable yard shows that the hunting hedge was already well formed. When he left Long Island for Maryland in 1929, he took his fox and hounds with him: the May 1936 issue of *Town & Country* notes that "on the driveway front [of Ladew's Pleasant Valley Farm] is a hedge, clipped in the shape of hounds following a fox, transported from his place at Brookville, Long Island."[84] Apparently when he added the present driveway and oval parking lot by the front door of the house, he planted a hedge along the parking area's western edge and set the fox and hounds into it to re-create a version of what had so captivated him in England. He probably had the hedge itself hauled down from New York, for a note from one Owen Flanigan of Brookville states, "The Triangle Nursery will dig and prepare the trees and load them at the rate of $2.50 each." Flanigan states that "there are twenty trees in all," that is, the seven topiary hunt figures, the shrubs that make up the yew hedge, and a tall, cake-stand topiary he placed near the farm's cottage.

At some point, Ladew decided to take advantage of the greater room offered in Maryland and moved the fox and hounds to their present site in a wide expanse of lawn between the house and the property's main entrance. It must have amused him to imagine motorists having to drive through the "hunt," as he placed the fox and one hound on one side of the driveway and the rest of the pack on the other. He also decided to enlarge the cast by adding a topiary horse and rider.[85] Ladew sculpted the huntsman so he was dramatically jumping a hedge—but the hedge was very angular, suggesting a yew snake fence. In the early 1970s he added a second horse and rider, rejuvenated some of the aging and ailing hounds, and straightened the "fence's" angles. (Plate 2.)

Jekyll warned that "in unpractised hands" sculptures in yew and box "might be dangerous" and should only be created by men and women endowed with "skill and fine taste," who would turn them into "right and fitting garden ornaments."[86] Surely "fitting" applies as the *mot juste* to a topiary hunt scene created by an MFH.

Once the fox hunt hedge suggested that topiary could make an expressive medium for his witty mind, Ladew set about his new art form in earnest. For a few years he continued to commission frames from Lady Blanche's artist but soon

While hunting in the 1920s, Ladew saw and was so impressed by Lady Blanche Scott-Douglas's topiary hunt (photographed in 1996) that he copied it at his Long Island estate. A later owner of Lady Blanche's house and grounds regretted that the topiary hedge had grown up and "swallowed" the animal's legs.

In 1929 Ladew brought his hounds and fox from his stable yard in Brookville, Long Island, to Maryland and placed them in front of his house.

During the 1930s, taking advantage of the greater space he had in Maryland, Ladew moved the fox and hounds to the grassy swath they still occupy and began sculpting a topiary huntsman.

Around 1971, an octogenarian Ladew began a second topiary huntsman, straightened out the hedge, and reworked the hounds. Finally, more than forty years in the making, his masterpiece was complete.

decided that since he himself "had studied painting and drawing," he felt qualified to make his own frames: "This has become a hobby I have greatly enjoyed. Among the topiary pieces there is an almost lifesize giraffe done in yellow privet, a unicorn, Churchill's hand giving the V for Victory sign, some seahorses, lyre birds, and so on. I am now planning to do some modern statuary—a family à la Henry Moore full of big holes in their anatomy—which I do not understand. Anyway, it will be fun. But someday someone may explain to me what it all means—if it means anything at all!" (Plate 9.)

In his typically generous way, Ladew prepared instructions for homemade topiary so that others could enjoy his hobby. He chose a swan as an example. Step one, he instructed, is to make a drawing "on a large piece of paper showing exactly how the topiary is to look when finished." "Suppose you want to make a life-sized swan. Draw him in profile first leaving two pieces of wire about a foot and a half long at the swan's base so that they can be inserted into a pipe which will hold the swan." Step two is to weld the various parts together to form "the bird's head, neck, and body." "It is not difficult to decide how wide these circles should be by anyone who can draw fairly well because when the plant is fully grown it should fill the circles. As the plant grows, you will readily see where it should be clipped. The yew should hide the wire circles entirely."

With the frame made, one should purchase an appropriate size shrub and "have a deep hole dug to plant it in." "Fill this hole with good topsoil and peat moss (to keep the soil damp). When and as you are placing your yew, drive a pipe into the ground within a foot and a half or two feet next to the center of the plant [and attach] the swan frame to the pipe. You will be surprised how quickly your swan will begin to take shape and soon be big and strong enough to drag Lohengrin off in a boat, away from his inquisitive and tearful bride. I have a circular yew hedge with twelve swans floating on a rippling hedge some distance away from an oval swimming pool and it has been thought very attractive. As time has gone on I keep making more topiary. It is a hobby, I suppose."

In 1930, Ladew hired a surveyor, "his only professional help,"[87] to lay out his planned paradise. To create the Great Bowl he needed someone to sculpt an indentation into the flat site. Accordingly, he hired a Mr. Kurtz, a local undertaker: "Harvey thought the funeral director would have a lot of experience digging," Leith Griswold recalled with a laugh. "I remember perfectly old Mr. Kurtz with his mules going round and round and round."[88] Ladew then fashioned the land between the house and the new bowl into the three transitional terraces and hired men to haul the excavated soil from there and the Great Bowl to other parts of the garden. "It was the Depression," he noted, "and I paid the men $2 a day. But $2 was something then and they were glad to get it." Then, with the stage set, he started planting.

He began his garden by planting the terraces and the hedges around the Great Bowl. Having completed that stage by 1937, the year he finished work on

Henry Moore was one of the few contemporary artists Ladew admired. Here the American pays topiary homage in his yew Man Walking a Dog. *Ladew sometimes said he based the "sculpture" on a photograph of his Uncle Berry walking his chow.*

the house, he started shaping the more distant "rooms." Bob Six, who left Harvey's employ in 1939, recently recalled that by the end of the thirties, "it was all pretty much in place."[89] Ladew chose two different evergreens for his hedges: yews (*Taxus cuspidata* Densiformis) for the swans and their waves, and hemlocks (*Tsuga canadensis*) for the walls that help form the garden's 1,100-foot main axis. When his hedges reached a certain height, he began to trim them into the desired shapes. And, to answer perhaps today's most-asked question, yes, *he* did the trimming. Bob Six recalled his employer as "a man on the go. He would be working in the garden at dawn"; Bibber Dow has stated simply that "Harvey was indefatigable in the garden." Indeed, even as late as 1967, Ladew could write his sister, "You can't imagine how hard I have worked and what wonderful things I have done. Today I clipped several miles of topiary for exercise and pleasure."[90]

He did more than clip his way into old age, however; he planned and planted as well. Shortly after he turned eighty, he wrote his sister, who had invited him to visit her in Westbury, that he couldn't make the trip: "I really have to stay here as I had ordered lots of plants from several nurseries and they are all coming *now.* . . . They have to be planted at once and I have to be here to tell Walter exactly where to put them," referring to Walter Preston, his gardening mainstay for dec-

While workmen smoothed out the newly excavated Great Bowl c. 1930, Harvey decided it was time to test his just-completed swimming pool.

ades. "If I am not here he will get everything mixed up and make a mess of the garden. He is very nice and a hard worker but he has *no notion* of where things should go." (Harvey later told his sister, "Walter is really wonderful and if I let him go I would have to give up this garden.") In the 1960s he acquired two Italian servants, Gina and Paolo.[91] Concerning the latter, he wrote his sister, "[He] is a great help to me and I hope he is as nice as he seems. I am sure he will help me a lot making wire frames for more topiary. What is awful is that I can't get a gardener to help Walter." Eventually he trained Paolo to work in the gardens, and life at Pleasant Valley bounced along for a few more years. Walter and Paolo reciprocated Ladew's fondness: "They loved working with him," Bibber Dow said.[92]

Ladew's choice of yew does not surprise. (Ironically, Ladew's great friend and virtual role model, the duke of Windsor, disliked "evergreens in general and any clipped yew or box in particular.")[93] He would have known, by perusing his copy of *Gardens for Small Country Houses*, that Gertrude Jekyll deemed yew "the favorite material for enclosure."[94] She also stated, "When our Tudor and Jacobean ancestors adopted a system of surrounding and subdividing their gardens with hedges of living greenery, they rightly chose yew as the tree that should conform to their will as green walls and ornaments in their gardens of formal design." Ladew wrote that he found the best thing to use was Japanese cuspidata yew or spreading yew. "Do not use Hicksii," he warned; "[it] grows in more of a column and has not nearly enough side growth for most pieces you want to make. English box is, of course, very beautiful and makes wonderful topiary, but unless you have the life expectation of Methusala you can not well use it as it only grows about two inches a year. The cuspidata is very quick growing and if you can plant a good sized one to begin with, you will have a finished piece in a few years and one that is even interesting to see as it is developing."

Ladew's topiary hemlock obelisks didn't just terminate the allée's walls; they also help frame all-important views. He recognized the need for frames and other eye-guiding devices, no doubt as a result of his artistic training. This knowledge possibly received reinforcement when he read what Shepherd and Jellicoe said in their definitive work, *Italian Gardens of the Renaissance:* "Limiting the lateral

View north through the arcade that connects the Oval Library to the Card Room, c. 1937. The house was finished; work on the garden could now begin in earnest: note that the hemlock topiaries on the terraces were coming along nicely, small hemlocks had been planted across the Great Bowl, the Swan Hedge is just discernible through the far right arch, but the main allée and Sculpture Garden had not been laid out.

In 1967 Ladew wrote his sister, "Today I clipped several miles of topiary for exercise and pleasure."

vision in a view greatly increases the effect," they write. The authors particularly cite the Villa d'Este at Tivoli, where the view towards the house from below includes "excited features building up and up, strongly framed all round by calm outlines," and the Villa at Caparola, where the owner carefully selected statues and other elements to "act as intermediaries between the spectator and the countryside and split up the view into a number of constantly changing pictures."[95] Ladew not only had his own copy of that monumental book, but he knew both of these glorious gardens firsthand.

Early-twentieth-century topiary gardeners in England often pierced their hedge walls with windowlike openings (called "*clairvoyées*"), finding them "extremely effective for focusing attention on a distant view." The element of surprise is important to a successful garden scheme, and it does make one gasp "when a solid wall of greenery suddenly gives way to a knee-trembling vista."[96] The godlike Jekyll used *Gardens for Small Country Houses* to praise the owners of one garden for cutting "a way through the middle of the old stepped hedge so that a vista might be secured." She explained, "A feature of this kind is very valuable in increasing the impression of distance and is attractive in its own right."[97] Thus, Ladew, who saw these windowed walls of yew in England and who knew his Jekyll by heart, clipped 4-foot-tall windows into the hemlock walls on the terraces to provide panoramic views of Harford's rolling hills. "There is a certain formality in the garden," he wrote of his Pleasant Valley creation, "but I never attempted to shut out the Maryland countryside, which I love." (Plate 13.)

Ladew also knew that a work of art—especially a three-dimensional work of

"Perfectly Delightful"

art—demands variety and excitement for success. Lutyens, for one, wrote that "the human mind adores to be tantalized, and eventually surprised and rewarded," and Jekyll, rather bluntly, stated that "the obvious in garden design is often dreary." Accordingly, Ladew designed his main allée so it bends slightly at the Temple of Venus end. He did so for reasons both practical (he needed a curved space for a skeet shooting range) and aesthetic, so he could achieve what Russell Page called "that valuable quality in garden design, viz., surprise." Curiously, when Page actually visited the garden in the 1970s and saw the bend in the hedge, he criticized it.[98]

Sometimes the Squire of Pleasant Valley created these touches of variety and surprise serendipitously. For instance, when he first envisioned walls along the terraces near his house, they were to be flat (except for the windows). But around 1950, in the midst of trimming the hemlocks, he stopped, stepped back, and discovered that he had been a bit sloppy: there were ripples on the walls. He immediately turned these "mistakes" into the swags that have become one of the terrace's most commented-on features. Happy accident? Perhaps—but it required someone with Ladew's trained eye to turn sloppy pruning into beautiful, Adamesque embellishment.

Early-twentieth-century topiary gardeners in England pierced their hedge walls with small windowlike openings. Ladew did the same at Pleasant Valley Farm. This photograph, taken looking into the Berry Garden from one of his grand terraces, also shows the hedges' serendipitous swags, the happy result of some of Ladew's own faulty clipping.

Ladew knew that his kind of informal formal garden demanded well-placed, well-chosen statues and other three-dimensional objects: they would contrast with the plants in material and hue; they would be amusing and/or beautiful in their own right; and they would add interest to the overall composition. For all these reasons Sir George Sitwell decreed that in "a pleasure ground, however small," sculpture "is to be regarded not as ornament, but almost as a necessity."[99]

Correct siting of statues was, as Jekyll told her readers, "of as much importance as their intrinsic merit"; Sitwell recommended putting them "in wall niches" clipped into tall evergreens such as yew. In this he was joined by Edith Wharton (among others), who credited the success of the "remarkable" gardens at Villa Valzanzibio to the contrast between the evergreen "pleeched alleys" and "wide *tapis verts*" of grass and the "statues charmingly placed in niches of clipped verdure."[100] Ladew read, remembered, and responded. (Or, more likely, he had *seen*, read, remembered, and responded.) Thus he trained a few of the hemlocks in the main allée to create spaces for his collection of eighteenth-century statues of peasants, placing the stone figures so they seem ready to dance off their bases and gambol through the garden.

Knowingly, he used other statues and three-dimensional objects in other ways—and to achieve other ends. When he planted his apple orchard, he dubbed it his Garden of Eden. To underscore the name (doubtless anticipating the arrival of the I.V.s), he found a concrete, near lifesize statue of Adam and Eve, which he placed amidst the trees. But Ladew's statue gives a new twist to the old story. Elizabeth Constable explains that yes, "Eve had the apple, and is handing it to Adam. But Adam has two apples in the other hand behind his back. Harvey loved that. I mean he just loved that joke." She added that "he left little jokes and messages" all around the garden. "You have to be alert to find them all."[101] The best of these must include the stone steps leading to the Rose Garden, on which he had inscribed "A Rose is a Rose is a Rose," and the sundial in the Yellow Garden, whose base he embellished with these lighthearted Hillaire Belloc lines, "I am a sundial and make a botch,/Of what's done far better by a watch." He enlivened the grounds near the house with three home-designed, home-built dove houses. He gave two, for unknown reasons, the form of pagodas, one three-tiered, one of a single story; he gave the other vaguely Gallic lines. But since lightheartedness governs Ladew's gardens, just as it did his life, perhaps a more representative sculpture is a fountain he contrived out of an old aquarium he found in a junkyard. Many fountains, he doubtless reasoned, have fish in their basins: so why not provide his fish with a sun-filled, above-ground aquarium? *Town & Country*, recognizing his playful nature at work, felt safe in calling the aquarium fountain "a characteristic detail" of Pleasant Valley.[102]

Ladew devoted a large swath of ground near the birdhouses to the bulb

Sir George Sitwell deemed statuary in a garden "a necessity." Ladew here demonstrates one of the reasons why—by clowning with his statuary twin at Pleasant Valley Farm, c. 1960.

Lycoris squamigera, possibly because he so delighted in the plant's common name, Naked Ladies. (Plate 2.) He wrote that he once spent a vacation with "an artist friend," Dean Faucett. The two were wandering through Faucett's garden one day when they "suddenly came upon a bed of bright pink lilies." "I though them very beautiful and asked Dean what they were called. He said 'Naked Ladies,' although they had a fancy Latin name which he did not know. I said I should very much like to get some of them and he told me they were planning to move this bed in the fall and that they would sell me some of the bulbs. If they decided to do so he would let me know. I had forgotten about this when one day months later a telegram arrived which my farmer's wife took down. It read, 'Can let you have fifty naked ladies, fifty cents apiece, if you can handle them.' I was very much

Eve tempting Adam in Ladew's apple orchard; she obviously does not realize that he already has two apples hidden behind his back. "Harvey loved that," recalled Elizabeth Constable. "I mean he just loved that joke."

amused and decided I must try to send him a telegram in return. My telegram read, 'Can easily handle fifty naked ladies but please be sure they are free from all diseases.' The telegram went through but caused a mild sensation as the different operators phoned it to each other."

Ladew clearly agreed with Jekyll when she deemed fountains and water "the soul of gardens,"[103] for water plays an important role in the most successful of his garden rooms, from the fountains in the Berry, Rose, Victorian, Water Lily, and Sculpture Gardens to the carefully controlled rippling streams of the Yellow and Iris Gardens. Indeed, water—in the form of a 70-foot by 30-foot oval swimming pool[104]—determined the very size and shape of the Great Bowl, the spiritual center of Pleasant Valley's garden. In the middle of the bowl is the swimming pool; in the middle of the pool is a fountain, whose single stream rises into the air like

"Perfectly Delightful"

an exclamation point, triumphantly and with eye-catching bravura marking the spot where the garden's two great axes meet.

Planting Out

In 1937, with the foliate "bones," water features, and sculptural accents in place or at least settled on, Ladew began planting in earnest. Or, to continue the metaphor that runs through this chapter, he began arranging the furniture in his garden rooms. In his choice of flowering plants, he no longer thought of Italy, partially because flowers play so small a role in Italian garden design, but relied instead on the romantic impressions scores of visits to England had left with him: "picturesque cottages with their silvery thatch roofs dappled with emerald green moss," he wrote; cottages with "wisteria, roses, clematis, morning glories growing along their walls" and with front gardens consisting of a riotous jumble of low-growing, flowering plants, with "delphiniums, lilies, and hollyhocks as a background, and, here and there in the beds, dark accents of topiary figures of yew or boxwood to give added interest." Accordingly, he filled his "rooms" with sweeping drifts of Japanese anemones, peonies, daylilies, pinks, roses, iris, and other cottage-garden plants Jekyll loved.

Appreciative as he was of the appeal of glorious mixings of hues, here and there Ladew deftly narrowed the spectrum to create his historically important single-color gardens. He enjoyed playing chromatic games and knew how various tones could be used to best effect. Bob Six recalls that during the 1930s Ladew had "a real black and white period": he picturesquely placed Holstein cattle and Hampshire hogs in the fields around his house and populated his birdhouses with black-and-white fantail pigeons. The hogs were soon shipped off to the Esskay meatpacking plant in Baltimore, but the pigeons proved of longer duration. (Elizabeth Constable remembers that he referred to them, with their black-and-white feathers, as "the nuns.") No wonder, then, that he planned and planted one of the first "white gardens" in the United States. (Plate 6.) He gave that space great prominence, too, for it plays a key role in the overall "floor plan" and serves as a sort of hallway to connect two of the most important "rooms," namely the Tivoli Teahouse and the Water Lily Garden.[105]

White as a color enjoyed tremendous chic during the 1930s, the very years Harvey was developing his Maryland garden. It was the "color of revolution," associated as it was with the Bauhaus school and the modern movement in all the arts. Many members of Ladew's artistic circle of friends placed themselves in the vanguard of this hoary sensibility: interior decorator Syrie Maugham created all-white rooms to shock; Elsie de Wolfe, the highly fashionable designer, became famous for her love of black-and-white color schemes; and Cole Porter immortalized de Wolfe in song:

She thinks black and white,
She even drinks Black and White,
That black and white baby of mine.

Constance Spry included a planting list for a white border in her 1937 book, *Flowers in House and Garden*, and in 1939 V. Sackville-West planned what she called "a really lovely scheme" for her renowned garden at Sissinghurst Castle in Kent: "all white flowers, with some clumps of pale pink. White clematis, white lavender, white agapanthus, white double primroses, white anemones, white camellias." She added, in a burst of romanticism which would have appealed to Ladew, "I cannot help hoping that the great ghostly barn owl will sweep silently across a pale garden next summer, in the twilight—the pale garden I am now planting, under the first flakes of snow." World War II kept her from actually beginning her white garden until 1949. Since that "room" has become the most famous part of one of the most famous gardens in the world, it seems worth noting that Ladew planted his white borders before Sackville-West planted hers![106]

Ladew didn't restrict himself to white borders. Nor did Sackville-West, who for years had a weekly gardening column in the English newspaper the *Observer*. She once told her readers, "It is amusing to make one-colour gardens." She added, however, "If you think that one colour would be monotonous, you can have a two- or even a three-colour, provided the colours are happily married, which is sometimes easier of achievement in the vegetable than in the human world."[107] Entering Ladew's magnificent Yellow Garden, perhaps the most successful of his "rooms," one does indeed feel, as Jekyll hoped, as though one is "coming into sunshine." The first known correspondence regarding the Yellow Garden dates from May 27, 1938, when Ladew ordered gold variegated privet for it from Enterprise Nurseries in Wrightsville, Pennsylvania, perhaps heeding the advice of the great Jekyll, who urged gardeners to use that underrated shrub because "its clear, cheerful bright yellow gives just the right colour all through the summer."[108] He continued to tinker with details here—indeed, in all his "rooms"—the rest of his life. After most of the initial planting was done, he "decorated" the Yellow Garden with some notable nonliving features including bee skeps, the Hillaire Belloc sundial (which both probably date from the 1940s), and the orange and yellow teahouse, whose flaring roof line all but screams a space-age sensibility. Even as late as 1968, he asked one poulterer for "the 'yellowist' pigeon" he had. "I want to put some in a yellow garden I have here."[109]

Pink—not a color one associates with Ladew except in hunting coats—dominates the garden at the Tivoli Teahouse. In 1948, when he learned that the eighteenth-century Tivoli Music Hall in London's Leicester Square was about to be demolished, he arranged to have the ticket office's wooden facade "moved lock, stock, and barrel, and set up down in the garden," as Leith Griswold recalled.[110] He covered the interior walls of his new garden house with a beautiful pink paint—

"Shocking Ladew Pink," Dee Hardie termed it[111]—and carefully drew deep blue birds and trees on the pink background to create "a sort of a copy of Chinese wallpaper," said Griswold. He then built a little garden below it, choosing plants whose flowers echo the colors in the teahouse. His garden notes include, under the heading "T. House," "pink and blue roses; standard geraniums in blue pots; lilacs; wild azaleas; iris." One photograph (c. 1950) shows Harvey in front of the little building, watering can in hand, having apparently just tended to the needs of some thirsty young clematis vines. (Clematis's fussy requirements quickly diminished his enthusiasm for the plant.) On the eastern wall, he made a window, Griswold recalled, "looking down over the valley—Pleasant Valley—and put a gilt frame around it. Underneath was the title, 'Ever-changing Landscape by H. S. Ladew.' That always caused a great deal of excitement."[112]

In addition to having favorite colors, Ladew, like most gardeners, had favorite flowers. But unlike the average gardener, restricted to a half- or quarter-acre plot, Harvey's 22-acre assemblage of garden rooms—one might call it a garden mansion—allowed him to set aside entire single spaces to preferred single flowers. For example, he truly loved roses and designed a special, brick-walled "room" for them. (Plate 4.) Typically effervescent at the prospect of a new project, he decided to act as his own mason. Elizabeth Constable recalled that "he worked very hard on that, but finally" got bored and "had to call in professional help to finish."[113] (One can still detect, sixty years later, the line between "his" few courses and the mason's work.) He placed a small fountain to mark the center of the "room," designed a niche in the wall to mark the beginning of the garden's cross axis, and divided the round space into quadrants separated by grass paths. He then planted his hybrid tea roses in these concentric, circular beds while his climbers clambered up and over 7-foot-tall metal arches placed to accentuate the entire design. In 1962, therefore, rather late in the Rose Garden's life, he decided to espalier pear trees to the brick walls; he ordered the trees that year from the Henry Leuthardt Nursery of Port Chester, New York.

The earliest documentation regarding the Rose Garden is dated August 7, 1937, and comes in the form of a letter from James Todd of the Conard-Pyle Company. In it, after expressing thanks to Ladew for his "excellent hospitality" ("I surely enjoyed the time spent at your home and in going over the Roses with you"), Todd offers several paragraphs of instruction regarding spraying, fertilizing, manuring, and other aspects of rose culture. Barbara ("Bunny") Hathaway, who restored the rose garden after the severe winter of 1994 killed off nearly every plant, examined Ladew's early rose orders and stated that "he certainly liked red!"[114] He also liked yellow, for a 1943 letter from Conard-Pyle acknowledges his purchase of "35 Editor McFarland" and "80 Soeur Theresa" plants and adds, "You cannot get varieties of yellow Roses superior in results [to those two]."[115] His Rose Garden color schemes changed often during the next thirty or so years: bushes would be killed by hard winters; he might find new varieties he liked; and,

The newly arrived Tivoli Teahouse, c. 1950. Ladew created a pink and blue hand-painted wallpaper for the teahouse and then filled the garden around the little structure with plants (among them lilacs and peonies) that blossomed in colors echoing the interior. One may also see here his gilt-framed "picture," Ever-changing Landscape.

Elizabeth Constable recalled, "when the Japanese beetle came, Harvey couldn't cope with that so he had all the roses dug up and planted zinnias."[116]

Predictably, Ladew's love of roses caused him to begin writing a history of the plant. He traced it at least as far back as ancient Rome, specifically to Pliny's garden, famous in its day for topiary. "But," wrote Ladew, "there was something else in the garden that was of far more interest to people" than topiary. "It was full of roses, flowers that had never before been seen in Italy. They had been brought to Pliny from Greece where they were plentiful. The Romans could hardly contain their enthusiasm for the beautiful, fragrant flowers. Before long, they put them into many practical uses, making perfume of them and also medicine in powdered and liquid form. The medicines were thought to cure a number of ailments such as loose teeth, watering eyes, and hangovers." Intrigued, Ladew "consulted the *Encyclopedia Britannica* to see if there was any truth in this statement and found that roses had been used in medicine and that in World War II rose

"Perfectly Delightful"

hips or fruits were a source of Vitamin C." He concluded, "I have a rose garden and, occasionally, I have a hangover, so if I ever have another one, I have decided to eat a few of my roses, though I will be careful to see that they have not been dusted with D.D.T.!"

When he stayed with Sir Harold and Lady Zia Wernher at Luton Hoo, he must have seen that estate's "imposing Italianate rose garden" (to say nothing of the "topiary and formal yew hedges").[117] The gardens had been laid out for Wernher's parents around 1910 "in the fashionable style of the day" with elaborate parterres and conservatories. Sir Harold and Lady Zia altered the grounds in the fashionable style of *their* day by adding "rooms" including separate spaces for terraces, a rock garden, and herbaceous borders. Lady Zia herself, "well known for her love of roses," designed Luton's rose garden. One wonders if Ladew ever planted shrubs of the hybrid tea "Lady Zia." Named for his great friend in 1959, it has been described as having "a beautiful bloom of real substance, rich rosy flame with outer recurving petals of a brighter and deeper fire. The flowers are always upright and the colour gets stronger and more glowing as they age."[118]

Just as Lorelei Lee loved finding new places to wear diamonds, Ladew loved finding new ways to grow roses. How he must have rejoiced when he read Jekyll's suggestion that gardeners train climbing roses so as to create living fountains of color. All one has to do is grow the climber straight up an iron pole for about 8 feet and then secure its branches to an inverted, dish-shaped frame attached to the pole so they "arch over and display the flowers to perfection." Ladew read about and created splendid "umbrellas" on the sides of his terraces, umbrellas composed of metal framework over and through which he trained rampant wisteria and rambling roses.[119] (Plate 14.) Pleased with the results, he created a similar effect on the terrace behind his house, where he planted wisteria at the base of an aged locust tree.

One of the great features at the earl and countess of Iveagh's garden, Pyrford Court in Surrey, a garden Ladew knew well, is its rhododendron grove. Many authorities, including Peter Coats, feel that the Iveaghs planted their shrubs according to advice given by their neighbor Gertrude Jekyll, who recommended using plants that flowered in a restricted range of hues—"not seventy different kinds," she wrote, "but, perhaps, ten of one kind, and two or three fives . . . always bearing in mind the ultimate intention of pictorial aspect as a whole."[120] Ladew, sparked by visits to Pyrford, planned a rhododendron garden for his new Maryland property, in part as a tip of the hat to his English friends, in part as obeisance to Jekyll, and in part sensibly wishing to take advantage of his farm's moist, acid soils. But one day in the early 1930s, while driving through Pennsylvania, he spied a nursery selling inexpensive azalea seedlings. Since it was the depression, he decided to substitute these budget-priced azaleas for the costlier rhododendron, an easy thing to do because both require similar growing conditions, and bought scores of the little shrubs to plant beneath the apple trees in his Garden of Eden.

And while he may have bought with cost in mind, he selected with color in mind, for the seedlings he planted—all whites, pinks, and pale mauves—perfectly complement the pinks and whites of the apple blossoms.

Ladew also had a great fondness for the genus iris and devoted one-half of the garden's cross axis to that plant. His iris "room" occupies a sloping site measuring roughly 50 feet wide and 200 feet long. (Plate 10.) Uncertain as to whether the room's stylistic inspiration should come from the Italian baroque or the Japanese, he compromised and borrowed a bit from both: the upper end, just off the Great Bowl, reverberates with suggestions of Piazza Navona—sweeping stairs, fish fountains, all drama and excitement—while the lower end becomes a place of quiet and repose: a topiary junk floats in a quiet pool; a bright red Japanese arch marks the middle background; and a Buddha in yew, approached reverently up four shallow flights of steps, contemplates it all. Ladew's notebooks show that he had clipped pictures of junks and arches from magazines; as ever, his research was thorough, but he used those examples for inspiration only: the final result was his own.

The Buddha, not incidentally, led to a near break with one of his oldest and closest Maryland friends, Alexander Brown ("Alec") Griswold. As one might infer from his name, Griswold was an heir to the Alex. Brown investment banking company. However, he chose not to spend his life in finance but to pursue his real love, the art of Southeast Asia. He became an internationally recognized authority on the subject and taught courses on the Far East at Cornell. He also assembled one of the most significant collections of Thai art in this country and built a museum wing for his collection at his house, Breezewood, about 2 miles from Pleasant Valley.[121] Griswold and Ladew had been friends since the 1920s: for years they guided the fate of the Elkridge-Harford Hunt (Griswold as treasurer, Ladew as MFH), and they shared a love of jokes and fancy-dress parties. Yet Griswold lost his good humor when it came to anything Asian. In 1967 Ladew wrote his sister that he wanted to show her his "latest living sculpture," the Buddha. "I will ask Alec to consecrate him with prayers and joss sticks." He did so—and immediately regretted it! In June 1970, he wrote to Virginia Sherwood, head of the ladies auxiliary for the new Greater Baltimore Medical Center, "I asked Col. Griswold if he would don his saffron robes and officiate at the ceremony to consecrate our statue, but he declined, saying that he thought the whole thing was 'sacrilegious' (!!!)"[122] Regaining his composure, Ladew replied that he did not agree with him and told Griswold he felt his topiary "Buddha far greater than any of the many in his collection." He explained, "Ours is a *living* Buddha, who continues to grow stronger and more beautiful every day while all his Buddhas are just as *dead* as the metal and marble in which they are fashioned." Feelings between the two men remained sour for some months.

But the sprightly octogenarian, never one to pout, quickly bounced back from the tiff with "Col." Griswold. He wrote to Sherwood to suggest, "Next spring you might elect a High Priestess from your group who could officiate at

"Perfectly Delightful"

Ladew's topiary Buddha, a feature of the Iris Garden, as it appeared about 1980. Much earlier Ladew's friend Alec Griswold, as an admirer of Asian culture (he once threatened to sue Rodgers and Hammerstein for the effrontery of The King and I*), had angrily, if briefly, split with Ladew over this creation, which Griswold considered sacrilegious.*

the consecration of the statue. Perhaps the first day of April would be a good date (April Fools' Day!). We could meet near the statue at Sunrise. I would have a lot of very good champagne there and the High Priestess could anoint our garden's deity with it. After this has been done, we could descend to the lawn in procession, kick off our sandals, and do ritualistic dances interspersed with champagne toasts to the God's success and happiness."

Ladew directed a little stream down the center of the Iris Garden and planted 10-foot-wide beds of iris on both sides of it with parallel beds to each side. In May 1967 he enthused to his sister, "I wish you would come down in about a week and see the Iris in bloom for I think that is the best time in my garden." It was indeed quite a collection: the American Iris Society visited Pleasant Valley and cataloged 112 different tall bearded and standard dwarf varieties and two species forms. (See Appendix.) They completely ignored his many Siberian varieties and probably would have quailed had they known that he had recently written his sister, "I now plan to go in for Japanese Iris. . . . There are some beautiful varieties."

This on-paper analysis of Ladew's garden was based on finding precedents for what he created. When one experiences the place at ground level, however, by walking through it, the strict geometry, so apparent in plan, fades to the background, and one's senses yield to the grand vistas and secret corridors, private jokes and hidden meanings, tunneled pergolas and quiet trysting places, all planted with a medley of colors and perfumes. Significantly, years of art school training made Ladew keenly aware of the sensations one feels moving from constricted to expansive spaces. Therefore, early in the garden's existence, he settled on the ideal route: he would begin in the Wildflower Garden; move on to the secluded nook that is the Victorian Garden; then go to the Berry Garden, made lively by birds and fountains; then proceed to the expansive Croquet Court; then, via the narrow Pink Garden, sweep into the Great Bowl with the Rose Garden, a private walled-in space, to the left; he then wandered along the looping paths in the Garden of Eden, giggled at the statue of Adam and Eve, straightened his posture for the highly formal Keyhole Garden, and waltzed into the Water Lily Garden, with its circular pools. After the dazzling experience of the Yellow Garden, he moved, via the Laburnum Arch, to the main axis with the Temple of Venus to the left, the Tivoli Teahouse (and Henry Moore topiary) dead ahead, and the White Garden veering off to the right. Proceeding south along the main axis, he quickly gained the Sculpture Garden, his magnificent collection of specimen topiaries that were hinted at by the "Henry Moore" *Man Walking a Dog*. Then down into the Great Bowl, deeper down into the Iris Garden, and, finally, back through the Great Bowl and up the terraces to the house. "That was the route he took," said Sibyl Brown. "*Always*." Significantly, Ladew's gardening god, Gertrude Jekyll, also felt strongly that one should have a set way of progressing through a garden, of "how the experience would be revealed." At her own garden, Munstead Wood, she organized her visits "around five paths radiating from the lawn near the house."[123]

The fascination of Ladew's truly beautiful creation lies partly in the fact that although it is historically important—perhaps the first garden in America to exhibit the English arts and crafts style, and with single-color "rooms" that predate Sissinghurst—it was never a period piece. Like a classic Chanel jacket, or in Ladew's case a Savile Row suit, it transcends the vagaries of fashion. Indeed, its quality of design has enabled it to absorb subtle alterations and additions, some made by Ladew himself, some made since his death in 1976. His thoroughly thought-out system of topiary forms and plantings achieves the effect of *distance* thanks to his long allées and vistas, of *variety* thanks to ingenious devices such as hedge "windows" and an orderly sequence of yew-lined rooms of different shape and size, of *unity* thanks to the seemingly continuous walls of hemlock and the wall-to-wall carpets of grass, and of *climax* thanks to the topiary-bejeweled terraces that cause the eye—and heart—to soar.

"Your old brother is a one!*"*

While Harvey Ladew kept busy during the 1930s redoing his new Maryland house and beginning its now famous garden, he also maintained the tradition of spending each fall and winter hunting foxes in England, a tradition he had been enjoying since 1919. (To avoid boredom, he varied the regimen with the occasional jaunt through the Arabian desert.) The outbreak of war in 1939, of course, rendered his old routine impracticable. But Ladew, nothing if not resourceful, soon created a new pattern for himself, one that would last him the rest of his life, namely, of wintering in Florida and spending several weeks in the summer—when he wasn't pruning his topiary—traveling, hunting, and generally having a high old time in Europe. Indeed, so lively did many of these adventures prove that he even impressed himself with his goings-on. Or, as he wrote to his sister in 1948, "Your old brother is a *one!*"[1]

GULF STREAM HAVEN

The deaths of his parents (his father in 1905, his mother in 1912) and his sister's marriage in 1914 abruptly ended the Palm Beach winters Ladew had so enjoyed with his family in the early years of the century. Just as he had closed his parents' gingerbreadish Long Island mansion and built himself a cottage of his own, so did he close the regimen of family Florida winters. When he decided to resume these stays in 1939, he settled not in Palm Beach, with all its past associations, but in Gulf Stream, a new community a few miles to the south near the town of Delray Beach.

If he was not to be in Palm Beach, Gulf Stream boasted an equine-based history that made it a thoroughly logical alternative. The community had, in effect, two mothers: the Gulf Stream Polo Club and the Gulf Stream Golf Club, incorporated in April and July 1924, respectively. Both organizations boasted officers and members Ladew knew and admired, and the community itself had been organized by brothers Howard and John S. Phipps, kin to Harvey through the Grace family.

The polo and golf clubs were initially planned for Palm Beach. But by 1924, that town had become too built up and no longer had the open space a polo field and golf links required. Moreover, the young, athletic Phippses probably viewed the older, somewhat stuffy residents of Palm Beach as inimical to the vigorous outdoors lives they wished to lead. These athletes wanted a place for *serious sports*. (More than one source has noted that by 1923 young golfers such as the Phipps brothers complained that the old duffers who played at the Everglades Club, which had the only course in town, slowed down the game.) Similarly, many of the older community's residents, "strictly formal" in dress and behavior, probably viewed the young men in their sweaty polo uniforms with disfavor.[2]

The Phippses also regretted the rapid, style-driven changes that came to the once low-key community. Did they really want to live next door to palaces designed by men like Joseph Urban, "architect to the Ziegfeld Follies"?[3] As the twenties wore on, the town became chockablock with Venetian *palazzi*, Tudor-English piles, and Gothic palaces—virtually anything and everything went so long as it was BIG. Or, as Ladew wrote in his unfinished history of the town, in the early twenties Palm Beach's movers and shakers had "'Castles from Spain' shipped across the ocean." Continuing, he observed, "Not only were the houses Spanish but all the streets began to have Spanish names—the Via This and the Via That"; and he winked that Worth Avenue, the community's main commercial strip, quickly boasted "what Anita Loos's blonde said of the Place Vendome when she first saw it—'all the classical, historical names such as Cartier.'"[4]

In fact, Peggie Boegner, John Phipps's daughter (who recalled that life at home "was pervaded by polo"), noted, "When Palm Beach started to become more fashionable, Mother and Father retired more into their own surroundings." She added that she herself "never liked the people in Palm Beach" and felt that her father and uncle were "most amenable" to refocusing their Florida lives to Gulf Stream.[5]

Ladew managed to maintain, in a bemused sort of way, his friendship with many of Palm Beach's plutocrats, including Marjorie Merriweather Post, whose enormous house, known as Mar-a-Lago because its 17 acres of grounds sprawl from the ocean to Lake Worth, dates from 1926. Ladew wrote that "Marjorie was divorced [from broker E. F. Hutton] and went on to a few more marriages. She was at one time married to Mr. Joseph Davies, who later became Ambassador to Russia." Harvey recalled that one night the Davieses were invited to dinner, "but Marjorie said she was very sorry they couldn't accept as Joe was making a political speech in West Palm Beach." Instead, they agreed that she should come to dinner and he could drop in later. Accordingly, Davies "arrived after the speech in white tie and tails." Ladew said, "[I] had never, in those days, seen anyone dressed

"Perfectly Delightful"

like that here. He also had on a top hat, carried a tall black cane with a gold top and was wearing an opera cloak lined with white satin. The man at the gate to the dining room said, 'We're not expecting the magician until twelve o'clock. Will you please go around to the back door and wait in the kitchen.' I suppose he thought there were rabbits and goldfish under the cloak."[6]

Ladew continued to attend such soirees well into the 1960s; sometimes they were in Palm Beach; sometimes they were in the exclusive community Hobe Sound, which he mischievously nicknamed "Hobo Sound." In a 1967 letter to his sister, he described "a small dinner party of sixty or seventy people" he'd gone to the night before at Mar-a-Lago. He called the evening "amazing" and noted, "We had every imaginable thing to eat except Post Toasties and Postum (which is a kind of Sanka—rather horrible)." He never ceased to marvel at the "great number of large and beautiful houses in Palm Beach" and the hosts capable of calling "in as many men as they need[ed] from different agencies for the evening" to serve. "These men are for the most part old time butlers or footmen and are perfectly trained. One meets them at every big party and they all know each person's

---

"Your old brother is a one!"

favorite drink without having to ask. Of course, they get an occasional shock when they bring the drink and find that the person has suddenly gone on the water wagon. (He or she probably had to.)"[7]

The architect of most of these "large and beautiful houses"—and of many of the "classical, historical" stores as well—was Addison Mizner, who gained his first Florida commission in 1918 when sewing machine heir Paris Singer asked him to design the Everglades Club. Mizner envisioned the club as a sprawling mélange of Moorish towers, loggias, and fountains—"a mixture built by a nun from Venice," with a "bit of new Spain from the tropics."[8] The club "became the new center of Palm Beach," and patron and architect worked to transform the quiet community, once characterized by its two frame hotels, into something "more glamorous." Ladew, who had known Mizner, felt that while "Addison may not have been a great architect, for he had completely forgotten to put a stairway to the upper floors of one house, he was a most amusing and witty person," famous for quips, such as "a word to the wise is resented."[9]

In 1924, Mizner designed the first building in the Phippses' new Gulf Stream community, a highly correct, Mediterranean revival–style clubhouse; nationally known golf course architect Donald Ross laid out the new fairways and greens.[10] While outside experts may have sufficed for the golf course, the Phipps brothers themselves took charge of the all-important polo grounds, eventually spending some six hundred thousand dollars on what the press dubbed "the Phipps Project."[11] Not surprisingly, given the brothers' almost hereditary interest in horticulture—John Phipps and his wife, for instance, created Long Island's internationally known Old Westbury Gardens—they spared no expense landscaping "their project" and even encouraged "one of the finest nurseries in the state" to relocate near the polo field. They embellished the grounds with "wide, winding bridle paths between rows of royal palm trees and Australian palm hedges," one reporter stated; the trails circled the polo fields and wound "in and out of the entire development, forming snaky lanes through the picturesque sports center." In all, the brothers planted some ten thousand royal palms, three thousand coconut trees, five thousand oleanders, seven thousand Australian pines, and uncounted numbers of hibiscus and crotons on the club's acreage.[12]

The polo club proved an immediate success and attracted most of the nation's top players, including, in addition to the Phipps brothers themselves, Stewart Iglehart, Stephen ("Laddie") Sanford, Raymond and Winston Guest (whose "original and imaginative"[13] mother, Amy, was a sister of John and Howard Phipps), and John Phipps's sons, Hubert, Michael, and Ben. By 1929 the club hosted forty-seven scheduled matches and stabled more than two hundred ponies. Whether or not "more polo was played on the Phipps field than anywhere else in the world," as one Florida newspaper trumpeted, no one—then or now—could dispute the club's claim that in the 1920s and 1930s, it reigned as the "Winter Polo Capital of the World."[14]

"Perfectly Delightful"

Some of Ladew's polo-playing friends (and, through the Graces, kinsmen), 1934. From the left are brothers Raymond (b. 1907) and Winston Guest (b. 1906) and their cousin Michael Phipps (b. 1910). The young men had just won a polo match at the Meadow Brook Club; their grandmother, Annie Phipps, presents them with their trophy. "Polo dominated our lives," Michael's sister Peggie recalled.

In addition to planning the polo field, John Phipps dabbled in local real estate. He bought vast tracts of open, sandy land and built oceanfront houses for himself, his friends, and his family in the subdivisions Gulf Stream Ocean Tracts (1935) and Gulf Stream Properties (1937). Again not surprisingly—given the family's fondness for the building arts—Phipps and his friends lured some of the era's finest architectural talents to Gulf Stream. Significantly, as was true with the Phipps brothers themselves, the architects for the community—once the venerable Mizner had completed the clubhouse—also represented the new generation. As discussed in Chapter 3, that generation of architects believed in designing houses that respected local building traditions. In Florida, that meant drawing inspiration from the sixteenth- and seventeenth-century structures Spanish colonists erected in places such as St. Augustine. Accordingly, Howard Major (born 1883) designed a clutch of Gulf Stream residences in the Spanish revival mode, including 2929 North Ocean Boulevard, built in 1925 for New Yorker Howard Whitney; Phillip Goodwin, a 1907 graduate of Yale's School of Architecture, designed the stuccoed 3145 North Ocean Boulevard for Howard Phipps in 1927; and Marion Sims Wyeth (born 1889) is credited with a dozen Gulf Stream mission revival residences.

For all the success those men enjoyed in south Florida, the architect best able to capture the era's zeitgeist was probably Maurice Fatio, dubbed "the new taste-maker for Palm Beach."[15] Born into a wealthy Swiss banking family in 1897, Fatio studied architecture at Zurich Polytechnic. Acting on his father's advice, the young architect moved to New York in 1920. The "charming and handsome" Fatio, de-scribed as "the quintessential society architect" and a man of "cosmopolitan glam-our and impeccable taste," gained so many commissions that in 1923 he was voted "the most popular architect in New York."[16] That year, developers hired him to design a speculative community in south Florida called Olympia Beach.

Olympia Beach failed, but Fatio stayed on and was taken up "by the socially powerful Phipps and Sanford families." He is said to have especially appealed to the Phippses because he eschewed "the extravagant magnificence of an Addison Mizner" in favor of buildings that suggested comfort and "family living."[17] Fatio opened an office in Palm Beach in 1925 and immediately became an integral part of Florida's new generation of architects. The tenor of his own life may be de-duced from this February 26, 1923, letter to his sister: "The climate is marvelous in Florida. I never put on a coat; you can dance outside in the afternoon and in the evening, and towards 3 o'clock in the morning . . . you can go for a dip in the sea, which sometimes is phosphorescent."[18]

In Fatio's first year of practice he designed a brace of relatively small Gulf Stream residences for members of the polo set. These cottages were located con-veniently near the playing field, not unlike the bungalows Harvey Ladew and oth-ers were building on the grounds of the Harford Hunt Club at exactly the same time. John Phipps himself commissioned one house from Fatio, a stucco and tim-ber dwelling located adjacent to the polo club and now numbered 3649 North Ocean Boulevard.

Concurrent with his work for the Phippses, Fatio helped Ladew's great friend Consuelo Vanderbilt Balsan escape the embarrassments of overheated Palm Beach. (She purportedly expressed her disdain for the town by stating that she only went there "to have her hair washed and to go to the bank.")[19] Consuelo Balsan bought the 50-acre Hypoluxo Island north of town and hired Fatio to remodel the exist-ing house on the property. Ladew's friends Horst and Valentine Lawford have described the Hypoluxo villa as "a rambling Hispanic retreat approached through a grapefruit and orange grove and backed by banyans and royal palms." Horst had particularly fond memories of "the palm-fringed pool," where "Jacques Balsan, well over eighty, regularly did his two lengths under water every morning and where she herself sometimes swam, in the quiet of the afternoon, wearing a wide straw hat."[20]

In sum, "by the 1930s Gulf Stream was firmly established as a winter resort for the wealthy."[21] As Pamela Murray told readers of the *Tatler* in 1941, the "attractive community [that had] sprung up around the Gulf Stream Club" was "much in favor." "The houses are small—none of your palatial Palm Beach sets—but they do not jostle each other."[22] So when Harvey Ladew started to look around for a place to buy in Florida, he didn't have to look long or hard. He simply settled on 3649 North Ocean Boulevard, the very house Fatio had designed for John Phipps.

After purchasing the beachfront villa, Harvey named the place Pied-à-Mer and immediately set about giving it his own highly individualistic imprint. (Billy Baldwin wrote that he "watched him make a gem out of his house in Delray.")[23] In 1958, *Vogue* ran an article on Ladew's "easy as an espadrille" beach house, and the anonymous reporter had nothing but praise for its "red and cream tile floors" and "compatible collection of French, Persian, Chinese, and modern furniture." The magazine especially liked his bedroom, calling it "a Chinese simplification: an ancient teakwood bed, hung with beige silk; off-white walls; and a beige fibre rug scored with black tape."[24]

In another bedroom, Baldwin detected similarities to "the beautiful decoration that Oliver Messel did for *House of Flowers*. The whole room, including the bed, was curtained in bright pink theatrical gauze."[25] (Others recall this as the "Watermelon Guest Room," as the rug, bed, and "all the accouterments" were "of watermelon flavor.")[26] Ladew also created a Green Guest Room, which he draped in filmy swathing to simulate an underwater atmosphere. This, too, left visitors "terribly amused and impressed": it "seemed to be practically in the sea. . . . Curtains of fishnets fringed with shells hung at the windows, and to enhance the room, Harvey had selected several Regency chairs in the form of silver shells."[27] It all suggests the contemporaneous work of Syrie Maugham, who declared in 1935, "I am specializing in everything to do with shells," and then went on to make great use of "shell motifs and Venetian grotto furniture, with its bizarre gilded oyster- and barnacle-encrusted rococo forms" in projects throughout Britain. Perhaps her most famous "shell" commission came from the aesthete Stephen Tennant for his house, Wilsford.[28]

All houses in Florida demand swimming pools. Ladew built his in a large coral outcropping and designed it to look "as though he had carved it out of giant rocks."[29] He decorated the pool with stone dolphins and pelicans spouting water and dotted his beach with other playful touches, such as a giant, inflatable crab to remind guests of the home owner's Maryland connection. Then when World War II ended, he brought over his Uncle Berry's blue-and-white-striped bathing machine from France. The *bon viveur* took especial delight in the *Tatler*'s coverage of the contraption: "There are no points of historic interest [in Gulf Stream]," its correspondent sniffed, "other than the bathing machine imported from Trouville

Merry Christmas, c. 1950, as Ladew and Santa toast in the holiday with a bottle of Johnnie Walker Black.

by Mr. Harvey S. Ladew. His neighbours are fascinated by it. Many have never seen one. Others, more cultured, at once offer to lend a polo pony to drag it into the sea."[30]

The magazine went on to call Ladew a "Bohemian figure," and nothing suggests he objected to that description. He built himself a little shed just north of the main house, connected the two structures by means of a loggiaed courtyard, and painted a mural of monkeys and trees on one wall. ("It was an outrage it was so bad," laughed one friend.)[31] He used the new room as a retreat where he could continue his sculpting and painting. In 1970 he wrote his sister, "I have improved my studio. The roof, facing the ocean, is now all glass and the studio looks like the one in the first act of La Boheme." Ladew truly reveled in the local art scene. He became a great patron of the Palm Beach galleries and a fixture at exhibit openings, often accompanied by Jacqueline and then Senator John Kennedy or by Joseph Hirshhorn.[32] Moreover, while Harvey never indulged in polo himself, he enjoyed the game and encouraged grooms and players to "ride their ponies over to his beach . . . to get water on their legs." He also seized the opportunity to make "some charming sketches and a very good painting of their activity."[33]

"Perfectly Delightful"

Shortly after completing the house, Ladew built a small rectangular pavilion a few yards away. It contained one large, oval-shaped room, "copied," according to one source, "from the proportions of his great oval library in Maryland."[34] It looked conventionally Floridian on the outside, with cream-color stuccoed walls, Mediterranean red tile roofs, and tall, arched windows and doors. But inside those doors came a surprise, for Ladew based the room's decoration entirely on playing cards. A *Vogue* reporter, in writing up this "House of Cards," found a rug stitched to resemble an enlarged king of spades; an arch of seashells and cards over a mirror ("in the manner of Grinling Gibbons"); a pair of nineteenth-century card presses gracing an agate-topped console inlaid with cards; an eighteenth-century Italian coffee table "with still more cards scattered, in scagliola inlay, all across the top"; a bathroom floor consisting of "tile canasta hands"; antique playing cards around the bathroom mirror ("with a row of poker chips to dot the edges"); and

The dining room at Ladew's Gulf Stream retreat. Billy Baldwin wrote that he watched his friend "make a gem out of his house in Delray." Note the small clamshell sconce on the wall echoing the monster clamshell that threatens from without.

"Your old brother is a one!*"*

Harvey Ladew's beach featured the nineteenth-century blue-striped bathing machine he got from his Uncle Berry and the inflatable crab he acquired to remind guests that he was a Marylander.

accent pillows with cards in needlepoint scattered about everywhere to "carry on the *jeu de cartes*."[35]

Ladew spent many happy hours at the bridge table either in his card room or in competitions. "Mr. Harvey Ladew," observed the *Vogue* reporter, "enjoys a game of cards as much as — and possibly more than — the next man," and he and his partners won several tournaments over the years. When the local magazine *Surf and Tide* reported one of his 1949 victories, it called him "Sir Harvey Ladew," an advancement in rank which pleased him no end.[36] "Your old brother has been knighted!" he delightedly wrote his sister. He was even more delighted to tell her that Charles Goren (no less) was numbered among the vanquished. Ladew pasted the tournament scores in a scrapbook, and Goren sportingly inscribed the page "with jealousy."

"Sir Harvey" made a garden in the space between the main house and card pavilion. Here his natural élan truly asserted itself, for he filled the space with a school of topiary whales he sculpted in Australian pine. He gave the whales electric light bulbs for eyes (the better for evening strolls) and installed an electronic sprinkling system that caused them to "spout" at the push of a button — all in all, "a long-distance echo," *Vogue* sighed, "of Mr. Ladew's famous Maryland topiary garden." On the small terrace leading from the card house to the "whales," Ladew placed twin tables shaded by "umbrellas copied, by long distance, from those at Lady Mendl's Versailles house." "Here . . . he gives his famous parties": luncheons featuring such Florida specialties as stone crab, pompano, and fresh strawberries and cocktail parties "with a special hors-d'oeuvre—tiny hot baked potatoes."[37]

It is possible to know precisely what he planted elsewhere around the house, thanks to—of all things—a particularly vicious storm that devastated south Florida in 1947. That September he wrote his sister, "I am rather sunk about my little house in Delray being so badly destroyed by the hurricane. I do not know all the details but that the house is damaged and Katie's house and the garage completely gone. . . . You know how I love being in Florida. Well, I will have to get a trailer and live at 'Briney Breezes'—and change the name of my place to Gone With the Wind." In the storm's aftermath, a Delray nursery man sent Ladew a list of what precisely was needed to "replace shrubbery, cacti, trees, palms, etc., destroyed by hurricane": thirteen palms of various kinds, one "Clump Bamboo," three citrus trees (two kumquat and one orange), and vines aplenty including five plumbago, a dozen bougainvillea, and sixteen sweet-scented jasmines.

A motorcycle proved a sensible, gas-saving way to get around during the war years of the early 1940s—but the beret?

"Your old brother is a one*!"*

195

In the midst of all this painting, bridge playing, and gardening, Ladew threw himself into the local scene with his usual flair and fervor. One suspects he may have indulged in a bit of willful eccentricity as well, for in the 1940s he took to commuting between Gulf Stream and Palm Beach on a motor scooter while wearing a beret. He claimed he chose the scooter to save on war-rationed gasoline— but the beret? The editor of the *Delray Beach News* enjoyed the idea of a motor-cycling aesthete and featured a cigar-smoking Harvey and his scooter (going "put, put, put") in a 1943 cartoon of local characters. The cartoon also includes Laddie Sanford, Stewart Webb, and a group of servicemen stating, "The town is full of nuts."[38] Ladew, in fact, contributed to the war effort by entertaining those (and other) befuddled servicemen. At the outbreak of hostilities, the Coast Guard requisitioned the polo team's Gulf Stream clubhouse and turned it into a barracks. According to the February 1943 issue of the *Maryland Horse*, Ladew's favorite American magazine, "Harvey S. Ladew . . . put in a busy Christmas day playing host to the fifty-odd men of the unit left at the base that day. The men, resplendent in dress blues, enjoyed to the full a complete Christmas menu," including "'lashings of beer' and a carton of cigarettes apiece. The dinner was served on the sunny patio of the Ladew home and was followed by songs and entertainments by the coast guardsmen."[39]

In 1942 Ladew (center in tropical shirt) did his bit for the war effort and had fifty-odd men from the neighboring U.S. Coast Guard station to his Delray house for Christmas lunch and "lashings of beer."

"Perfectly Delightful"

During the forties and fifties Ladew kept his winters busy organizing tableaux vivants, *including this homage to Renoir, for Palm Beach's Society of the Four Arts.*

Since there was no foxhunting in south Florida, there was no Elkridge-Harford Hunt Club for Harvey to guide and fret over. But he did find a good substitute in Palm Beach's Society of the Four Arts.[40] He immersed himself in the society's goings-on, partially because he found so many old friends among the organization's directors, including Michael Grace, Marjorie Merriweather Post Davies, and Amy Phipps Guest. Ladew, as chair of the committee on "Drama and Moving Pictures," used his Hollywood connections to ensure that Palm Beachers saw first-run films. He also urged the club to sponsor the amateur theatricals he so enjoyed. In 1949 he wrote a friend to thank her for helping him "with the Tableaux." "If we can get the right people to be in them I think they will be very attractive and that it will be a bit of a novelty for Palm Beach. I would like you to be Chairman of the Casting Committee and think the girls you suggested would be fine, if they will do it," and he mentioned Mary Sanford, Amy Guest and a "Mrs. Rockefeller."[41]

As had so often happened before, when Ladew truly enjoyed something, he wrote about it. In 1946 he became *Town & Country*'s reporter for the area, and (again as so often happened before) once he filed his story, he grew bored and looked for new amusements. But in that one piece, he was pleased to tell readers that polo was "in full swing" at Gulf Stream and he "hoped" that Winston Guest,

just out of the army, might be playing at Delray "before the season is over." Drawing comfort from the fact that there had been "such an influx of British nobility
lately that the social columns in the Palm Beach papers read very much like the
Court Circular," he noted the presence of the duke and duchess of Sutherland (at
whose coronation ball he had shone so brilliantly), the duchess of Westminster,
Lord and Lady Astor, and Winston Churchill, who had "spent his vacation quietly
with his ex-relative and friend Mme. Balsan."[42] Ladew was saddened, though, to
note that after forty-seven years, Bradley's had "closed its doors for good." He

*As this page from his Delray guest book suggests, Ladew enjoyed his usual mix of friends in
Florida with names ranging from European aristocrats to the toasts of Broadway and Hollywood: Note Zia Wernher (born a Romanov) and her husband; "Dicky" Adare, eldest son
of the Irish earl of Dunraven; playwright Terence Rattigan, comedienne Beatrice Lillie, and
actor Clifton Webb.*

"Perfectly Delightful"

knew that the end of Bradley's, a gambling house established during Palm Beach's early, informal years, also ended an era: "Somehow," he wrote, "the place will never seem the same without it."

Billy Baldwin has probably provided the best vignette of life with "Sir Harvey" at Pied-à-Mer. During World War II, the decorator enlisted in the army and found himself stationed in Florida. Once in late 1943 he managed to obtain a weekend pass to visit his longtime friend. "We had a wonderful lunch," Baldwin wrote, "and I was taking a real siesta on the soft coral rocks at the pool." He continued,

Harvey at that time was painting everything he could lay his hands on, and that day he decided to paint a portrait of me. He said, "You'll be glad to know that what I want to do is to paint you in the nude lying on your stomach. I want you to spend the afternoon as though you were alone. First of all, I want you to get very comfortable so you won't have to change your position."

I said, "Sure, Harvey. But don't you think I'll get a wild sunburn?" That consideration didn't seem to bother Harvey, and the sun wasn't all that hot, so I posed and Harvey painted.

While he worked, I slept, lying with my head turned on its side. I got quite pink from the exposure, and when it was very nearly done he said, "I know one thing without doubt. Anybody who sees this who knows you at all will undoubtedly say, 'That is Billy Baldwin.'"

I got up and walked over to see it. The picture was small, about ten inches by twelve inches. My sleeping pink form was surrounded by white rocks and incredible colored hibiscus. In one of those moments when everything works, Harvey had caught me: the line of my shoulder, the line of the thigh, my head shape, hair, the whole thing.

I said, "Harvey, I've never asked you to give me anything, but I would like that portrait."

Harvey said, "Oh, William. I couldn't do that. It's going to be one of my treasures."

"Can you do another?" I asked.

"No," he said. "It's been done."

It would have been fun to have because it was a very amusing thing. He painted very well; not as well as he thought, but still it was as amusing as the dickens. I often wonder what became of it. After Harvey's death and the Delray house was sold, I'm sure that it was probably sent to an auction house where it was sold, or it might simply have been destroyed and is in ashes.[43]

Pace, Mr. Baldwin. The little painting survived deaths and auction houses to find its way to Maryland, where it now rests safely at Pleasant Valley Farm. (Plate 18.)

With the end of World War II, Ladew, eager to return to the England he had known and loved, booked passage on virtually the first ship he could find to Southampton. "When the boat train deposited me late one evening at Victoria Station," he wrote, "I felt an indescribable thrill for, after all the long years of war, I was once again in my favorite city." He had accepted an invitation to stay with his old friends the Wernhers, and the couple's "lovely apartment in Grosvenor Square, full of Rembrandts, Franz Hals, Hoppners, Romneys," delighted him, especially after they put "their Rolls-Royce and chauffeur" at his disposal. After he unpacked, he found himself "far too excited to think of sleep," so he "tore out into the street."

But a series of unpleasant surprises awaited. "The Ritz, as I passed it, had a gloomy, unfamiliar look, for its lower floor, where the shops had been, was still blocked up with cement." He found "the Cavendish Hotel still there, with the big white lettered signs that had been painted on its walls at the beginning of the war, 'Business as Usual,'" and he pictured "Rosa Lewis sitting in her office unmoved, though possibly not unshaken, as the bombs dropped around her." After he climbed around "many signs of the Blitz and several demolished houses" to get to Berkeley Square, he was appalled to find "that once perfect example of 18th century London" completely "ruined." Seeking some creature comfort, he repaired to his prewar favorite restaurant, Pruniers, for plover's eggs but was served seagull's eggs instead, "a very poor substitute." He wrote his sister that the rest of the "indigestible" meal consisted of "Portuguese oysters, probably full of typhoid germs, and cold coquille of lobster, a glass of beer, coffee, and four crackers. Well!" Ladew found matters no better at his club, Boodle's. "There *is* food here—but nothing substantial—all very sick-making." Still, he admired the English for refusing to succumb to the black market, and he contrasted this with Paris, "where the 'Bon Marché noire' [was] openly indulged in and where a friend said to [him], 'I get butter and eggs from my coiffeur and meat at my modiste's.'"[44]

Still not everything about the city depressed him. The theater remained strong, as he wrote in his unfinished autobiography, and he saw a revival of *Lady Windemere's Fan* (Cecil Beaton sets); *The First Gentleman*, in which Robert Morley "seemed the very incarnation of George IV"; a Beatrice Lillie revue ("amusing as ever" even though "most of her songs and numbers were old ones"); and *Big Ben*, a "new Cochran show . . . lavishly staged" and featuring Hermoine Gingold, whose brand of humor he deemed "not as subtle as Lady Peel's" but "nonetheless most amusing." One English friend asked him how the West End's offerings compared with Broadway's. Harvey said he found them similar but that New York boasted more long-running plays, "including *Life With Mama*." "Don't you mean *Life With Father*," his friend said. "Oh yes," Ladew replied. "I must have been thinking of *Oedipus Rex*."

Royalty remained an attraction, too, even though his favorite, Queen Mary, showed signs of age. Invited to a garden party at Buckingham Palace a few years later, Ladew recalled standing in line as the young Queen Elizabeth II progressed from guest to guest. At one point near him she stopped, and he saw the chamberlain whisper something to Her Majesty. Cocking his ear a little, Ladew heard the queen say, "Oh, you are a photographer. What a coincidence. My brother-in-law is a photographer." "A coincidence, indeed, ma'am," came the courtly reply. "My brother-in-law is a queen."

Finally, he learned that Myrtle Farquharson had been killed in an air raid. Without Farquharson, that dear friend with whom he had shared many a giggle at the royals' expense, Ladew knew London was no longer for him.[45] Seeking refuge in the hunting field, he drove to Northamptonshire to rejoin the Pytchley. The first day he "had lunch with Colonel Lowther, who had been MFH for twenty years" but had recently resigned. "I found many other changes. A number of the men I knew had been killed or badly wounded, the large estates were being split up, and the country was a network of barbed wire." The new Labour government, swept into office in 1945, had pledged to end all "bloodsports," and the pitiful state of hunting must have made it seem an easy victim: "The lodges emptied, the grooms, stablemen, and servants went, never to return," one historian has written. "A deserted Melton was like a town of ghosts."[46] Even though Colonel Lowther assured him that the Pytchley would carry on, if at "a much reduced scale," a sad Ladew concluded, "It is no wonder that there has been an exodus of English people to Ireland."

He decided to join that exodus. He contacted some prewar friends, "Dicky" Adare and his wife, Nancy. This couple, who had stayed with him in Florida, proved the ideal hosts in Ireland. On September 23, 1947, Harvey wrote his sister from the Dunraven Arms Hotel in the village of Adare, "Here I am in Eire—getting comfortably settled in this little apartment, which couldn't be nicer. I have a small sitting room, with really good central heating—and a peat fire. A nice bed room and my own bathroom—a room for Ned [Ned McDermot, his new valet] and a large pressing room. The food is delicious—plenty of eggs, bacon, chicken, lamb chops, vegetables—well cooked. . . . The Adares just couldn't be nicer to me and I like them so much." He included "a photo of Dicky's father, the Earl of Dunraven," with the letter and noted the earl was ninety-four years old. "He called on me today, which I must say I think was terribly nice." Ladew also got in touch with his American friend George Garrett, an investment banker who served as U.S. ambassador to Ireland from 1947 to 1951.[47]

Ladew adored Ireland and the Irish—the landscape, the citizens' good nature, and the love of hunting which permeated the entire countryside: "It is indigenous to the soil and bred in their bones," he wrote. He relished the tale of one farmer who had hunted all his life until he realized he had simply grown too old for the sport. But, even though the farmer no longer rode, he still drove upwards of 50 miles to see a hunt. Ladew said that he told the old man, "Why, Pat, you must be mad to come such a distance." To which the countryman replied, "Ah, well, me Lord. Sure if we were all out-and-out *sane*, there'd be very little fox hunting." Even the clergy, Ladew gaily informed his sister, thrilled to the hunt, although because of postwar austerity, the Vatican hierarchy only allowed "the priests to keep one horse each." He found he almost envied the Irish clergy: "They have a grand time here. They golf, shoot, go racing, breed greyhounds and of course race them, fish. One priest likes bridge and was playing with Mrs. Luke Lillingston. He loves to win and was furious because he was having very bad cards. Mrs. L. said to him, 'Well, never mind. You know, unlucky in cards lucky in love'—and then she hurriedly added, 'Oh, I forgot, you can't do *that!*'"

At first, "Dicky" Adare let Ladew choose horses from his own stable. But the American, increasingly enamored of Ireland and all things Irish, decided to acquire three mounts of his own. He told his sister, "There is a black mare called 'Dark Anne' that I love. She is a grand hunter, big and strong. I think I will buy her and bring her back as she jumps walls so well . . . and she would make a grand brood mare." He did and soon proudly reported that the duke of Beaufort offered to buy the horse for a sum that would mean "a hundred pounds profit." Harvey didn't sell.[48]

Out in the field, he found it "10 times as hard to cross this country" as it was to ride in America over post and rails. "Everything you come to here is *different*." Still, he felt "it great fun and perfectly delightful." Even so, the days were not without incident. In October 1947 he wrote his sister, "We had a terrific hunt last Friday. People were lying all over the fields and people and horses were stuck in boggy ditches. It looked like a battlefield—when the battle was over." Far more typical, however, was the evening he wrote to say, "Just back from a day's hunting. . . . We jumped all sorts of things that were new to me. I went back to tea with the hunt Secretary and his wife, Mr. and Mrs. Waller. It was really a huge meal: boiled eggs, ham, muffins, tea. On reaching home a boiling hot bath with a cake of pink Bendel soap floating in it—What could be a nicer day?!"

Once again, Ladew's new enthusiasm lured him to the typewriter. He wrote his sister excitedly, "Well—Carmel Snow wants me to write up two Irish hunts and I am doing Limerick and Tipperary. Harper's Bazaar in Paris has flown a French photographer over and I have brought him here to take the pictures—He is M. Tabard, and very nice. He paints and writes and has good manners." He had reason to be excited about working for Snow, editor in chief of *Harper's Bazaar* from the 1930s to the 1950s and a woman Horst described as "brilliant." She had "a rare nose for new talent and an instinctive sense of the temper of the times," the photographer reminisced, and an ebullient personality that served as "a source of inspiration and encouragement to the artists whose work she used." Ladew, who knew Snow socially as well as professionally, actually completed two articles for her.[49]

"Perfectly Delightful"

Ladew and his fellow sportsmen preparing for a day out with the Tipperary Hunt in the fall of 1947.

The first was the piece on Irish hunting. In it, he traced the history of the sport to 1734, when twelve men got together to form the Limerick Hunt. He recounted the tale of a particularly colorful whipper-in, one John Kennedy, whose front teeth had been knocked out in a fall. To compensate, Kennedy wore dentures, but they proved ill fitting and fell out of his mouth at the slightest bump or shake. Thus, whenever he knew the hounds had found a fox, Kennedy removed the plate and prepared for a mad dash across the rough field. "This became a sort of signal to the field," Ladew reported, "and just before the start of a run, one would hear the remark, 'Lookout, Kennedy has pocketed his teeth!'"[50]

Generally, Ladew tried to hunt three or four times a week. On other days he busied himself with golf and fishing. As he wrote his sister, "Lord Dunraven has a private golf course on his place right near the Inn. . . . It is one of the prettiest courses you can imagine. There are two ruined abbeys on it and views of the Manor House and river." On November 5, 1947, he wrote her begging, "Do me a favor and send me right away some golf tees? I can't get the long ones here," and he enclosed a sketch of what he needed. In another letter he said that Dunraven had let him fish in the river Maigue, a famous salmon stream that ran through the earl's estate. Ladew had taken up rod and reel back in his Long Island days. Typ-

Carmel Snow, the legendary editor in chief of Harper's Bazaar, *here seen as photographed by Horst, who called Snow "a source of inspiration" to artists. She must have been so, for she coaxed two complete articles out of Ladew, a man who rarely finished any literary project.*

ically, he bought every book he could find on the subject, but he admitted that the tomes on salmon fishing proved "a bit unsettling as all the authorities seemed to differ in what flies to use and methods to employ."

On November 1, 1947, Ladew wrote his sister to say he had decided to give a big cocktail party "here at the Inn some time in January." He wondered if she could send him "some original cocktail party invitations," observing, "I don't think people over here send them out and it would be rather a novelty for them." He recalled that "Abercrombie & Fitch did have an amusing one with a man falling off a horse into a brook": "It says 'Come to my cocktail party and you'll get something better than water.' I dare say I would have between fifty and eighty people." He ended that note telling her that he planned to return to America "some time in February and would like to go to Florida." He hoped to book passage on the February 13 Cunarder crossing for McDermot, "the car, and the trunks." He himself would fly to Miami "a few days after that."

But on December 4 Harvey wrote with the bad news that the Irish idyll was over—and ignominiously too. A few days earlier, while he was out with the Galway Blazers, a horse kicked him. He decided to ignore it, remount, and continue the hunt, which he did "for five hours, . . . leading the field." ("Dicky now calls me 'Iron Man.'") On his return to Adare, he decided to have some x-rays taken,

"Perfectly Delightful"

"as it hurt a lot." They revealed that the kick had broken his leg "straight through." "At the moment my leg is all bandaged up, rather painful, and I can't get a shoe on. What a nuisance!" He then limped to Dublin and moved into the consulate with George Garrett and his wife, Ethel. He also saw "a good surgeon" who taped his leg and told him "not to hunt any more this season." He and the Garretts must have made quite a trio: "Ethel, you probably know, fell down a flight of stairs and had a bad concussion. She came to dinner for the first time last night—but had to be carried."[51] So he never had his cocktail party and had to return to America, hobbling, two months early.

Still, even that abrupt end couldn't dampen his enthusiasm for Ireland. As he wrote in his *Harper's* article, "The people one meets driving their little milk carts along the road still have a delightful old-world politeness, and they will return your nod with a cheery smile and the spoken wish, 'May the saints preserve you.'" He concluded the piece by observing, "In many ways, Ireland seems to be about fifty years behind the rest of the world—and fifty years ago is a nice time to be today."

ANTIBES, VENICE, AND GREECE: "ALL GREAT FUN"

Just as the general postwar cutting back of English hunting as he had known it led Ladew to cease his outings with the Pytchley and sample the sporting life in Ireland, so memories of "absent friends" caused him to abandon the London social scene and look elsewhere for convivial companionship. He had spent his happiest moments in London, and many of his deepest friendships had evolved there. Now, the restaurants and theaters he had once so enjoyed were darkened by associations with the dead, of those killed either in the war like Myrtle Farquharson or immediately before it like T. E. Lawrence. It seems only human that when Ladew resumed his transatlantic holidays in the 1940s, he chose to avoid England and its painful memories and instead make new, happy memories elsewhere. Prolonged stays in France and Italy allowed him to do just that.

In the summer of 1947, for instance, he spent ten days with the duke and duchess of Windsor at their villa Château de la Cröe on Cap d'Antibes. "I did not expect to stay so long," he wrote his sister, "but Wallis insisted." He described the château as "large and beautiful, full of their own furniture and things." "It's right on the water and has a swimming pool cut into the rocks above the beach. We bathed there every day." The duke and duchess "entertained a great deal," and Ladew and the Windsors went to many parties. "Moi and Lady (Sheila) Milbank were houseguests" (he had known Milbank from various hunts in England), along with "a most attractive young French couple, the Baron and Baronne de Cabrol." Ladew immediately warmed to the Cabrols. Then in their mid-twenties, the couple radiated youthful animal energy and healthy high spirits. The baronne,

"Delightful," "old-world," and "cheery" are some of the words Ladew used to describe Ireland and the Irish. He especially loved scenes such as this one—a donkey-powered milk cart jingling down the main street in the village of Adare.

Daisy, was called "one of the most fashionable young married women" in post-war France, and her husband, Alfred, was an avid sportsman and talented amateur artist. No wonder Ladew told his sister he found that stay "all great fun."[52] (Plate 17.)

One night the group went to dine with Somerset Maugham at his nearby villa, Mauresque: "very beautiful, set in a lovely spot overlooking the hills and plain below," Ladew recalled. "After dinner we went to have our coffee in a lovely drawing room. At one moment the Duke was asked if he would do a little act that had amused many people. It was an imitation of Queen Mary when asked to a house that contained many beautiful objets d'art. The idea was that the Queen admired some priceless object and, as this had been a frequent occurrence, she said how she longed to have one like it. The hostess said, 'We would love to give it to your Majesty. We will send it.' The Queen said, 'Oh no, I will take it right along with me in my car.' I suppose it was rather amusing and the Duke carried it

"Perfectly Delightful"

off very well. His audience laughed—but I thought it was in very bad taste to do such an imitation of his wonderful mother."

Ladew had met Maugham years before in London through a mutual friend, Charles Towne, editor of the *Smart Set*. Towne had come to England to secure contributors for the magazine. He asked Harvey if he'd care to attend a planned lunch with Hugh Walpole, Edith Sitwell, and Maugham. "Of course I was delighted to accept and it proved to be a very interesting experience." Ladew noted that the writer "was at the time married to Syrie Maugham," a decorator who "specialized in having everything white," as is discussed in Chapter 4. "Of course her own house was as white as the scenery surrounding the North Pole. There were even polar bear rugs on the floor and the flowers were all white. It sounds a bit like the decor of a very sanitary hospital, but it didn't look a bit like any hospital and everything in the house was very grand and beautiful."

While he was staying with the Windsors, Ladew's keen fashion sense made him greatly interested in the latest style in women's bathing suits on the Riviera: "things called 'Bikinis'—practically *nothing*—a little bra and something lower down about the width of a necktie showing their navels and derriere. We never

Baron and Baronne de Cabrol photographed in 1948. Ladew had met this "most attractive young French couple" the year before.

"Your old brother is a one!"

could decide how they kept the lower part on." He jokingly wondered if they "were the result of the war and the shortage of material (?)"[53]

In another letter, he described how he accompanied the Windsors to a cocktail party given for officers of an American warship anchored at Nice. The evening proved successful, and the duchess asked the officers if they'd care to visit the Windsor compound to swim, have cocktails, and relax. "They accepted gladly," Ladew wrote.[54] The next day "several attractive young Americans" landed their dinghy on the Windsors' beach. The duchess went down to meet them, "dressed up in a Japanese kimono with large chrysanthemums in her hair and carrying a Japanese parasol." She greeted her guests bowing and saying, "Welcome. I am Grandmama Butterfly." Ladew noted that "the boys" joined them "at the swimming pool above the rock and a jolly time was had by all."

One day, Ladew left the Windsors and drove to Monte Carlo to retrieve the personal property left by his Uncle Berry, who had died there during the war. He wrote his sister that he found five trunks. "The first one I opened a cloud of moths, the size of eagles, flew out: all the clothes destroyed. The other things were all

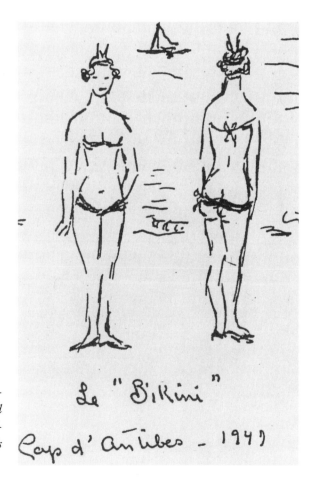

The bathing suits Ladew saw on the Riviera in 1947 fascinated him ("things called 'Bikinis'—practically nothing"), and he illustrated what he meant in a letter to his sister.

"Perfectly Delightful"

In 1947 the duke of Windsor asked Ladew to accompany him on an inspection tour of a British warship. The officers look a bit apprehensive.

right and I can arrange to give some of them—shoes and hats—to the Red Cross. One trunk of nice clothes I am sending to Paris and will give to musicians and people like that, through an address someone gave me. Uncle Berry's watch and the gold cigarette case I gave him in 1919 were there as well as a few studs, etc. I am bringing them back. I suppose Uncle Berry sold all Lomie's jewelry. I have the list, but nothing was there."[55] He added, "Uncle Berry had 2 Vuitton trunks— one was 37 years old and Vuitton said not worth repairing so I left it with them. The other is quite good, but needs repairs." He told his sister, "I would like this trunk, if you don't want it, as I have no really good trunks now and they can't be bought."

To thank the duke and duchess for a most enjoyable week and a half, Ladew gave a dinner for twelve at the Palm Beach Casino in Cannes on August 30. With war-deprived London on his mind, he was pleased to write his sister, "There seemed to be all the food around anyone could want." The party at the casino consisted of, among others, the earl and countess of Dudley, Prince Pierre of Monaco (father of Prince Ranier), Lady Milbank, and his new best friends, the Cabrols.

When it was time to leave, Harvey was delighted to find his old friend Elsa Maxwell, and her companion, Dickie Fellowes-Gordon, in the south of France. The women planned to drive to Venice and asked him to join them. Ladew, in turn, brought along a companion of his own. As he wrote his sister, "In Antibes I met a fellow called Hon. John Young. He had been in Russia as aid to the Admiral. He is pleasant and knows lots of people I do."[56] Perhaps it was the new friendship that made him rave about the trip through Italy. Maxwell had packed "food and wine and we had a delicious picnic lunch on the road. Spent the night in Turin, which couldn't look a more prosperous city: beautiful clothes, leather things for sale, plenty of *delicious* food, a fine modern hotel. I have never seen Italy look so prosperous—wonderful roads, fine crops everywhere, everything being rebuilt and painted. Lots of servants. Everything here much better than France or England." In another letter he crowed, "[Italy] is *perfect*—and BEAUTIFUL I have *never* seen it in such good condition and it has everything to offer that I love."[57]

Twenty-some years earlier Maxwell and Fellowes-Gordon had treated a young Noël Coward to his first trip to Venice. The playwright found the city "much to his liking. In this fantasy setting, frivolity prevailed." For example, Fellowes-Gordon encouraged Oliver Messel to perform mime acts at parties: "He did an Italian tart with an English colonel. . . . And then he'd do a child being given an enema, and you'd have sworn that was true." Coward felt that the elegant Fellowes-Gordon (composed of "social and Bohemian graces tactfully mixed") perfectly complemented Maxwell. For while the American Maxwell had a saloon-singing background, "Fellowes-Gordon was the real thing: she came from a rich, titled Scotch family"[58] ("who regards all English kings after the House of Stuart as German upstarts"),[59] and she had money to bankroll her party-giving pal. "A tall, stunning girl," Maxwell described Fellowes-Gordon, "the best and most helpful friend I have ever known."

In Venice, Ladew and Young found rooms in the Europa e Britannia, because "all the good, old hotels like the Danieli and Grand [had] been taken over by English and American armies." The duo certainly entered into the social swing. "Lots of fun with Elsa, who is an old friend of mine," he wrote to his sister. "She knows everybody and has lots of small parties all the time."[60] And of course there was Harry's Bar ("where everyone meets for drinks"). "We dined (John and myself) with Elsa last night. She is having a big dinner Saturday. John is having a dinner to-night and then we go to the movies." He then described the renowned Venice Film Festival, founded in 1932 and in 1947 just getting back on its feet after the war. "They are having a week of movies—competition to select the best," Ladew wrote home. "We will have a supper party after."

He indulged in some serious sight-seeing, too, and he wrote that he and Maxwell spent one day "motoring to Vicenza to see the Palladian architecture."

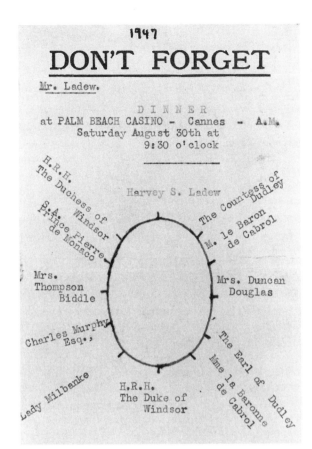

1947

DON'T FORGET

Mr. Ladew.

D I N N E R
at PALM BEACH CASINO - Cannes - A.M.
Saturday August 30th at
9:30 o'clock

Harvey S. Ladew

H.R.H. The Duchess of Windsor

S.A. Prince Pierre de Monaco

The Countess of Dudley

M. le Baron de Cabrol

Mrs. Thompson Biddle

Mrs. Duncan Douglas

Charles Murphy Esq.,

Mme la Baronne de Cabrol

The Earl of Dudley

Lady Milbanke

H.R.H. The Duke of Windsor

Seating arrangements for the dinner Ladew gave for the Windsors to thank them for a most enjoyable ten-day visit. Whoever prepared the plan tactfully called the duchess of Windsor "Her Royal Highness" (H.R.H.), something her royal in-laws never did and something she and the duke very much wanted.

He toured Palladio's Villa Barbaro with Horst, who was photographing it, and left deeply impressed by the richly symbolic Nymphaeum and its pool, which Palladio had designed for the villa's garden. (The visit caused him to resolve to rethink the system of pools, streams, and fountains at his Maryland garden, but he never got around to it.) Ladew experienced Palladio again in 1951 when he stayed at the celebrated Villa Malcontenta on the Brenta Canal as a guest of international businessman Bertie Landsberg. Harvey's scrapbooks are filled with images of shirt-sleeved luncheon parties and other festivities including a private August 31 concert given at the villa by the Boccherini Quintet.

Clearly smitten with the city—"Venice is perfect"—he decided that he and his sister should rent a palace the following year "for at least six weeks or two months." After hours combing the canals for a suitable place, he wrote her that he had narrowed the list down to three: one unnamed *"beautiful* palazzo" ("although I suspect all the bath rooms might not always work"); another "belonging to an American, Mr. Curtis" ("which they say is lovely"); and a third possibility, "a haunted one that Barbara Hutton had." But if none suited Elise, they "could book rooms in the Grand Hotel"; that, at least, would allow "for trips to Florence and Rome" and days swimming at the Lido (although on the 1947 trip he complained that the

"Your old brother is a one!"

Adriatic "looked like a lukewarm, vegetable soup, with things floating around in it").[61]

Evidently none of the choices pleased his sister, and a few days later he wrote excitedly, "*Eliza*, I found a DREAM [palazzo]. It belongs to the Princess Chavchavadze, who is an American." Continuing, he explained, "[It is] the Palazzo Polignac about the middle of the Grand Canal—on a bend, so you look down to ends of the Canal. *Nothing could be so beautiful!* I had tea with the Princess and she asked me to dine. She is married to Prince C, the famous Russian pianist. . . . She thinks she might rent the palazzo—you would love it. It has one HUGE salon two or three times as big as your 'music room' that runs the entire length of the palazzo—with a big window and balcony on the Grand Canal. They dine at the other end by a huge window overlooking the garden—although there is a dining room. This room is QUITE beautiful with lovely old things—two big sofas owned by Richard Wagner—a huge piano." "The Princess took me all over and I can't believe any of the other palazzos are as comfortable. It has 9 bedrooms and *six* bathrooms. If she decides to rent it, she will leave linen and servants—an excellent cook, a butler, etc., and two gondoliers. Wouldn't it be fun to have the palazzo next August or September?"[62]

Ladew closed his letter telling his sister, "The Princess will be in America and Elsa Maxwell said she would ring you up and ask you both to lunch. . . . I think it is a mistake to always do the same thing—and just wait for new grandchildren to be born. (I never do!)" He reassured "Eliza" that she would like Elsa. "She is not a bit frightening, has lovely manners, loves beautiful things and amusing people of all sorts. She would make us a visit—if we wanted her—and it would be fun as she knows everyone in Europe." If, however, Mrs. Grace balked at mixing with café society, Harvey wrote that he "would be perfectly happy without lots of people around as [he] would love to paint."[63]

As mentioned, on this trip Ladew ran into his old friend Horst, who spent the summer of 1947 photographing in Venice and the south of France for *Vogue*. The men not only visited the Villa Barbaro together, they also stayed at the same hotel in Venice, the Europa e Britannia, and mixed with many of the same people. Horst's comments say much about Ladew's playmates. He photographed Princess Elizabeth Chavchavadze on the balcony of her "dream" palazzo and wrote that he found her "a discriminating but generous hostess in the days when Venice was still a favorite holiday resort for the fashionable and the intelligent and the young." Of Elsa Maxwell, "born (allegedly in a theater box) in Keokuk, Iowa," Horst noted that she was "known as an inspirer and an inspired giver of parties." Although she had become the butt of many jokes by the 1940s, "few of those who knew her well [could] quite bring themselves to forget her, perhaps because, for all her failings, she consistently tried so hard to achieve the impossible: to give away more than she possessed."[64]

Ladew's last known visit to La Serenissima came in 1955 and was, suitably

Horst's 1947 photograph of Princess Chavchavadze on the balcony of, as Ladew wrote, her "DREAM" palazzo.

enough, sparked by Maxwell, whom the queen of Greece had asked to help publicize Hellenic tourist attractions. Maxwell listened—and acted. She cajoled shipping magnate Stavros Niarchos to lend her his yacht, the liner *Achilleus*, if she could assemble "120 of the international set's most solvent globe-trotters for a see-and-be-seen tour of Athens and the Greek islands."[65] Niarchos also agreed to underwrite the venture's entire cost, purportedly $110,000.

"Suiting action to the thought," *Time* magazine's incomparable prose notes, "the yeasty 72-year-old Elsa went to work" and drew up her guest list. Since the trip was intended to give a public relations boost to Greek tourism, she reasoned that she needed to get maximum press coverage of the outing, "and that could not happen unless the *Achilleus*'s passenger list included celebrities who were worthy of newsprint."[66] Further, since the queen "wanted people who would spend money," Maxwell decided not to invite any royalty ("since royalty, alas, has no money"). Other titles, however, abounded, and Maxwell saw to it that the state-rooms and decks of the *Achilleus* glittered with coronets: at the head came a trio of duchesses (Argyle, de Brissac, and Westminster) followed up by an assortment of other lesser *noblesse*, including the comte et comtesse de Lagarde, the vicomte et vicomtesse de Ribes, Marchesa Assaro, Conte e Contessa Guido Brandolini, Conte Cigogna, Conte e Contessa Crespi, and Marchese e Marchesa Salina. Maxwell also managed to squeeze in a few nontitled (but still newsworthy) souls, including Cynthia Balfour, Olivia de Havilland and her husband, Pierre Galant, Perle Mesta, Cesare Sieppe of the Metropolitan Opera—and Mr. Harvey S. Ladew. (*Time* reported that "Mr. Ladew found Miss de Havilland to be 'charming and awfully nice.'")[67]

Reviewing the list, Ladew, who joined the group breathless after a week of music at the Salzburg Mozart Festival, told a reporter from the *Baltimore Sun*, "I'm the only unimportant person on this cruise."[68] He was not, however, without friends, for, in addition to Maxwell herself, the ship would be filled with laughter from such cronies as Gilbert and Kitty Miller, Vicomte and Vicomtesse de Noailles, Baron and Baronne de Cabrol, Conte Lanfranco Rasponi, Margaret Case, and Dickie Fellowes-Gordon.[69]

After a few days "of elegant parties and an elaborate ball" in Venice, Maxwell and her guests boarded the *Achilleus* and set sail down the Adriatic. The hostess, no stranger to staging elaborate events, had obviously given some thought to logistics. Realizing that her 120 guests might get on each other's nerves if kept at close quarters for two weeks, she devised a system to ease any possible tensions. "If you wear your hat with the brim turned to the side," she told them, "it will mean 'Don't anybody speak to me. Just don't talk to me.' That way I think we will enjoy our days together more." She also insisted that the trip have its serious moments and told *Time*, "Oh, we will play a little bridge and do a little dancing—and Spyros Skouras has sent us 20 new movies to show. But everybody will have to be in bed by 12 and up at 8. There'll be a gong to wake them."[70]

And enjoy the trip they did—or at least "world-traveller, fox-hunting authority, topiary expert, art connoisseur, sometime author" Harvey S. Ladew did. He told the *Sun*, "No one could have ever seen the islands in such comfort and luxury—and no one will again." He deemed the *Achilleus* "the most beautiful yacht" he had ever seen and felt that just the chance to look at the ship's art collection, including three paintings by van Gogh and two by Renoir, "made the trip worthwhile."[71]

The ship anchored at a different island each day, and guests were put ashore by motor launch to be met by limousines, mules, or buses to take them inland to see the sites. Maxwell hired four archaeologists, "two of whom spoke English, two French," to explain the highlights of the trip. What Ladew called "the famous phallic monuments at Delos," however, required no explanation. While most of Maxwell's coterie, including Ladew, enjoyed that stop and spent many happy

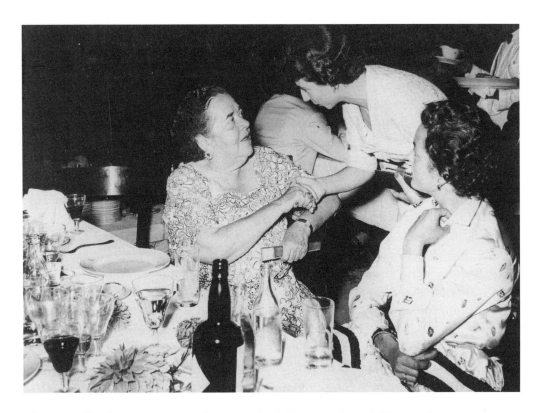

Elsa Maxwell on board Stavros Niarchos's yacht the Achilleus *at the end of her 1955 Aegean cruise. "No one could have ever seen the islands in such comfort and luxury," Ladew told the* Baltimore Sun, *"and no one will again."*

hours posing and snapping photographs, the duchess of Argyle told their hostess "she did not feel her young daughter should view them."[72]

On reaching Athens, the group took two days off to attend a reception given by the king and queen of Greece and to see a special production of *La Clemenza di Tito* on the Acropolis. (Ladew never could get enough Mozart.) On the last night out, Maxwell threw a costume ball, and Harvey, long practiced at fancy dress, "requisitioned several sheets which, with the aid of safety pins, he fashioned into a reasonable facsimile of a Greek toga."[73] At the end of the evening, he and his fellow guests toasted their hostess in six languages. "I don't think there was a person on the cruise who didn't enjoy it and thought it was the most wonderful thing he had ever done," a still-dazed MFH told the *Sun*.

"'Chasser'-ing" at Chantilly

When Ladew met the sports-loving Baron et Baronne de Cabrol on his 1947 stay with the Windsors, the couple invited him to return to France for some hunt-

---

ing. He immediately wrote his sister that that was one thing he "certainly want[ed] to do!" Never one for idle wishes, Ladew arranged to visit France the following year. (The sexagenarian couldn't avoid a bit of boasting: "Imagine, at my age, dashing through the forests after wild boar and stags!") Ever thorough, in June 1948 Ladew arranged to meet the comte de Roualle in New York. "He is MFH of a pack near Paris and says he will take care of everything." Harvey had been introduced to de Roualle by a mutual friend, Matilda Whitridge, formerly of Baltimore but then living in France "in a really lovely old house at the edge of the forest de Chantilly." "Lady Dianna Cooper is her neighbour. She has a horse to hunt, two or three servants, and delicious food." Ladew admitted that life in the forest sounded good: "if I get hard up — or, I might say, harder up — I might settle there and have a horse and studio, a garden and lots of beautiful models."[74]

Not surprisingly, Harvey found more to amuse him in France than wild boar. One authority has called postwar Paris "an escape for those who could afford it, with unrationed food and drink and the liberated atmosphere of a city which knew how to enjoy its victory"[75] — just what Ladew craved. Duff and Lady Diana Cooper, installed in the British Embassy, "presided over a social renaissance,"[76] and Janet Flanner, the *New Yorker*'s Parisian correspondent for decades, recalled those years as ones "of elegant, aristocratic hedonism."[77] Nor was the hedonism restricted to Anglo-Americans, for, as Horst observed, "the French aristocracy in

Baltimore's Matilda Whitridge (to Ladew's left) *and Harvey hunting stag in the forest de Chantilly, 1948.*

"Perfectly Delightful"

"Rather beautiful and very impressive" is how Ladew described his 1948 stag-hunting foray in France. He also very much enjoyed the posthunt celebrations and here (center) leans towards a bottle of Champagne in keen anticipation.

the twentieth century had an intrepid appetite for what was avant-garde" and happily threw themselves into the postwar social whirl.[78]

De Roualle kept his promise to arrange everything, and records show that he opened an account for Ladew at the Morgan Bank, conveniently next door to the Ritz Hotel, where he had booked rooms for the visitor. The Frenchman also hired a Citroen, a groom, and two horses for his American friend. "I don't expect to have a chauffeur," Ladew boasted to his sister in November 1948, "but will attempt to run the Citroen myself." He liked his "nice little room" at the Ritz—"it *is* little, for all my malles, but the valet de chambre tells me it is one of the plus chauds chambres in the hotel. There is lots of heat, I must say, and we have had some cold days, but my chambre got so chaud that I had to ouvrir les fenetres."

On November 3 he wrote his sister from Paris, "I have been on the go ever since I arrived . . . lots of things to attend to about my hunting plans." He arranged for his horses to "go by train to Chantilly for [his] first chasse on Saint Hubert's Day." He himself had "been riding every day in the Bois to get 'entrainee,'" as he hadn't ridden since Ireland and "the jambe casse." He had his first outing on the 13th and couldn't wait to tell her about it. "I am back about an hour ago from a long hunt in the forest. We galloped for hours after a stag—Finally he went into a little pond and was killed. (That was rather sad, and horrid.)—the Comte gave me 'l'honeur du pied'—They only give one foot—I got it on account of being an Xmaster and visitor. They played tunes on the big hunting horns throughout the chasse—and after the stag was killed they all stood around—about two dozen people—and played for nearly half an hour in the forest. Rather beautiful and very impressive."

Naturally, he found time "in between 'chasser'-ing" (as he put it) to take advantage of the dazzling social life that Paris offered anyone with wit, cash, or connections. Fortunately, Ladew had all three. He attended a session of the United Nations with the duchesse de la Rochefoucauld, who invited him "pour les cocktails in her beautiful home." (He laughed to his sister, "I will sound just like Uncle Berry if I go on this way.")[79] Another evening he went to "a lovely party" given by the David Bruces. "They had a lot of people there—Margaret Biddle, Eve Curie, Lady Diana Cooper, etc. I am getting to like this life in Paris."[80]

He also saw a lot of the Windsors, who, too, had rooms at the Ritz. "I asked them to lunch but Wallis said the Duke never lunched out—however SHE would lunch with me. We lunched *alone* at Maxim's—but not in a 'Cabinet Particulier.' Can you imagine how everyone stared?! Wallis had never gone out to lunch without the Duke before. Wouldn't Cholly Knickerbocker like this bit of information! Well, we had a lot of good laughs." He and the duchess spent the rest of the day shopping: "I went with her to a wonderful dealer in a private house where he had the most beautiful china things. Two pugs, I think like the ones you have on brass stands. Wallis loves china and bought quite a number of things for her table." Pleased with the day's purchases, the duchess asked him to cocktails to introduce him "to quite a few *Chasseurs a Courre*"—"and the first thing you know, your brother will be visiting all the nobility all over France."[81]

On November 13 he wrote, "Wallis W. has asked me to take her to Noel Coward's opening—He is playing in one of his plays *in* French—The Duke disapproves of Noel's morals and won't go." (When Ladew met Coward in the 1930s, it was widely rumored that the actor was enjoying a love affair with Prince George, duke of Kent, the youngest brother of the duke of Windsor.) The play Ladew was referring to in this letter to his sister was *Present Laughter*, translated by Coward into French as *Joyeux Chagrins*.

Before leaving New York, Ladew had talked to Carmel Snow at *Harper's* about writing a piece on French hunting. She liked the idea and arranged for him to meet the magazine's Paris contact, Marie-Louise Bousquet. It came close to proving a match made in heaven. "What a wonderful person," Ladew wrote on December 6 to thank Snow for leading him to Bousquet. "She certainly knows *everyone* in *all* sets in Paris. She has taken me to all sorts of previews and openings. Yesterday we motored to Rambouillet with the Duchesse de Brissac and had lunch in their wonderful hunting-box that belonged to the Duchesse d'Uzes." (One need hardly add

"Perfectly Delightful"

that the duc d'Uzes stands as the premier duke of France.) "It has a big hall with hundreds of stags' antlers all over the walls *and ceiling*." On another day, his "Boss" took him "to the preview of Picasso's show" and even introduced Ladew to Picasso—but that didn't change Harvey's misgivings about the artist.[82]

Bousquet, "the eccentric *'concierge de Paris'*" according to Flanner,[83] held a salon each Thursday at her "delightful little house in the rue Boissiere. . . . Because of her impromptu wit and fearless comments, hers was the salon most frequented by Academicians." Ladew, invited to the rue Boissiere, delighted in the experience: "She mixes every one up," he wrote his sister, "la noblesse, writers (like me), painters (like me), actors, prize fighters, politicians, etc. Her Salon is famous." He sensed she had "plans" for him—"so it looks as though I will be on the move"—and he (not unreasonably) concluded, "I do think it is going to be fun and different from what most people generally do."[84]

A few days later he wrote, rhapsodically, that Marie-Louise Bousquet was "the greatest gal" he had ever known. "She has been wonderful to me and she says she has never known a foreigner who has read as much French literature as I have—and she wants me to come *every* Thursday 'pour son jour.' You just see every sort of person at her jours—great fun." He described one "*most* amusing" afternoon there with "the David Bruces, the great French writer Colette whom [he had] always admired—and read nearly all her books—Bébé Berard and Jean Cocteau." (Harvey liked to describe "the best way to eat snails": "with Colette, in bed.") Since Horst, also in Paris in 1948, called Cocteau "the most vulnerable, provocative, original, versatile, productive, scintillating, and sociable Frenchman of his time," one wishes that Ladew's impression of him had survived.[85]

On another day, Mme. Bousquet ("my *divine* French boss") introduced Harvey to the vicomte and vicomtesse de Noailles, whom Horst deemed "the most intellectual" Parisian society figures of the 1930s and 1940s.[86] Even in the midst of the others Ladew met on that trip—Cocteau, Picasso, Colette and the rest—the "eccentric, vigorous" Noailles must have seemed impossibly romantic and appealing. Marie-Laure de Noailles's ancestry included three divergent literary figures: Petrarch's beloved Laura (for whom she was named), the marquis de Sade, and Chevigné, the model of elegance who inspired Proust's duchesse de Guermantes. A keen amateur painter (and the aunt of Philippe de Montebello, current director of the Metropolitan Museum of Art), the viscountess produced works of "loose structure, rather like Turner's visionary canvases." She wrote three novels that Aldous Huxley deemed among the few contemporary works of fiction destined to endure, and her revolutionary gardening efforts were described in Chapter 4.

The vicomte Charles de Noailles was himself a figure of no little interest. During the 1930s, photography and the making of private films became the rage among the Parisian beau monde. According to Horst, "Hollywood movie stars . . . imperceptibly assumed the place left vacant by Europe's vanished or vanish-

Marie-Louise Bousquet, Harper's *representative and Ladew's "divine French boss," beams out to the world from her 1949 Christmas card to him. "She knows everyone in Paris," Harvey wrote his sister—so many people that the* New Yorker's *famed Janet Flanner dubbed Mme. Bousquet "the concierge de Paris."*

ing Royalties. Whatever the *grandes dames* of the Faubourg St.-Germain might say among themselves about the absurd vulgarity of Elsie de Wolfe, the fact is that some of the crustiest dowagers of the *monde* were seen at Lady Mendl's dinner in honor of Gary Cooper." Interestingly, he observed that "even the Vicomtesse de Noailles was not above spending several days at the Hotel Trianon-Palace at Versailles because she heard that Marlene Dietrich was staying there." A creature of that cinema-crazed era, the vicomte underwrote several epochal films, including Bunuel's *L'Age d'Or*, Bunuel and Dali's *Le Chien Andalou*, and Jean Cocteau's "hermaphroditic, perverse, traumatic, highly poetic" masterpiece, *Le Sang d'un Poete*.[87] The Noailles, to whom Cocteau dedicated his play *La Machine Infernale*, lived "in an inherited family treasure house on the Place des États-Unis. It was the outstanding house in Paris for intelligence, modernism, art, and sharp conversation," Horst observed; it also served "as a home-away-from-home for the good-looking."[88] Thus one can only raise one's eyebrows at Ladew's comment to his sister, "Well, I certainly have enjoyed this little trip."[89]

Small wonder the next summer found him back in France. This time Harvey took rooms at Uncle Berry's favorite hotel, the Meurice, and set out to do everything he had left undone the year before. For instance, in 1948 he had written his sister that he particularly wished to attend the art students' annual Quatres Arts Ball; in 1949 he wrote, "Now I have a chance; it is difficult to get an invitation—but we famous artists have a pull." So it proved, for "one of the architectural students at the Beaux Arts" took him. "I expect it will be a riot."

It turned out to be all that he'd hoped for—and possibly a bit more. On July 12 he wrote his sister that he "couldn't begin to describe le Bal des Quatres Arts": "It was really too rough and you would be horribly shocked to think your old brother had been to such a dreadful orgy." But, obviously titillated and delighted with himself, he proceeded to tell her quite a bit about it. "I brought a costume—made by a 'little woman' in Maryland—but I only wore the hat and belt; they told me to bring some striped material and I undressed in the loge of the directeur, who made a pair of 'diapers' for me out of half the material. He then painted all of me brilliant blue! I was glad to have the other half of the material which I am sure kept me from having pneumonia, as it was a very cold night and I am not used to going to a ball in diapers. . . . I arrived at the ball at 5 in the afternoon, as the directeur thought I might not get in if I arrived later. No one was allowed out until 5 in the morning—so I was there for 12 hours!" Coy about revealing exactly what occurred, he did describe the antics of "one American girl who was *very* drunk had *all* her clothes pulled off." "I saw her making 'amour' in a dark corner of the balcony."

Exhausted but elated, he staggered back to the hotel the following dawn. "The night porter at the Meurice didn't recognize me—and, as I couldn't go to bed with all the blue paint on, I had to soak in a bath for about an hour."

He enjoyed more conventional amusements as well. One day he and Mme. Bousquet "motored out to lunch with Elsie Mendl" (the former Elsie de Wolfe) at Le Petit Trianon. Another evening he had dinner with Baron and Baronne Cabrol, "the most attractive young couple" he knew. "They have never been to America but may come next year to stay with me in Florida." (They did.) He hoped his sister might invite them to New York: "You must meet them—and I do hope you will show them a bit of L.I. life. They would love it." Another day he wrote, "Hoytie [Wiborg] is having a party July 14th—the national holiday. A lot of people going to her apartment to see the fireworks—Suzy Solidor singing afterwards."[90] Horst, who often photographed Solidor, described her as the "outstanding Paris cabaret performer" of the era, "renowned for her tough

Ladew uncaps his lens, probably in the mid-1950s, and casts about for a good image. He retained an interest in photography all his life and self-mockingly wrote his sister in 1949 that "famous artists" such as himself "have a pull" at wangling social invitations.

sailor songs" but equally popular with "a more restricted audience consisting of intellectuals and members of the *monde*," including Berard, Cocteau, Dufy, and Picabia.[91]

On July 26 Ladew wrote, "Tonight Matilda Whitridge is dining with me in the Champs Elysee and we will go to the ballet—to-morrow she motors me out to visit Fountainbleau for the day and then we go on to her house at Chantilly where I will spend the next day [and attend the Hunt Ball]." He wrote his sister in eager anticipation that the ball "should be a wonderful night—and tres chic." Once he went "to the Comédie Française next door to see 'La Parisienne,' . . . beautifully done"; another day he sipped "cocktails with the Windsors in their new house"; and on yet another he "gave a luncheon at the Mediteranee"—"Millicent Hearst, the Jack Lowthers (he is MFH of the Pytchley), Bert Taylor and wife, Dorothy Frasso and my Harper's editor." He even found time for "a little painting—one of the Moulin Rouge. Had lots of fun going up to Monmartre to do it from a sidewalk cafe."

"Perfectly Delightful"

Thrilling as the "tres chic" Hunt Ball undoubtedly was, and as amusingly risque as the Quatres Arts Ball proved, the highlight of the trip—"one of the most wonderful experiences I have had in my life," in fact—came when he and Mme. Bousquet attended a white-tie benefit performance at Versailles "in 'le theatre de la Reine'—the tiny little theater built for Marie Antoinette at the Trianon—where she herself acted and sang in little operettes." On July 12 he wrote his sister, "The theater only holds 250 people. It is hung with blue brocade and the seats are blue velvet—you can't imagine anything more lovely. . . . The allees and fountains were all lighted—simply beautiful—and there were powdered and liveried footmen standing about. They gave one of the operettes that Marie Antoinette had played in—and a ballet with music and costumes of the period." Then came "a supper with champagne . . . served in a little rotunda lighted with candles as it was in the 18th century." Ladew's Maryland neighbors Millard and Eleanor Tydings, along with Mrs. Tydings's father, Amb. Joseph Davies, and stepmother, Marjorie Merriweather Post Davies, also attended the benefit. Eleanor Tydings remembered it as "the most memorable occasion. . . . Invitations were much sought after by the haut monde."[92] While Harvey was always pleased to see Sen. and Mrs. Tydings, Eleanor Tydings's stepmother generally left him both impressed and bemused: "Marjorie Davies was there," he wrote his sister, "dripping with enormous emeralds and diamonds—I'm sure Marie Antoinette never had any jewels to compare with them."

In the midst of all this, Ladew actually managed to complete the article for *Harper's* on French hunting, which appeared in March 1950. Surprisingly, the piece has a sour tone. He complained, for example, that while he found the French "very polite and extremely kind," and while he "enjoyed the experience thoroughly," the Gallic sense of superiority irritated him: "They did not hesitate to say that they thought their hunting was far more scientific and that their hounds were better trained than others." For his part, Ladew fussed—in print, not to his hosts—about hunting in the forests of Rambouillet, where they never had to jump any obstacle: "As far as I am concerned, that detracted greatly from the sport. . . . I missed our American post and rails, the stout hedges and ditches and brooks of England, and the formidable banks and stone walls of Ireland." And, dandy that he was, even he found the French a bit much when it came to costume etiquette. "No one," he wrote, "is allowed to wear the hunt uniform until he/she is formally presented with 'le Bouton,' the hunt button, by the Master. One day the daughter of the French president appeared to hunt at a pack I was with. She had never hunted with them before so, of course, she had not been presented with the Bouton." When she "appeared, perfectly turned out" but wearing the hunt button, "the field were greatly shocked. The gossip never ceased."

With that off his chest, Ladew admitted that he was glad he had hunted stag in the French forests. He wrote that he "never galloped so much and so long" as he did in Rambouillet, and he likened the French *chasse* to "hunting to music."

"Certain members of the hunt are allowed to carry horns and there are various tunes that they play which tell the direction in which the stag has turned, etc." Tellingly—and notwithstanding his grousing about Gallic foibles—when he learned of one place "in France where they hunt in the Anglo-American manner," complete with "imported fox hounds from England" and an American huntsman, Ladew felt "no desire to go there," since "it was in no way typical of French hunting," a not at all surprising reaction from one who devoted his life to the pursuit of as many—and as varied—happinesses as he could.

6

"America is going to HELL!"

The struggle to preserve his Maryland garden provided Harvey Ladew with one pleasant and positive outlet for his energies as he lived through his seventh and eighth decades. Diverting as clicking glasses with the Windsors and cruising the Aegean with Elsa Maxwell and all those duchesses may have been, by and large those years found him fretting over shaky finances, declining health, servant problems, and a general belief that the country was in decline; or, as he wrote his sister in 1967, "America is going to HELL!" Later that year he sadly told her, "It really interests me in a macabre way to witness The Decline and Fall of the whole world." For example, he took one disgusted look at the squalid condition of the city of his birth and grumbled, "As far as I go they could give NY back to the Indians—but I doubt if they would take it. Indians love fresh, pure air and clean water. Fortunately I never worry."

Money had been a worry at least as far back as 1947. That year a hurricane battered his underinsured Florida retreat, and the repair bills left him reeling. He hit on the idea that his sister might prove his salvation and wrote to suggest that, should she predecease him, she ought to remember him in her will. That October he wrote her, "You do not say if you are leaving me something to support me . . . and it looks as though I will need it. I don't want to end up in the poor house." He concluded his pitch rather pitifully, "Well, maybe I will be so old and ga-ga I won't know what goes on." In 1949 he wrote, "Don't say I make you 'laugh about your will.' I really am spending my money and I am sure you would hate to think of me ending up in the poor house. Just remember how we supported Uncle Berry for years. All you have to do is put in a little codicil in your will to say that, if I am without funds, you want me to have enough for a room at the Ritz, a nice trained nurse, doctors' bills and a few clothes. A car and chauffeur would be nice. At any rate, write the children a note to tell them not to let their Uncle Harvey starve," that last a probable reference to the dying words of Charles II (Ladew's favorite monarch), "Let not poor Nelly starve."

He knew he had to budget for "a nice trained nurse" because he found himself increasingly beset by one ailment after another. Sometimes old riding accidents flared up; sometimes new and more mysterious illnesses incapacitated him. In October 1969 he wrote, "I must have done something to my head—it feels as though I had a little volcano in it that is constantly erupting lava into one ear. This has been going on for a month—and in that time there has been enough 'lava' to cover Pompeii *and* Herculaneum." Continuing, he said, "Something in connection with all this is so awful but so funny that, having a sense of humour, I can't help laughing. I bought a tube of some ointment—the chemist said it would disinfect the cuts. I put it on all the cuts and it dried like hard white enamel all over my face and I have not succeeded in getting it all off though I have tried alcohol etc. . . . You can imagine that I haven't felt much like going out. But I did go, for a short time, to a dinner and dance (costume). I went as Bluebeard and had of course a blue beard stuck on to my varnished moustache." He concluded the letter tellingly: "It takes a lot to depress me."[1]

The following May he wrote to thank his sister "for putting [him] up and putting up with [him]." "It made the trip to the doctor so much easier. He is at the Harkness Pavillion—on 165th Street, which is some trip. . . . Dr. Savelli is the 15th doctor I have seen and the ONLY good ear Doctor. All those other idiots said 'There is nothing in your ear, Mr. Ladew' and after three months one of them pulled out two inches of surgical gauze and wasn't sporting enough to say 'I apologize because I was wrong.'"[2]

A month later he returned to New York. Since he had sold his pied-à-terre, he booked rooms at the Sherry-Netherland and readied himself for another trek to 165th Street ("it is almost like going to Europe from here") and for a steady decline that saw him become more or less confined to his bed. At some point his doctor told him he had diabetes, a diagnosis he chose to ignore until he fell in and out of diabetic comas and eventually was put under round-the-clock care of nurses.

But if these maladies broke his health, they couldn't break his sense of humor and joie de vivre. "It does not worry me in the least whether our souls hang together and go on after death," he wrote in 1960. "I see no reason why mine should go on, but, if it does, that will mean new and, probably, wonderful experiences; if it does not go on, that will mean a deep sleep. I have always loved travel and new experiences and I have always loved a good, sound sleep. So there it is."[3]

Servant problems worried him the most—even more than his own failing health and (largely imagined) financial crises. The last of the fabled "Ladew Girls" died in the early 1960s, leaving him without domestic help for the first time in his life. "He'd been brought up in a sort of belle epoch," Leith Griswold explained, "where there were hot and cold running chamber maids all over the place. He just didn't know how to get along with having to do a lot himself."[4]

Finally, a few of his Maryland friends managed to find two Italian immigrants who would see him through to the end: "Paolo was an electrician and he

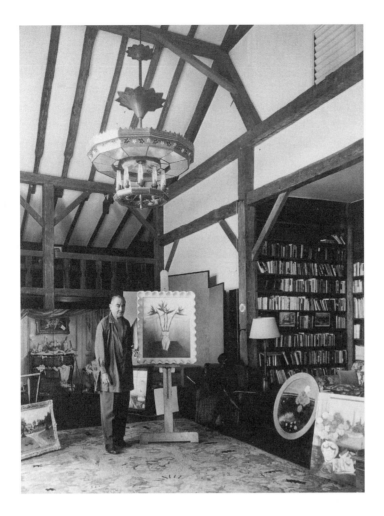

Oils and canvas provided Ladew with an escape from the world's ills well into his seventh decade. Around 1960 he wrote that if people didn't like his masterpieces, he took "the attitude of other moderns": "[I] say, as witheringly as possible, that if they do not understand or feel what I have expressed, I fear there is nothing I can do to help them." In 1964, A. Aubrey Bodine photographed Ladew in his Pleasant Valley studio.

knows all about radio, t.v., etc.," Ladew enthused to his sister. "He drives the car well—he isn't happy unless he is *working*—a great help in my garden. Gina, no relation and older, charming, . . . is a good cook—she does all the laundry, sheets, towels, my shirts (beautifully)." Paolo and Gina "even started a vegetable garden." Ladew decided, "[If they ever] leave me, I will follow them to Italy, not to live in but to die comfortably!" And because Paolo and Gina spoke "not a word of English," they presented him with a serendipitous benefit: "my Italian has improved so much that I have nearly finished Dante's Inferno, Purgatorio, and Paradiso—in the original Italian."[5]

In the midst of all this he decided, "It is high time I had a dog," as he wrote his sister in 1968. "I thought I would get a dachshund as they have short hair and can stand the heat better. There is a kennel in Pennsylvania which I motored to yesterday. I had been told they have the best in the country. I bought a lovely little red girl puppy." He "wanted a good German name" for the puppy and settled on Marlene Dietrich, or "Lena" for short. That nickname, though, proved difficult—"My Italian maid (who does not speak a word of English with the exception of 'Good Morning') is named Gina. So when I call one of them, their names are so alike that both Lena and Gina come running to me."

"Lena" immediately became the joy of his life, the delight of his old age. "I have only had her two days," he wrote his sister on September 27, 1968, "but she is *amazingly* intelligent—*so* beautiful. I am mad about her—she is very affectionate and seems actually to understand what I say to her. As I am not sure if she is house-broken, I have rolled up all the rugs from the floor—but I am told if anything happens to quickly pour *white vinegar* over it or a bottle of club soda." Then, beaming with this domestic knowledge, he smugly asked Mrs. Grace, "Never knew that before, did you?"

"We are crazy about each other," the besotted Ladew wrote of Lena a week later. "She doesn't want to leave me for an instant and cries and howls if I have to put her in a pen—or even in my bathroom at night. Very flattering, of course. . . . She is really beautiful and sweet—a most lovely animal—so clean. She always comes and asks when she wants to go out. How did I ever go 30 years without a dog?" In the fall of 1969, before embarking for what proved his last Florida winter, he bred Marlene. A few weeks later he wrote his sister from Pied-à-Mer, "Marlene never had any sex education that they give children in schools to-day—so I can't imagine *what* she thought was happening—but *now* she knows": she had grown "enormous." "She looks like one of those Goodyear Blimps. We are all terribly excited."

Then, as puppies started arriving, he started what became a stream-of-consciousness letter:

> I was terribly worried about her as I really love her. I was going to have a veterinary here for the accouchement—but it does not seem necessary. . . . [The] first baby arrived and rather painlessly, I think, as she didn't cry. Gina, who loves her, is kneeling by the basket watching her clean off the baby, which is quite large—How she will love her puppies. I enclose a clipping saying how quiet everyone must be before babies are born—and we have made no sound whatever.
>
> I won't have the heart to give *any* of them away and will have a pack of Dachshunds. This afternoon I will be working on an article for "House & Garden." Horst has already taken the photos and the article is called—"An American Topiary Garden." I feel better—but have no desire to see the Jet Set in Palm Beach. (Now I must see if there are any more new puppies—Lena has washed the

first one carefully.) We now have 3 puppies! . . . Well, the Birthday party is over. NOW we have 7 puppies—with Gina, who loves Marlene, kneeling on the floor—helping!

On January 20, 1970, he wrote to thank his sister for her christening present: "Marlene was delighted with the little milk bottles. Much nicer than the one I found in a toy shop here. I am glad to say that her puppies are alive and well—but as yet their eyes are not opened." Four days later he wrote, "Missy [a great niece] made a mistake in addressing the letter to *Miss* Marlene Dietrich because she is *married*—and has SEVEN children, two daughters and five sons." As for the milk bottles, "We tried them out at once. Marlene didn't like the idea at first (you see these are her first children) but feeding them all was really too much for her and now she lets Paolo and Gina feed the children twice a day—I will hate to let any of them go but I don't suppose I can keep a whole pack of hounds who are meant to hunt rabbits."

When Susan Sage interviewed Ladew at Pleasant Valley in the spring of 1970, she began the tape announcing, "Harvey had just come back from Florida and hadn't been awfully well, but he had all of his usual good humor." The interview proceeded, and towards its conclusion he told her, "Before you leave me I want you to see my puppies. I have a lovely dachshund bitch. She's about a year and a half old. She's never been shown. But the papa and the mama are both champions and her puppies are by a grand champion. She had seven and we had to sit up all night feeding them. I had to get a U-Haul to bring them back from Florida behind my car."

"FOR THE ENJOYMENT OF PEOPLE"

About the time he began worrying about his own insolvency, Ladew started to look for a way to preserve his celebrated Maryland gardens. He particularly hoped that men, women, and children from all walks of life might visit his creation: "All they [the public] have to do is give me a call," he told a reporter for the local weekly, the *Ægis*. "I'd love to have them come and visit my garden. I created it for people."[6] Or as his longtime friend Pattie Penniman recalled, "Harvey wanted people to discover the pleasure he derived from learning to create. He thought that there was a need to stimulate other people's imagination and hoped that his creation would become a center for educational pursuits."[7]

He first offered the property to the city of Baltimore "as well as a maintenance endowment, if enough public interest were shown," he told a reporter for the *Sun*. "I'd like to think that these gardens which have given so much pleasure to my friends and interested visitors could be preserved as a park for the enjoyment of people who live in the city and surrounding areas." The paper also announced that Mayor Theodore Roosevelt McKeldin hinted that the "proposed endowment for maintenance made the 300-acre [*sic*] garden additionally attractive."[8]

But not attractive enough, evidently, for nothing came of the idea. So Ladew decided to approach the state. His friend Dee Hardie wrote a column for the *Sun* headlined "A Shrine to Beauty Can Be Maryland's."[9] But nothing came of that idea, either.

Then on November 28, 1960, Julia Cameron, executive secretary of the Harford County Gardens Trust (a short-lived consortium of the Garden Club of Harford County, the Country Garden Club, and the Evergreen Garden Club), wrote to thank Ladew for his "superbly generous offer" of Pleasant Valley Farm. She said members of the trust were "unanimous in their enthusiasm and appreciation of [his] offer of an endowed Garden Foundation": "[They] feel it would be a wonderful thing for both Harford County and the whole state of Maryland if your lovely house and gardens could become a permanent museum and landscape center." Mrs. Cameron talked to the county commissioners about the proposal. In response, they showered Ladew with fulsome letters, letters that were appreciative in tone but vague in content. And nothing came of *this* idea, either. Perhaps that mounting frustration explains why Leith Griswold commented that Ladew, in his later years, "hated politicians, per se. He said, 'I don't want any politicians here.'"[10]

Discouraged, on August 12, 1963, he wrote Benjamin Griswold to thank him for offering to help him in trying to leave his house and the gardens to Maryland.[11] He concluded his letter by saying, "Actually, I no longer care what happens to the place. My furniture & china collections and paintings will go to my family and any cash from the land to hospitals and the Four Arts Society (which I have worked with for years) in Florida."

In early 1965 he wrote Griswold from Florida, "I plan to keep the place going through 1966—when the Garden Club of America are coming." Then, "I will sell the land and house—or tear the house down. If only I had a lovely, capable wife like Leith to engage servants (and phone the police to remove the drunken ones) I could possibly remain the rest of my days 'Pleasantly'—but otherwise I would end up in a padded cell." That March he wrote, "I think very seriously of getting out of everything in America—then have a chauffeur-valet and spend most of my time at the Ritz in Madrid. It is no fun trying to run a house any more. I would keep this place in Florida, which is comparatively easy to run—well, I am forgetting Hurricanes."[12]

In one last attempt, around 1967 he asked Griswold if "it might be possible to get some big foundation to take over the Garden—like the Ford." That got Harvey thinking about foundations in general and specifically about creating one of his own. He told the Griswolds that he would like to rewrite his will "leaving the house and garden and an endowment (really quite a large one)" to such a foundation. "I felt it would give many people pleasure—also I felt I would like to do one nice thing in my life."[13]

Intrigued by the project, the Griswolds, and a handful of other of Ladew's farsighted Maryland neighbors, rallied and lent their talent and energy to the cause. Eventually through trial and error these men and women—amateurs in the best Jeffersonian sense of the word—made the garden not merely endure, as Faulkner could have phrased it, but prevail. They created the Ladew Topiary Gardens, Inc., a body corporate to guarantee and guide Pleasant Valley's survival into perpetuity, a foundation "to be run," as Leith Griswold importantly explained, "by people who knew him and knew his desires and dreams for the future."[14] Fortunately, Ladew himself lived to witness—and take part in—that victory.

As an aside, it may be worth noting that even as Ladew's horticultural masterpiece has its own firm place in the history of gardening, so does his foundation have its place in the history of the preservation movement. In England and America people began to understand the need to preserve significant gardens in the 1960s, just as Harvey entered the fray. When he started to think about his garden's future, he charted new territory, for no endowed gardens—as opposed to gardens coincidental to historic houses—existed in Maryland at the time: in 1967, for example, Annapolis's now famed Paca Garden was a parking lot. Even the concept of garden history as a discipline was, at most, as dormant as a tulip bulb in February: England's pioneering Garden History Society dates from 1965; the Garden Conservancy, dedicated to preserving historically important American examples of the horticultural arts, dates from 1990.

Recently, aided no doubt by the wider environmental movement, preservation of historic gardens has become a virtual growth industry. Ladew himself was something of an early environmentalist. His letters from the era defined by the publication of Rachel Carson's *Silent Spring* (1962) and the celebration of the first Earth Day (1971) show him fully aware of the dangers that DDT, carbon monoxide, and toxic runoff posed to his world, a world where beauty and order mattered above all else.

HARVEY LADEW: *BENEFACTOTUM HORTICULTURUS*

Before committing himself to a legally charted foundation, Ladew wanted to see if people would actually drive out and pay money to see a garden. He began his experiment by opening the garden to the public two weekends in 1968, for the benefit of the new Greater Baltimore Medical Center (GBMC). Nan Black represented the hospital board, which was a comfort to him because she (born Nan Byers) was a sister-in-law of his niece Alison Byers. (Black initially began her letters to him, "Dear Mr. Ladew." He didn't care for that formality and wrote her, "All Elise's children call me Uncle Harvey," and so should she. He added that his sister's chauffeur also calls him Uncle Harvey, "but I don't think he means to be cheeky.") On January 25 of that year Black wrote, "We are more than grateful to you and will make all arrangements that you require."[15] Even though he was in Florida, 1,000 miles from Pleasant Valley, he threw himself into the project with his customary verve, and he focused his keen, intelligent interest on every detail, no matter how small. In late January 1968, he suggested opening the place on weekends in May when the irises were in bloom. "That is when my garden looks best. If you and Mrs. Brown [Sibyl Brown] could talk over about dates it would be a good idea. She knows so much about gardening." He also suggested having "five or six gals in different parts of the garden from 10 until 1 and another five or six from 1 until 6." "We could have chairs for them so that they would not have to stand all that time. I will feed any gals you bring to help and also give them booze." He also suggested she get in touch with Josephine Doak and Pattie Penniman, and he counseled "not making the admission too high—might attract more people."

On February 19, Black wrote to say she and "Jeanne Baetjer [had] been in long session in hopes of making [his] garden parties a tremendous success." She added that Tilton Dobbin, former chairman of the hospital's Executive Committee, would ask Governor Agnew to open the garden. ("Tilton happens to have managed Agnew's campaign.") On February 28 Ladew suggested that Black's husband, Gary, whose family owned the *Baltimore Sun*, "write a letter about getting notices in the paper." He urged the Blacks to use the talents of Dee Hardie, "a very clever girl" on the paper. "I think she could write this tour up in an interesting way. She has worked on Garden Tours of my place for many years and knows it very well." He also suggested that "Mayo [McIntosh Bryan] could give a lot of information and help"; pointed out that articles on him had appeared in the *Sun Magazine* in 1957 and 1965; and felt "sure Aubrey [Bodine] would have a lot of photos that were not used . . . and a few of them could be shown." The important point, he stressed, was "to have it *well advertised*." He wanted everyone to come and wondered if the Blacks knew someone "in the Hearst paper—which the lower class read": noblesse oblige à la Harvey Ladew.[16]

On March 20, Nan Black wrote to him in Delray confirming the weekends of May 11–12 and May 25–26. She added, "Gary and I are dining tomorrow with Bill Schmick, publisher of The Sun, and I will speak to him personally about how they might handle publicity. Also, I'll ask Bill's advice as to who to go to at the News Post [the "Hearst paper"]. I am quite sure that Dee Hardie is quite clever. I love the way she writes." Hardie's article, which ran in the May 20 *Sun*, began by saying, "Sometimes, if you're lucky—and being good has absolutely nothing to do with it—something nice happens like lunch with Mr. Ladew. He is kind and witty . . . [and] looks like a mischievous Somerset Maugham with a dash of Douglas Fairbanks, Sr., and he twinkles." She told her readers, through dramatic use of ellipses, that if they should run into Ladew while on the tour, they shouldn't "forget to ask him about Lawrence of Arabia . . . or Edna Ferber . . . or Cocteau . . . or those pink lilies . . . or almost anything, including Today."

It proved a roaring triumph, and, when it was all over, a tired but happy Ladew wrote his sister, "The garden tour—four days—for Nannie's hospital was a great success—sunny weather—hundreds of people and we made over three thousand five hundred dollars. If the new taxes break me, I think I will go into garden tours as a business!"[17]

On May 26 Virginia Sherwood, president of the Board of Trustees of the GBMC, wrote a thank-you note to Harvey Ladew, their "*Benefactotum Horticulturus.*" (In 1927 Sherwood's father-in-law, who shared Ladew's passions for horticulture and conservation, began the celebrated Sherwood Gardens, whose 7 acres of tulips, daffodils, and spring-flowering shrubs form one of the glories of north Baltimore.) Her note took the form of a poem:

> We propose a toast to Harvey Ladew,
> Who fashioned a garden of privet and yew
> Into long-necked giraffe and swans afloat.
> He even included a Chinese boat
> 'Mid borders of tulips and iris and roses,
> Before banks of lilacs to pleasure our noses!
> Rhododendron, azalea, golden chain trees
> Harbor houses for pigeons and hives for the bees.
> Wisteria drips and pond lilies float,
> Where a brazen bullfrog emits a rude croak,
> As visitors wander in obvious glee,
> While happily sipping a glass of iced tea.
> Then on to the house with its pleasures galore—
> So many have ne'er seen like treasures before—
> As paneling, paintings and books all arow,
> Where china and silver reflect candles' glow,
> And huntsman's horn, stirrup cup, spurs all attest
> To the might of our host as a sportsman—the best!
> A toast we proposed, and a toast we will give,
> To Mr. Harvey Ladew, Long May He Live—
> To open his place so that hundreds may see,
> While filling the coffers of GBMC!"

Ladew, never one to miss a chance to indulge in a bit of doggerel, responded (in part):

> Your poem is wonderful,
>   It's made me most conceited.

"America is going to HELL!"

I read it after gardening,
    When tired and depleted.

I've found a handsome frame to hold your poem;
    It will be read by all who come within my home.
(You may not think that "Poem" and "home"
    Rhyme well—and it is too Nash-ish—
Or perhaps you think that I have had
    An overdose of hash-ish?)

Now, pleased by the success of the GBMC tour and confident that a nonprofit garden foundation could work, on December 22, 1969, Ladew signed a deed of trust to his four nieces and nephews, and to the Marine Midland Bank, all acting as trustees for "a public park and museum to be known as the Harvey Smith Ladew Topiary Garden." (That year, Walter Mather, vice president of Marine Midland Bank, innocently estimated the foundation could run the garden successfully on "$50–55,000 per year,"[18] a figure that can only cause pitying smiles from those who manage the place today.) Significantly, if the trustees ever deemed the project no longer viable, they were empowered to sell the property in whole or in part and divide the proceeds among three Palm Beach charitable institutions, Good Samaritan Hospital, St. Mary's Roman Catholic Hospital, and the Society of the Four Arts.

The deed of trust also set up a local Advisory Committee consisting (alphabetically and as they appear in the deed) of Mrs. Sloan Doak, Mrs. F. Warrington Gillet, C. A. Porter Hopkins, D. Luke Hopkins, Mrs. Peter Jay, Mrs. J. Reiman McIntosh, Mrs. William McMillan, Mrs. Elizabeth Wickes Nichols, Thomas S. Nichols, Mr. and Mrs. Nicholas Penniman III, John D. Schapiro, and the Honorable Joseph D. Tydings, in addition to the Blacks, Constables, and Griswolds. Gerard L. Carroll, Ladew's New York attorney, was retained as the group's lawyer.

On June 3, 1970, Carroll wrote the Benefactotum Horticulturus to announce that "after many years of endeavor," he was "happy to advise" him that the IRS had "formally approved the Harvey Smith Ladew Topiary Garden Foundation." Luke Hopkins quickly penned a note to say, "I think it is just wonderful that you have persevered in the ideas you had for so long in making it possible that the lovely place will be one of the green spots of the world."[19]

Ladew hosted the Advisory Committee's first meeting, held, appropriately, at Pleasant Valley. He appointed Benjamin Griswold chairman, Nicholas Penniman vice chairman, and Elizabeth Constable chairman of the Garden Committee. Members then elected Mayo McIntosh secretary and Luke Hopkins treasurer.[20] Endearingly, Ladew felt that the foundation was fine but was not as important as Marlene Dietrich's puppies. In the spring of 1970, as the group was planning to open the garden for regular tours, Ladew told Susan Sage, "They are going to

"Perfectly Delightful"

Plagued by ill health, servant problems, and financial worries, Ladew managed to keep his effervescent good humor into his old age, as his 1965 Christmas card suggests.

have cold drinks and I thought I'd put up a sign because I could sell two or three dachshunds. I would say, 'Champion-bred dachshunds for sale; inquire at gate.' Then I'm going to put: 'Cold Drinks and Hot Dogs For Sale but we do not guarantee the hot dogs will be champion-bred.' Don't you think that will be quite funny?"[21]

During the foundation's first years of existence, with Ladew still very much on the scene, simple good manners required the Advisory Committee to move gingerly. "We obviously had to be diplomatic," Sibyl Brown recalled. In 1973 the committee met to set regular hours for visiting the gardens: weekends from one o'clock to four; other times by appointment. Mather encouraged the committee to target tour groups, deeming them "not only essential for admission income, but even more valuable for public relations." In May of that year Treasurer Hopkins announced he had started a local bank account to enable the committee to function more smoothly: the first contribution (one hundred dollars) came from Ladew's great-nephew Augustus Paine; Alexander Brown Griswold and his brother, Benjamin, quickly added two hundred and five hundred dollars, respectively.[22]

Not content with individual contributions, the Advisory Committee also organized benefit parties. One of the more successful of these was held in June 1975.[23] The event proved to be the last social function the invalid Ladew attended. But he did enjoy it! As Louise Ingalls, society reporter for the *Baltimore News Post* observed, "there was more than a hint of the good old days as well as the ambiance of an English countryside" that evening as "large floppy hats and soft floaty gowns worn by many of the ladies" suggested—to Harvey's delight—"that the mid-70s [were] enjoying a renascence of things ladylike, genteel, and elegant."[24]

"America is going to HELL!"

"My garden isn't finished yet," Ladew wrote his sister in 1969. "I have only worked on it fifty years and it will take another fifty years for my friends to finish it." The new foundation began that fifty-year project largely under the direction of Leith Griswold, president of the board, and Elizabeth Constable, vice president and chairman of the Garden Committee. Both women had known Ladew since the early 1930s. Their earliest memories seem thoroughly in keeping with his effervescent spirit. Constable said that she first met him as a young girl on the dance floor in the ballroom of Baltimore's Belvedere Hotel. Griswold loves to describe how she met him one winter in London when she was attending a girl's boarding school and he was in the midst of an English hunting season. Her parents, Jack and Arabella Symington, among Ladew's first Maryland friends, asked him to look their daughter up and take her to an educational play if he ever got to London. "He picked me up in a yellow Rolls Royce," she recalled, "and we went to dinner. Then we went to a theater and took our seats. The play he chose was the FILTHIEST thing I ever saw—before or since! He kept whispering in my ear, 'Remember, we're seeing Shakespeare; we're seeing Shakespeare.' I loved him immediately."[25]

Despite, or perhaps because of, their long familiarity with Ladew and the garden, both women deemed their task "pretty daunting," as Constable has said. They and the board adopted a policy of working to keep the *spirit* of the place alive and intact, but not necessarily each variety of every one of Ladew's original plants. Every visitor during his lifetime commented, as the Garden Club of America had, on Pleasant Valley's innate good humor; or, as one member wrote him after the 1966 visit, "When I first heard that yours was a topiary garden I was not enthusiastic, because my immediate reaction was to remember the stiff, overly formal effects. But how wrong I was! The fox-hunt running across your lawn, the beautiful hedge of life-like swans on their rippling base will never be forgotten. It was all so delightful and such *fun*!" Dee Hardie sensed that spirit, too, and through her monthly *House & Garden* column told the nation about it: "Harvey was endlessly entertaining," she wrote. "He was the first to teach me that gardening could not only create a pretty picture, but an amusing one as well, filled with imagination."[26] Thus the amusing futuristic teahouse in the Yellow Garden will always be there, even though it runs against the "good taste" of many visitors (and board members) and Adam will always have those apples behind his back.

Accordingly, the Garden Committee felt free to plant more disease-free and blackspot-resistant roses, for instance, in place of Ladew's often troublesome hybrid teas. Similarly, although the Yellow Garden will remain *yellow*, it will not, perhaps, always achieve that color using the exact same plants Ladew chose. This willingness to experiment not only makes common sense but makes historic sense as well. Ladew himself continuously tinkered with the garden's details. His papers contain hundreds—literally hundreds—of notes to himself: "Add Siberian Iris Croquet Court"; "Move hydrangeas croquet court"; "If pink hydrangeas turn blue—remove them"; "Find shade loving plants croquet court"; "more GREY in borders"; "Remove Naked Ladies"; "Water garden—Can I get seed of different small sedum to plant between flagstone? Fill open spaces—pepper bush"; "More Autumn flowers—Hardy Asters, Boltonia, Lobelia cardinalis, Scabiosa"; "Plant a few lotus"; "Move Ballerina rose"; "Orchard: Move mock orange trees"; "White Border—White sweet peas—look up planting directions"; and on and on and on. In 1970, he decided to add his "latest thing": stone steps here and there engraved with appropriate messages and witty sayings such as "A Rose is a Rose is a Rose," which is carved into the three granite steps that carry one from the Great Bowl into the Rose Garden.

At times his notes suggest the activist approach FDR took to battle the Great Depression: "Try something," the president famously wrote. "If that fails, try something else—but try *something*!" Similarly, one finds in Ladew's notes instructions to himself to "Try some Anemone Cormaria"; "Try Sweet Peas on poles"; "Tennis Court—Try Climbing Hydrangeas"; "Try grape hyacinth"; "Berry Garden—Ask Kingsville Nursery for ideas"; and "Yellow Garden: might order some Yellow Hollyhock seed"—*might*: he himself wasn't certain it would work, but he would *try* it. Moreover, his lively brain kept coming up with ideas for new yew sculptures, including "Queen Elizabeth on horseback," a "Velasquez Infanta," and a "J.F.K. Memorial Topiary." (Although the slain president's politics left Ladew cold, he keenly admired Jacqueline Kennedy, whom he had met in Palm Beach.) Sometimes his notes contain ideas that seem doomed at the start. What on earth was he thinking when he scribbled, "Orchard—Tulips"? That idea couldn't possibly have worked because there was no room to plant the bulbs: the paths were narrow, and he couldn't plant them among the azaleas because those shrubs have such shallow roots. Finally, there were notes to correct past mistakes, such as "Do not put pansies in border."

Now and then, the new foundation's Garden Committee felt that some of his favorite plants had to be eliminated altogether. He struggled for decades trying to nurse delphiniums through Maryland's hot summers. One of the most dog-eared books in his horticultural library is *How to Grow Delphiniums*, and he ordered a dozen plants from his favorite source, Wayside, in 1959; another "3 Doz English Delphiniums" in 1965; and two hundred (!) more in 1969. He no doubt fell in love with them in England, where they thrive in the cool dampness. (Recall that he listed delphiniums among the plants one associates with English cottage gardens.) But Maryland's Augusts do not suit them at all. And although he was free to struggle with them ("Try to save old delphinium plant," he wrote himself in one note; "Try to save delphiniums," he wrote in another), a nonprofit foundation simply couldn't afford the luxury of treating those majestic plants as expensive annuals.

"America is going to HELL!"

On July 28, 1976, Harvey Ladew died peacefully at Pleasant Valley Farm. On November 18 of that year, Crocker Luther, Ladew's executor, called a special meeting of the foundation's Executive Committee at Nicholas Penniman III's law office in Baltimore. Penniman, Ladew's local attorney, reported that the will had been probated and that he was making arrangements to have the contents of the house inventoried and appraised. After a few other preliminary announcements (Ladew's relatives had taken charge of his personal effects; various pieces of art were stored at the Walters Art Gallery; Gina was given Marlene Dietrich and one puppy; and so on), Luther turned the meeting to a discussion about restructuring the hitherto loose organization into something capable of running and maintaining a 230-acre property with 22 acres of formal gardens, a twelve-room manor house, and a half dozen outbuildings.

In 1967, just as Ladew was endeavoring to find a way to preserve his garden, in England Nigel Nicolson, younger son of V. Sackville-West and Harold Nicolson, gave the gardens his parents had created at Sissinghurst Castle to the National Trust. In his preface to a recent history of Sissinghurst, Nicolson offered some good advice and sound thoughts to those who manage historic gardens:

> People who like to boast of their long and deep acquaintance with the place are apt to say that Sissinghurst is no longer what it was "in Vita's day," implying that it has lost something of its serenity and betrayed her genius. Let the reply be: that no garden is, or should ever be, what it was, since it is a living, growing, changing thing, and it would be foolish, unimaginative and actually treacherous to Vita's own conception of a garden to replace every plant that dies and every tree that topples by the same plant or same tree. This of course applies provided that nothing is done that conflicts with the architecture of the place, or its colour-scheme, and that everything new should be in spirit faithful to the date of the garden's origins, mid-twentieth century.[27]

The trustees of the Ladew Topiary Gardens, Inc., have done precisely that. They have also, intentionally or not, responded to the thoughts of one visitor who, after the hospital-benefit tour, sought out Harvey to thank him and to tell him, "[I] loved the Ladew Gardens and will be very sorry when they are Ladone." He replied that she should take heart: the gardens weren't going to be "Ladone" when he was alive and would never be "Ladone" in the future.

"Perfectly Delightful"

EPILOGUE

Although Harvey Ladew lived to see his gardens become famous, since his death, the foundation he established has seen to it that they have become exceptionally so. Studied, written about, and admired by cognoscenti from five continents, Pleasant Valley Farm is now visited by more than thirty thousand pilgrims each year and supported by seventeen hundred foundation members.

Shortly after Ladew died in 1976, members of the foundation he had created met in the Baltimore law offices of Nicholas Penniman III to discuss the future of Ladew's legacy. They asked attorney George Constable to prepare a reorganization plan based on that day's conversation. He proposed the foundation adopt a three-part structure consisting of a twenty-one-member board of trustees (including Ladew's nieces as ex officio trustees); an Executive Committee consisting of the chair and vice chair of the advisory board, the recording secretary, and the chairs of the Garden, House, and Education Committees; and an open-ended Consulting Committee. The trustees would meet quarterly, the Executive Committee monthly. Marine-Midland Bank would continue to oversee the organization's finances and would send a monthly stipend to the foundation's local bank. The minutes show that "his proposal was gratefully accepted."[1]

The trustees also formulated this mission statement to guide their actions and the actions of those who will follow:

The mission of the Ladew Topiary Gardens, Inc., is to maintain and promote the gardens, house, and facilities in keeping with the creative spirit of Harvey S. Ladew for the public benefit and for educational, scientific, and cultural pursuits.

As gardens are continually growing and changing, the aim is not only to restore or simply preserve, but to nurture Ladew Gardens, always keeping in mind Mr. Ladew's over-all design.

Ladew Topiary Gardens, Inc., shall develop and operate diverse projects to broaden the appeal of the Gardens, to secure the financial stability of the organization, and to maintain the gardens, buildings, and facilities in the best possible condition to accommodate the public.[2]

Under the 1976 plan, volunteers began work to prepare for the grand opening of the house and garden the following April 24. Ground-floor rooms were to be repainted (using paint donated by Oliver Reeder and under the supervision of House Committee chair Eleanor Constable Weller), the old service wing of maids' rooms would be turned into an office wing for staff, and a newly formed Library Committee, headed by Mac Griswold, started to catalog Ladew's thousands of books. On other fronts, William Voss Elder III, curator of decorative arts at the Baltimore Museum of Art, went through the house room by room with Pattie Penniman to "give his opinion as to what should be done."[3] Because the foundation relied heavily on Ladew's neighbors and friends to maintain the property, a Committee for Volunteers became necessary; it has been gently and effectively chaired by Martha Robbins.

The trustees also formed an Education Committee. Its first chairs, Nancy Brewster, Bibber Dow, and Nancy Symington Perrin, set out to prepare a slide lecture about the grounds which could be sent to garden clubs throughout the United States. In 1980 Pattie Penniman succeeded the trio as chair of the Education Committee; she decided to begin a lecture series, which under her direction and that of Alice Ober (who has chaired the committee since 1985) has gained national renown, bringing luminaries such as Rosemary Verey, Caroline Seabom, Bunny Williams, and Joe Eck and Wayne Winterroud to speak in Ladew's studio.

In addition, Ladew's old friend Billy Baldwin agreed to serve on the Consulting Committee, to assist in preparing a story about the property for *Architectural Digest* (which never materialized), and to help write a visitor's guide for the gardens. He also generously said he would oversee all restoration work on the house and grounds he had known so intimately for more than forty-five years. This incalculably important offer was, of course, quickly accepted, and before his death in 1983, Baldwin supervised the restoration of Ladew's bedroom and sitting room (most significantly the aubergine enamel paint) and the hand-painted "Ladew pink" wallpaper in the Tivoli Teahouse.

Outside, Elizabeth Constable, whom Ladew had chosen to head up the foundation's Garden Committee, had been busy since the early 1970s. In June 1973 she reported that she and her co-workers felt they should initially conduct "a holding operation" to prevent any further deterioration of the landscape. Accordingly, during that year they bought some chrysanthemums and "a few roses" to fill in gaps. She also decided to experiment with "some white geraniums for the Rose Garden" as an environmentally safe method of repelling aphids. In addition, the Iris Garden had been dug and its soil tested, irises had been divided and replanted, and six dozen new irises had been added to Ladew's collection. "Rank growth" in the Yellow Garden had been removed; lilacs got pruned; and Bunny

Hathaway volunteered to contribute seven hundred tulips for the Pink and White Gardens. In addition, the Garden Club of Twenty quietly worked to restore the "Woods Garden," adding *Phlox divericata* and ferns.[4]

In 1974 the Garden Committee replaced sixty roses that had been winter-killed, a half dozen ailing espaliered apple trees, and some clematis vines that had succumbed to "wilt." Committee members also bedded out 170 chrysanthemums. The same year the American Iris Society agreed to take on the Iris Garden as a project, and the Guilford Garden Club agreed to superintend the Rose Garden. The following year the Garden Committee planted a dozen *Rhododendron maximus* to screen the "Woodland Garden" from the increasingly busy Jarrettsville Pike; members also planted a further five espaliered pears to replace more dead ones on the Belgian fence and dug in eight hemlock trees between the Croquet Court and Pink Garden.[5]

In 1977 Nancy Brewster, a longtime member of the Garden Committee, drew up a plan for replanting the Berry Garden with hardy berried shrubs as Ladew intended. The same year committee members planned a background fence or hedge along the Jarrettsville Pike "to carry out the plan originated by Mr. Ladew." They recommended that "all weed trees and brush interfering with the original plan of the garden . . . be removed"; and, at the strong urging of Mayo McIntosh, they insisted that "the poor drainage in the area of the Topiary Fox Hunt" be corrected. (One hound had already "drowned.") "The postponed restoration of the original design of the Fox Hunt should not be continually by-passed," they declared. "It is the first thing visitors see on arrival and the last thing as they leave!"[6]

Seeking expert, professional advice, the board asked authorities from Maryland and adjacent states, including Liddon Pennock, Russell Page, Mrs. Alfred Bissell, Ms. Landon Scarlett, Dr. Darrell Apps, Dr. Marc Cathey, and Edward Hogarth, to join a Visiting Horticultural Committee, which would come to the gardens once a year to note progress and offer suggestions.[7] After their first visit, Mayo McIntosh, recording secretary, reported that the committee had recommended filling in the outside circle in the Water Lily Garden with earth and then planting it with woodland plants.

That garden, with its central fountain (which Ladew purchased in England in 1939 for ninety pounds from Crowther of Syon Lodge), perimeter pools, and slate "floor," had had an eventful history. Elizabeth Constable recalled that in its day, it was "simply beautiful," as Ladew had planted "little tiny Alpine plants" between the slate stones. Unfortunately, one day a group of schoolchildren, who had volunteered to weed during Ladew's last illness, "pulled out every one of the Alpine plants and all of the Johnny-jump-ups—they made a clean sweep of it." Then there was the matter of the pools: Ladew, being "no engineer or contractor," felt that an inch and a half of concrete would suffice for the pools' walls. "After fifteen years of course the whole thing cracked up and all the water went out."[8] Fortunately, however, the board reconsidered the idea of filling in the ponds and instead voted, as the minutes record, that it "must be restored . . . [because] it is the hub of the Yellow Garden, White Garden, and Orchard Garden, all of which start or end there." Thanks to a grant from the Abell Foundation—"Gary [Black] was very kind to see that we got some money," Leith Griswold recalls[9]—the committee relined the ponds, relaid the slates ("Tom Hunter, a builder, did a beautiful job there," said Elizabeth Constable), replaced plants between the stones, and got it "looking almost the way it was when it was at its height, when it was so beautiful."[10] (Plate 5.)

On another sojourn, the Visiting Horticultural Committee focused on Ladew's Iris Garden, planted, in his day, in one wide central swath of iris with narrower parallel beds to each side. When Ladew planned the garden, he knew it would look spectacular for two weeks in May and then could be completely ignored for the rest of the year. This, while fine for a private garden, simply would not do in a place open to the public from April to October: "When people drive 50 or 100 miles to come here, we have an obligation to have something for them to see," Elizabeth Constable remarked. Then there was the matter of upkeep. As Mrs. Bissell and the Visiting Committee pointed out, "You could easily spend all your time and money on iris." Consequently, the Garden Committee, guided by Edward Hogarth and Anne Donnell Smith, removed the parallel flower beds and replaced them with mixed flowering shrubs; they also added various ornamental grasses from Blue Mount Nursery at the foot of the central swath; finally, they replaced most of the demanding (if beautiful) bearded irises with low-growing shrubs, daylilies, and less labor-intensive Japanese and Siberian irises.[11] That decision might strike some as heretical, but recall that Ladew himself had written his sister that he planned "to go in for Japanese Iris." Moreover, the Taylor Publishing Company, producers of a respected series of garden books, liked the result so much it used a Derek Fell photograph of the new Iris Garden for the cover of the fourth edition (1988) of their tome *Garden Design*.

Other changes came about for other reasons. Across the stream from the Yellow Garden—just west of the allée leading to the Temple of Venus—Ladew created what he called his "Mimosa Pie," a space filled with privet planted and clipped to resemble four Chinese chops, each with a mimosa tree in its center. Shortly after Ladew's death, the mimosas died, and the Garden Committee decided not to replace them because the trees tend to be so short lived. Also across the stream—but on the eastern side of the main axis—Ladew began another allée bordered and formed by yews and what had become, by the 1970s, "ratty-looking hydrangeas." Well before his death, Ladew had lost interest in this part of the garden—"Harvey had all kinds of ideas, but so many were never executed," said Elizabeth Constable. She and Leith Griswold toyed with the idea of cleaning out "that no man's land" and placing an obelisk at the end of the allée, a cenotaph to Ladew. They felt that other matters were more urgent and dropped the idea—"but the yews are still there if anyone in the future wants to revive the plan!"[12]

"Perfectly Delightful"

The foundation-renovated Iris Garden, photographed by Derek Fell in 1987. Of all the Ladew "room gardens," these beds have grown to be some of the most interesting to horticulturalists, professional and amateur alike.

Back in the main section of the garden one finds the tiny Keyhole Garden. Here the committee replaced "an unsafe rickety old wooden bench" with a safe "visitor-friendly" iron one. Otherwise the rosey-hued planting scheme is maintained with Pissard plum (*Prunus cerasifera*), red barberry (*Berberis thunbergi atropurerea*), and brilliant red dahlias.

The Rose Garden has proved a perennial source of headaches, but as Elizabeth Constable pointed out, "You can't have a garden open to the public without roses—and Harvey did so love roses."[13] When the Japanese beetle first hit America, Ladew, always reluctant to use chemical pesticides, grew discouraged when he saw the beetle-eaten shrubs. His solution—a drastic one—was to dig up the roses and replant the round "room" with zinnias. The Garden Committee decided to remove the zinnias (or, rather, just not replant them) and fill the spaces with roses. At the Tivoli Teahouse garden, the Garden Committee kept Ladew's scheme of plants that bloomed in pinks and blues to echo the wallpaper he designed for the folly's interior. In Ladew's day, this space was largely a highly scented spring garden filled with peonies and lilacs; the Garden Committee simply added summer-blooming (and highly fragrant) oriental lilies.

Ladew's use of hemlock to form the main allée's walls plagues those who manage the garden today. Most agree that he chose hemlock because he was middle aged when he started the garden, didn't know how long he'd live, and wished to get fast results. But over the years the severe clipping necessary to turn a 70-foot-tall tree into 15-foot walls stressed the hemlocks and left them easy prey to disease and parasites, as if a horticultural sword of Damocles hung over the garden.

The sword finally fell in the late 1980s, when the woolly adelgid (*Adelges tsugae*) arrived. This parasite, a native of Japan, particularly relishes hemlock, as the modifier *tsugae*, derived from the Latin for hemlock, *tsuga*, suggests. The vermin, Mike Klingamen colorfully wrote for the *Baltimore Sun* of October 4, 1993, "attacks with a one-two punch that is half vampire, half viper: The bug sucks the trees' sap while injecting a lethal spittle." Many of Ladew's stressed hemlocks quickly succumbed to the ravenous parasite; others lost whole limbs as garden staff removed adelgid-ridden sections of the plants. Because the scale and the trimness of the hedges have always been among the key elements of the garden, creating, as they do, its "bones," the hemlocks' apparently inevitable demise seemed catastrophic. But after the situation was analyzed, it was decided to replace the dead or hopelessly diseased hemlock with yew and arbor vitae (avoiding another monoculture); other trees, less infected, are being nursed along to prolong their lives as long as possible.[14]

The board and Garden Committee also had to deal with the effects Ladew's once private paradise would suffer by becoming public, for visitors bring welcome revenue but cause physical problems as well. Thousands of pairs of feet can turn every path and large stretches of lawn into vast quagmires. The foundation has coped with this by installing bits of paving at highly traveled spots, such as the gates to the Rose Garden and the terrace behind the card room.

Finally, there was the question of how to treat the front of the house, where guests would enter for tours. Ladew had a kennel built there for his dachshund, and that proved a sticky point. "Harvey didn't design the place as a showplace," Elizabeth Constable remarked. "It was his home." But other board members felt that most visitors would be less than thrilled by an unused kennel by the entrance door. (Restocking it with dachshunds was ruled out as an impractical alternative.) So the committee hit on an ingenious solution: remove the kennel but put a doghouse, topiary dog, and punning sign ("a place to pause; a place to rest my paws") in its place to honor the original spirit of the space.[15]

During 1974, garden tours and gifts (from 62 garden clubs and 365 individu-

Ladew and polo remain linked, even after his death. The Maryland Polo Club still plays on Ladew Field in a corner of Pleasant Valley Farm. Here Harvey's niece, Patricia Corey (fourth from right), and her polo-hall-of-fame husband, Alan (far right), congratulate winners of a match held to benefit the gardens. From the left, players on the Capital City Mortgage team included Tom Nash, Alan Nash, Rick Barrow, and Martin Astrada; between Mr. and Mrs. Corey stand Jack Burlbaugh and Marcos Bignoli.

als) generated income of $46,507, very near the figure Mather had predicted would cover operating costs. The following year the Advisory Committee decided to open the *house* for tours; because its owner was ill, members voted to limit tours to once a month. Even so, income from house tours in 1974 totaled $8,000.

Notwithstanding the income generated by benefit parties and tours, the garden's finances remained precarious. In 1980, the foundation felt forced to hold an auction. Patricia Hughes, wife of Maryland's governor, acted as honorary chair. The auction caused some dissention among the members of the Advisory Committee about the pros and cons of selling Ladew's personal property. As if to defray criticism—from within and without—they carefully pointed out in the catalog that articles sold came "primarily from Mr. Ladew's properties in New York and Florida and from several rooms at Pleasant Valley" not normally open to the public. In addition, several friends contributed "special donations" to be sold for the benefit of the gardens;[16] among these lots one finds five Thai bronze Buddhas dating from the fifteenth to seventeenth century, donated by Alec Griswold. In all

Epilogue

In the late 1970s, the foundation established by Harvey Ladew experimented with the idea of a summer concert series at the Great Bowl. It proved a success and now attracts hundreds of picnicking music lovers on Sunday evenings in July and August.

the auction netted approximately $66,000—a most gratifying sum. Even so, one person involved with organizing the auction recently said she wondered if it was the right thing to have done. One fund-raising effort no one at the garden regrets today was the 1993–97 capital fund drive—nicknamed by co-chairs Ned Daniels and Wendy Griswold "A Hedge for the Future"—which created an endowment of just over $2 million.

The 1976 reorganization improved conditions for a while, but the board continued to operate in what might be called excessive informality, and in October 1978, George Constable and Nicholas Penniman prepared a memo stressing their lawyerly "concern about proper and orderly procedures." After some discussion and innumerable meetings, Constable suggested that the foundation be reincorporated thusly: a set number of corporate trustees to make policy; a board of trustees to vote on policy; and a nonvoting consulting committee to assist as needed. The new corporation became a legal entity in 1981, and in 1982 the 1969 trustees transferred 227.59 acres to the Ladew Topiary Gardens, Inc. During the years of uncertainty and reorganization which characterized the foundation in the 1970s, stability came in the presence of John Robbins Jr., who, as pro bono director, provided much-needed continuity. The new corporation, however, required

"Perfectly Delightful"

a full-time, paid director; that came in the presence of the indomitable Lena Caron, who superbly filled the role from 1981 until she retired in 1996.

Slowly and determinedly, the foundation and its Garden Committee proceeded with their work, and through the extraordinary efforts of Ladew's friends and acquaintances, his horticultural masterpiece was eventually brought back. Care was taken to preserve the original integrity of the overall plan. Existing structures were repaired (notably the Tivoli Teahouse) while others were adapted for new uses: the garage, for instance, became the visitors' center and shop; the studio—scene of those wonderful costume parties—became a lecture hall; and the stables became the Ladew Café. That last venture was one of the first projects taken on by Director Caron. She completed it in 1983, and at the following April's board meeting, members praised "the entire Garden Staff on the stupendous and backbreaking job they did" laying the brick in the restaurant courtyard and observed that "Lena's design has resulted in something very elegant."

More recently, in the 1990s the Maryland Polo Club asked for—and received—permission to construct a playing field on a remote part of the property. The club holds weekly matches there in summer; not only has this proved mutually beneficial to both organizations, but it is also—clearly—in the spirit of that keen equestrian Harvey S. Ladew. Horses brought Ladew to Maryland in 1929, after all, so it seemed highly fitting that the hoofs still pound Pleasant Valley's acres. Coincidentally, at about the same time, the trustees of Old Westbury Gardens decided to bring polo back there. Thanks to people such as Ladew's own brother-in-law, William Russell Grace, polo matches characterized Long Island's North Shore in the 1920s and 1930s. But as those original players aged, the game diminished in importance in the Great Neck–Westbury area. Today, as Peggie Phipps Boegner has written, "Polo is becoming popular again and returning to Long Island and even to Westbury House. Following an international match at the Meadow Brook Club in the summer of 1985, the house and gardens again rang out with the laughter and conversation of a gathering of polo enthusiasts."

In recognition of the board's success, the Garden Club of America presented 1990's Distinguished Achievement Award to Leith Griswold for ensuring that "Ladew Topiary Garden is now an internationally known attraction and a tribute to the time-honored tradition of topiary art." In response, Griswold thanked the club for "the thrill of a lifetime." She also acknowledged "Harvey Ladew's dedicated friends and neighbors," the "tireless labors of the director and her staff," and the support of the extended Ladew-Grace family. "The Garden has now obtained worldwide recognition, visited and enjoyed by thousands of people from all walks of life and all parts of the globe. Please," Leith Griswold said, in words that might conclude this section of the book, "give us the opportunity to welcome each and every one of you to America's most renowned Topiary garden in the near future."

APPENDIX

Harvey Ladew's Iris Garden

Exhausting as it seems, the following list, as compiled by the American Iris Society in 1974, does not include all the irises Ladew grew in Pleasant Valley Farm's Iris Garden. For instance, period photographs clearly show clumps of Siberian and Japanese irises mixed in with the bearded varieties cited in the list; many surviving nursery receipts further document their presence and offer specificity as to variety, for example, "5 Japanese Iris Mahogany Giant" (from Fairmount Gardens, in Lowell, Massachusetts, dated September 30, 1943) and "100 Iris Siberica Snow Queen" and "100 Iris Siberica Caesar's Brother" (both from Springbrook Gardens in Mentor, Ohio, dated October 10, 1960). In addition, among his undated, random gardening notes is this bit of self-instruction: "Iris Garden—More Siberian Iris."

Finally, Ladew did not dream of segregating his irises in a single "garden room." His notes show that he thought about planting yellow and gold varieties in his Yellow Garden, and there is the dream-making scrawl "Pink Iris–Tea House—150." While nothing suggests he carried out that latter plan, how his mind's eye must have enjoyed the vision of the Tivoli Teahouse sitting amidst 150 billowy pink-blooming irises!

TALL BEARDED VARIETIES

Ad Astra	Belle Prairie	Chinese Coral
Allegiance	Blue Hawaii	Chosen Beauty
Ancient Amber	Blue Shimmer	Christmas Time
Andalusian Blue	Bright Cloud	Cinnamon Tart
Angel Lyric	Camelot Rose	Cliffs of Dover
Apple Valley	Campus Flirt	Cloud Capers
Arctic Fury	Cape Ivory	Coffee Royal
Astronaut	Capt. Jack	Congo Song
Azure Lace	Caroline Jane	Corduroy with Lace
Bar Harbor	Centurian	Craftsman

Debbie Rairdon
Deep Space
Delicious
Dreamy
Eleanor's Pride
Ever & Ever
Faustina Walker
Flagship
Flame and Sand
Flaming Dawn
Fly Away
Fond Wish
Frontier Marshall
Gay Paree
Grand Alliance
Grand Baroque
Helen Louise
Hot Spell
Idaho Gold
Irene Neece
Irish Lullaby
Jan Hess
Java Dove
Jilby
Laurie

Lilac Champagne
Lonely Sea
Lord Baltimore
Lovely Light
Lute Song
Madam Butterfly
Margaret Zurbrigg
Margarita
May Romance
Mexicali
Miss Idaho
Mission Sunset
Miss Saltillo
Mulberry Wine
New Harmony
Orinda
Pale Cloud
Pink Horizon
Pinnacle
Punchline
Radiant Bride
Radiant Sun
Ribbon Round
Rippling Waters
River Styx

Rococo
San Leandro
Sapphire Shores
Scarlet Ribbon
Silver Shadows
Snow Tracery
Spooned Phantom
Star City
Star Shine
Stepping Out
Sudden Spring
Tawny Mink
Tonga Moon
Velvet Dusk
Victorian Veil
Wasatch
Wenatchee Valley
West Coast
Wild Apache
Wild Plum
Windy
Winter Dreams
Yokayo

STANDARD DWARF VARIETIES

Crown
Gingerbread Man
Marinka

Royal Fairy
Snow Troll
Spring Laughter

Stockholm
Tomingo
Twice Blessed

BEARDLESS AND SPECIES FORMS

Blue Roof Iris (*Iris tectorum*)
Dorothy K. Williamson (Louisiana Iris)

Notes

Prologue

1. This and other letters by Ladew to his sister may be found at the Ladew Topiary Gardens (hereafter cited as "LTG").

2. Elizabeth Constable, Elizabeth ("Bibber") Dow, and Leith Griswold, interviewed by Charles Camp, December 21, 1991, tape and transcript at LTG.

3. Dee Hardie, "Still-Life Foxes and Swans Cavort on Maryland Farm," *New York Times*, April 26, 1970.

4. Federated Garden Club of Maryland, *1960 House and Garden Pilgrimage* (Towson, Md.: Federated Garden Club of Maryland, 1960), 61; Mary Frances Wagley, "Pleasant Valley Farm," unpublished information prepared about outstanding houses and gardens in Maryland for participants in the Garden Club of America's annual meeting held in Baltimore in May 1966.

5. Henry Francis du Pont to Harvey S. Ladew (hereafter cited as "HSL"), May 7, 1956, LTG; Diany Binny to HSL, May 12, 1967, LTG.

6. Sibyl Brown, nomination of Harvey Ladew for Distinguished Achievement Award, April 1971, Archives of the Garden Club of America, New York, copy at LTG.

7. Garner Ranney, conversation with author, September 10, 1997.

8. Michael P. Chrismer, "Pleasant Valley Farm," *Ægis*, October 5, 1961.

9. HSL to Betty Blagden, October 21, 1969, LTG; HSL to Mr. and Mrs. Benjamin H. Griswold III, August 18, 1964. All letters to the Griswolds are located at the family home, Fancy Hill Farm, Monkton, Md.

Chapter 1   *"I loved seeing all my young relatives"*

1. HSL to Nicholas Penniman III, October 21, 1968, LTG.

2. Billy Baldwin, *Billy Baldwin Remembers* (New York: Harcourt Brace Jovanovich, 1974), 217.

3. *Tatler*, August 30, 1939, clipping at LTG. Baldwin, *Billy Baldwin Remembers*, 224.

4. HSL to Elise Ladew Grace (hereafter cited as "ELG"), April 1, 1967, LTG.

5. HSL to ELG, March 14, 1967, LTG.

6. Harvey S. Ladew, *Random Recollections*, ed. Martha Frick Symington (Monkton, Md.: Ladew Topiary Gardens Foundation, 1980), 1.

7. HSL to ELG, October 5, 1967, LTG.

8. HSL to ELG, June 20, 1967, LTG.

9. Baldwin, *Billy Baldwin Remembers*, 218.

10. Patricia Corey, conversation with author, January 11, 1998.

11. HSL to ELG, December 8, 1949, LTG.

12. HSL, interviewed by Susan Sage (now Dillon), April 1970, tape and transcript at LTG.

13. *New York Tribune*, March 11, 1888; obituary of Harvey S. Ladew, LTG.

14. Hoyt later served two terms in the Connecticut legislature. Frank W. Norcross, *A History of the New York Swamp* (New York: Chiswick Press, 1901), 98.

15. Ibid., 103.

16. Ladew obituary; *Cumberland Daily News*, March 12, 1888.

17. Norcross, *Swamp*, 103.

18. Fayerweather left the bulk of his wealth to various colleges, but "the litigation over his will became a *cause celebre*" and no institution of higher learning ever saw anything of the once-great fortune. Ibid., 102.

19. HSL to ELG, September 27, 1968, LTG.

20. Baldwin, *Billy Baldwin Remembers*, 217.

21. The inventory was presumably made for insurance purposes. It is at LTG.

22. Anita Leslie, *Edwardians in Love* (London: Hutchinson & Co., 1972), 323–24.

23. Edna Ferber to HSL, January 4, 1947, LTG.

24. HSL to ELG, December 8, 1949, LTG.

25. HSL to ELG, January 20, 1967, LTG.

26. HSL to ELG, September 2, 1947; July 12, 1949, LTG.

27. HSL to ELG, November 27, 1947, LTG.

28. HSL to ELG, October 21, 1947, LTG.

29. He said he initially found this livery, the first he had seen in America, "extraordinary" but that in time he got "used to it." One day he asked the footman how he powdered his hair. The servant replied that he washed his own hair with soap and water "and that before it dried he sprinkled it with powder."

30. HSL Papers, LTG.

31. "The Barlow Place at Glen Cove Sold," unidentified newspaper clipping, LTG.

32. Flagler's railroad eventually reached Key West in 1912.

33. Peggie Phipps Boegner, *Halcyon Days* (New York: Harry N. Abrams and Old Westbury Gardens, 1986), 218.

34. "How Mrs. Ladew Made a Million Dollars as a Factory Boss," undated clipping from unknown newspaper, LTG.

35. Harold Acton, *Memoirs of an Aesthete* (London: Hamish Hamilton, 1967), 208.

36. "New York Travellers Trail Phileas Fogg around the World," *New York Herald*, Sunday, April 6, 1913.

37. *New York Times*, June 12, 1913; *New York Herald*, June 11, 1913.

38. HSL, Sage interview.

39. Miscellaneous clippings, LTG.

40. HSL, unpublished, untitled typed note, LTG.

41. Berry Wall obituary, LTG.

42. "Elsa Maxwell's Party," undated clipping from unknown newspaper, LTG.

43. For instance, Evelyn Laye "sang several of her numbers from 'Bitter Sweet'"; that Noël Coward smash-hit operetta about Old Vienna opened in New York November 5, 1929. Ladew was photographed at the party by Edward Steichen.

44. Dee Hardie, *Views from Thornhill* (New York: Atheneum, 1988), 167. Other sources place the dinner jacket's debut in Tuxedo Park, New York, which explains the jacket's nickname.

45. Ladew, *Random Recollections*, 2.

46. The only other surviving story concerns Mr. Crimmins' funeral, which Ladew attended because he was a close friend of a Crimmins grandson. Harvey wrote about another grandson, "[He] had recently made a marriage to a very pretty chorus girl. It had not been received very enthusiastically by the family but of course she was with them draped in black crepe at the funeral. When the body was removed from the high altar the family followed it down the aisle. At one moment the recent bride seemed to stumble but did not fall. However, from under all the crepe a pair of bright pink silk panties dropped down and remained in full view. . . . They must have been quickly removed by someone but I do not know by who since I had my face covered with both hands to stifle the laughter that I could not control. I have not been in the cathedral since then."

47. On September 2, 1947, Ladew wrote his sister from Monte Carlo, "Just remember how we both supported Uncle Berry for years."

48. Berry Wall obituary.

49. Patricia Corey, conversation with author, January 21, 1996.

50. "New York Society," *New York Tribune*, April 26, 1914, LTG; *Chicago Tribune*, April 26, 1914, LTG.

51. Boegner, *Halcyon Days*, 176.

52. Ibid., 173.

53. Ibid., 176.

54. Boegner, *Halcyon Days*, 210.

55. E. Berry Wall, *Neither Pest nor Puritan* (New York: Dial Press, 1940), 101–2.

56. "Germans Take Auto of Honeymooners," miscellaneous clipping, LTG.

57. Wall, *Pest nor Puritan*, 101.

Chapter 2   *"Happiness comes in absorption"*

1. Ladew liked to tell of one famous society hostess who had a passion for boxing and once even staged a prize fight in her barn. "She gave a dinner party that night and said nothing about the fight which was to be a surprise to her friends. It certainly was." Yet everyone "seemed to enjoy it"—Ladew "certainly did," even "though a certain amount of blood and teeth flew out among the audience." Ladew papers, LTG.

2. Baldwin, *Billy Baldwin Remembers*, 217–18.

3. Monica Randall, *The Mansions of Long Island's Gold Coast* (New York: Hastings House, 1979), 109–12. On Ambrose Clark's death in 1964, the estate was broken up: horses were sold at auction, furniture was given to Lenox Hill Hospital in New York, and the horse paintings went to the racing museum in Saratoga. The house and grounds were bought by the State University College of Old Westbury; in the midst of adapting the mansion to academic use, it caught fire and burned to the ground, and in 1980 only "an empty shell, some charred brick walls, and twisted steel girders" remained to hint at the place's former glory.

4. Edmund Morris, *The Rise of Theodore Roosevelt* (New York: Coward, McCann & Geoghegan, 1979), 315.

5. "Cabaret As Ladew Home Is Destroyed," *New York Enquirer*, May 30, 1915.

6. Aunt Lomie was awarded the Croix de Guerre for her war efforts. Patricia Corey, conversation with author, January 12, 1998.

7. "Headquarters of a Hunting Sportsman," *Town & Country*, undated clipping, LTG.

8. Frederick N. Reed, "The Problem of the Sleeping Porch," *House and Garden* (June 1914): 462; Charles Keefe, *The American House: Being a Collection of Illustrations & Plans of the Best Country & Suburban Houses Built in the United States during the Last Few Years* (New York: U.P.C. Book Co., 1922), 15; plates 51–54.

9. "Headquarters of a Hunting Sportsman," *Town & Country*, undated clipping, LTG. The eight-bedroom house, recently restored by Mr. and Mrs. Alex Nichols, was featured in the Sunday *New York Times* of December 24, 1995; see "A Manor House Wrapped for Christmas."

10. Under his system, all the horses he bred at home were given names incorporating the word "home," as in Home Made, Home Brew, Home Wrecker, and Home Spun.

11. Quoted in John E. Mack, *A Prince of Our Disorder* (Boston: Little, Brown and Co., 1976), 215; Patricia Corey, conversation with author, November 2, 1997.

12. He traced the terrier family back to a fourteenth-century illuminated manuscript depicting three men armed with a hunting horn accompanied by a terrier; the next reference he found was in the writings of "the 15th century sportswoman Dame Juliana Berners, Abess of Sopewell, who alludes to her terriers, or 'teroures,' in the chapters devoted to hunting."

13. Sir Osbert Sitwell, Bart., *Noble Essences* (London: Macmillan & Co., 1950), 133; Helen Worden, "This and That about Society," undated clipping, *New York World*, LTG.

14. Philip Hoare, *Noël Coward* (New York: Simon & Schuster, 1995), 122.

15. Randall, *Mansions*, 10.

16. The Duke of Windsor, *A King's Story* (New York: G. P. Putnam's Sons, 1947), 199–201.

17. Ibid., 200; Wall, *Pest nor Puritan*, 101–2. One of the Graces' three daughters questions this tale and suggests that it shows that Uncle Berry loved a good story more than he valued historical accuracy. Corey conversation, January 12, 1998.

18. Windsor, *King's Story*, 201; the Prince of Wales to HSL, September 22, 1924, LTG.

19. Ladew, *Random Recollections*, 10.

20. That duo visited Ladew at his Florida house in 1947; Lillie stayed one day—March 28—but Webb remained until the 30th.

21. Elsa Maxwell, *R.S.V.P.* (Boston: Little, Brown and Co., 1954), 83–85.

22. Weissmuller made his first Tarzan film in 1932.

23. Harvey Ladew, "The Roman Hunt," *Harper's Bazaar* (March 1952): 159–61, 222.

24. Elsa Maxwell, *The Celebrity Circus* (New York: Appleton-Century, 1963), 102.

25. Ladew, "Roman Hunt," 160.

26. Ibid., 159.

27. Edith Wharton, *Italian Villas and Their Gardens* (New York: Century Co., 1904), 93, 84, 94, 117, 120.

28. HSL to ELG, June 10, 1966, LTG.

29. Worden, "This and That"; Acton, *Memoirs*, 49.

30. Worden, "This and That."

31. Ibid.

32. "Mrs. Cornelius Vanderbilt" refers to Mrs. Cornelius Vanderbilt III, née Grace Wilson (1873–1953). Her husband inherited 640 Fifth Avenue, which had been built by William H. Vanderbilt in 1881, from George W. Vanderbilt, youngest son of William, uncle of Cornelius III, and builder of Biltmore in North Carolina. Grace Vanderbilt was nicknamed "the Kingfisher" because of her love of scooping any visiting royalty she could. The noted hostess entertained ten thousand people a year at her homes in New York and Newport and on her yacht; one frequent guest was former president Theodore Roosevelt. One evening Mrs. Vanderbilt was perplexed by protocol—who got precedence, Roosevelt or the mayor of New York. Roosevelt told her, "By all means put the mayor on your right. A live dog is better than a dead lion any day." See Arthur T. Vanderbilt II, *Fortune's Children* (New York: William Morrow and Co., 1989), 205–10.

33. *Town & Country*, undated clipping, LTG. The world of gardening remains wonderfully close. The internationally known Belgian landscape architect François Goffinet had an uncle who was "Comptroller to Prince Charles at about the time" the prince befriended Ladew. Anthony Hamilton-Little, business manager of François Goffinet, Ltd., letter to author, November 22, 1994, LTG.

34. Horst, *Salute to the Thirties*, foreword by Janet Flanner, photographs by Horst and George Hoyningen-Huene; notes on the plates by Valentine Lawford (New York: Viking Press, 1971), 178.

35. Ladew, *Random Recollections*, 19–20; HSL to ELG, July 12, 1949, LTG.

36. Baldwin, *Billy Baldwin Remembers*, 217.

37. Quoted in ibid., 224.

38. Simon Blow, *Fields Elysian: A Portrait of Hunting Society* (London: J. M. Dent & Sons, 1983), 23, 25, 98.

39. "Burnaby's fame dated back to the 1890s when he had won the Moonlight Steeplechase. It was an idea of the moment and all the participants had ridden with

night-shirts over their scarlet coats and breeches. But Burnaby had forgotten his night-shirt and he had won the race in a pink, beribboned night-dress lent by Lady Augusta Fane." Ibid., 98.

40. Windsor, *King's Story*, 195.

41. Blow, *Fields Elysian*, 125.

42. The twelfth earl of Airlie was born in 1893.

43. Constable, Dow, and Griswold, Camp interview.

44. Blow, *Fields Elysian*, 107, 110, 112.

45. Baldwin, *Billy Baldwin Remembers*, 218.

46. Blow, *Fields Elysian*, 105.

47. Ibid., 61–62.

48. Corey conversation, January 21, 1996.

49. Blow, *Fields Elysian*, 24.

50. Robert Pearsons, Susanne Mitchell, and Candida Geddes, eds., *The Ordnance Survey Guide to Gardens in Britain* (Twickenham, England: Country Life Books, 1986), 311.

51. Peter Furtado, Candida Geddes, Nathaniel Harris, Hazel Harrison, and Paul Pettit, eds., *The Ordnance Survey Guide to Historic Houses in Britain* (Twickenham, England: Country Life Books, 1987), 170.

52. Nikolaus Pevsner, *Northamptonshire* (London: Penguin Books, 1951), 101.

53. Acton, *Memoirs*, 208.

54. Michael Hall, "Making the Bourgeoisie Sit Up," *Country Life*, October 27, 1994, 60.

55. Acton, *Memoirs*, 204–5. For their undoubted eccentricity, the Sitwells brought the scorn of the British art establishment down on their heads. But Acton felt that "Sitwell-bashing" had a pettier motive than mere artistic disagreement: "That they had private incomes was the root of the grievance. . . . Poets were meant to starve" (205).

56. Ibid., 205. Sacheverell and his wife visited Ladew at least twice in Florida. Their longest stay was in 1952, when Sacheverell was on a lecture tour in the United States—and presumably needed some time away from the podium.

57. Sarah Bradford, "Childhood at Renishaw," in *The Sitwells and the Arts of the 1920s and 1930s* (London: National Portrait Gallery, 1994), 16.

58. Sarah Bradford, "Sacheverell," in *Sitwells*, 200.

59. John Pearson, "Osbert," in *Sitwells*, 166.

60. Bradford, "Sacheverell," 200–201.

61. Ibid., 196. Weston, Sacheverell Sitwell's own country house in Northamptonshire, is remembered as being "cluttered with historic bric-a-brac." Acton, *Memoirs*, 206.

62. Michael Urwick Smith, *Luton Hoo: The Wernher Collection* (London: Pitkin Pictorials, n.d.), 20. When the Wernhers opened Luton Hoo to the public, Ladew's favorite, Queen Mary, was the first visitor. Julius Wernher was one of five Life Governors of DeBeers; regarding the name of the estate, it lay near the town of Luton, and "hoo" is Old English for "hill."

63. *Ordnance Survey Guide to Historic Houses*, 212.

64. HSL to ELG, June 20, 1961, LTG.

65. Ladew, *Random Recollections*, 23.

66. Maxwell, *Celebrity Circus*, 26–27.

67. Charlotte Mosley, ed., *The Letters of Nancy Mitford and Evelyn Waugh* (New York: Houghton Mifflin Co., 1995), 31.

68. Miscellaneous clipping, LTG.

69. Ladew, *Random Recollections*, 10.

70. Miscellaneous clipping, LTG.

71. *Tatler*, August 30, 1939, clipping at LTG.

72. Lawrence James, *The Golden Warrior: The Life and Legend of Lawrence of Arabia* (New York: Paragon Books, 1983), xi, 220.

73. Ibid., 18.

74. Ibid., 330.

75. Ibid., 120.

76. Malcolm Brown, ed., *T. E. Lawrence: The Selected Letters* (New York: W. W. Norton & Co., 1988), 443, 176. Westminster later gave the portrait to the Tate Gallery, which made a best-selling print from it; this is the print Ladew owned.

77. Hoare, *Coward*, 224.

78. Brown, *T. E. Lawrence*, 443.

79. Ladew, *Random Recollections*, 62.

80. James, *Golden Warrior*, 341.

81. Brown, *T. E. Lawrence*, 468.

82. James, *Golden Warrior*, 281.

83. Harold Orlans, ed., *Lawrence of Arabia, Strange Man of Letters* (Rutherford, N.J.: Fairleigh Dickenson University Press, 1993), 27.

84. James, *Golden Warrior*, 281.

85. Jeffrey Meyers, "His Letters," in *T. E. Lawrence: Soldier, Writer, Legend*, ed. Jeffrey Meyers (New York: St. Martin's Press, 1989), 24. Lawrence, according to Meyers, wavered "between asceticism, masochism, homosexuality, and an idealistic longing for spiritual unity with another man" (25). Meyers adds, "Military service, for Lawrence, had the positive advantage of severing him from women, who often made threatening sexual overtures." In 1933 Lawrence wrote his friend and confidante Lady Astor, "People seem in my judgement to lose their heads rather than their hearts. Over the Christmas season two men and four women have sent me messages of fervent love. Love carnal, not love rarefied, you know: and I am uncomfortable." Mack, *Prince*, 397.

86. "Cholly Knickerbocker Says," undated clipping, LTG.

87. Brown, *T. E. Lawrence*, 160.

88. Quoted in Mack, *Prince*, 310.

89. T. E. Lawrence to HSL, January 10, 1922, LTG.

90. T. E. Lawrence, introduction to Charles M. Doughty, *Arabia Deserta* (London: Medici Society, 1921), iii.

91. Harold Orlans and Bonnie Schriefer, conversation with author, August 17, 1997. The notes contain such bits of arcane information as "Bedou ask for cigarettes"; "The Bedou can get on promontories and fire down upon caravans"; "Some camels

will step 50 and some 60 times in a minute"; "to violate the guest of Allah is the great offense"; "anthropomorphic"; and "gazelles have same colour as desert."

92. T. E. Lawrence to HSL, January 24, 1922, LTG.

93. T. E. Lawrence to "K.C.," March 7, 1922, LTG; T. E. Lawrence to "Graves," March 9, 1922, LTG; T. E. Lawrence to HSL, n.d., LTG.

94. E. Alexander Powell, *By Camel and Car to the Peacock Throne* (Garden City, N.Y.: Garden City Publishing Co., 1923), iv, 356, vi.

95. E. Alexander Powell, *Free Lance* (New York: Harcourt, Brace and Co., 1937), 150.

96. Powell, *By Camel and Car*, 3.

97. Ibid., 4–5.

98. Powell, *Free Lance*, 167.

99. Powell, *By Camel and Car*, 5.

100. Powell, *Free Lance*, 176.

101. Powell, *By Camel and Car*, 62–63.

102. Ibid., 78–81.

103. Ibid., 86–87.

104. Ladew, *Random Recollections*, 10.

105. Powell, *By Camel and Car*, 86, 89.

106. Ibid., 140–41, 181.

107. Russell Page, *The Education of a Gardener* (London: Atheneum, 1962), 223.

108. Powell, *By Camel and Car*, 310–11.

109. Ibid., 322.

110. Powell, *Free Lance*, 269.

111. Ibid., 272.

112. Powell, *By Camel and Car*, 323; HSL to Martha Symington, n.d., LTG.

Chapter 3 *"A foxhunter's earthly heaven"*

1. Being accepted by the cotillon caused "the greatest excitement. . . . This was something not easily done . . . because, quite frankly, the board was made up of southern gentlemen who were not particularly interested in a northern colonel." Baldwin, *Billy Baldwin Remembers*, 221.

2. Constable, Dow, and Griswold, Camp interview.

3. "Sportsmen Seek State's Horsey Lands," *Baltimore Sun*, November 10, 1929.

4. Quoted in "Dallas Leith and the Elkridge-Harford Hounds," as told to Harriet Iglehart, privately printed memoirs, 11.

5. J. Rieman McIntosh, *A History of the Elkridge Fox Hunting Club, the Elkridge Hounds, and the Elkridge-Harford Hunt Club* (Monkton, Md.: privately published, 1978), 62.

6. See Harford County deeds 213/406 from Harry C. Scarff and Marguerite Scarff, both unmarried, for 110 acres; 213/407 from Hannah Cochran, widow, for 51.4 acres; 213/408 from Anna E. Thompson for 42.6 acres; Ladew made further purchases of land in 1937, 1945, and 1973.

7. "Maryland Meeting," *Sports Illustrated*, November 26, 1956, 69.

8. Leith, "Dallas Leith," 25.

9. An undated *Sunpapers* story notes, "Mr. Chalmers Wood, of Syosset . . . possesses the most attractive bungalow ever designed by a certain MFH."

10. HSL, Sage interview.

11. See C. Milton Wright, *Our Harford Heritage* (Bel Air, Md.: privately published, 1967), 390–92. Scarff's fellow directors included Dr. M. L. Jarrett and Samuel Street.

12. Alva Mary Amoss and Alice Harlan Remsburg, *The Gateway* (Fallston, Md.: privately published, 1976), 46–47; the quotation in the following paragraph is also taken from this source. See also John McGrain, "Molinography of Harford County, Maryland," unpublished typescript in files of the Harford County Department of Planning and Zoning; Wright, *Our Harford Heritage*, 146.

13. *A Portrait and Biographical Record of Cecil and Harford Counties* (New York: Chapman Publishing Co., 1897), 144.

14. HSL, Sage interview.

15. Construction of the school buildings began "in 1921 from plans by James W. O'Connor." *The WPA Guide to New York* (1939; reprint, New York: Random House, 1982), 527.

16. Collette O'Connor, conversation with author, December 17, 1993. Randall, *Mansions*, 219.

17. John Taylor Boyd, "The Country House and the Developed Landscape: William Lawrence Bottomley Expresses His Point of View about the Relation of the Country House to Its Environment in an Interview," *Arts & Decoration* 31 (November 1929): 98.

18. Ibid., 99; Fiske Kimball, "The American Country House," *Architectural Record* 49 (October 1919): 397–99; Clive Aslet, *The American Country House* (New Haven: Yale University Press, 1990), 31; Boyd, "Country House," 54, 100.

19. James O'Connor, "A Modest Georgian Residence in East Norwich, Long Island," *Architectural Record* (February 1926): 111, 121; two years later O'Connor wrote of his work on another project that he tried to create a design "reminiscent of Colonial days . . . [including] wood panelled walls and rough ceiling beams . . . [which] recall the hand work of the times when mouldings were run out by hand and standardization by machinery was unheard and unthought of." James O'Connor, "Traditions Associated with Site Give Character to Design of This House," *American Architect* (May 5, 1928): 613.

20. See "House of J. P. Grace, Esq.," *American Architect* (January 29, 1913): 103–5; "Residence of H. W. Warner, Esq., Syosset, New York," *Architectural Record* (May 1918): 274–76; and "Cottage on the Estate of G. E. Fahys, Esq.," *American Architect* (January 29, 1913): 103. There is the occasional anomaly: note O'Connor's neo-Tudor brick mansion for L. H. Shearman in Lakeville, New York, with its clustered chimneys, casement windows, and castelated courtyards. See *American Architect* (August 31, 1921): 57.

21. Quotations in this and the succeeding two paragraphs draw from Baldwin, *Billy Baldwin Remembers*, 219, 220, 200.

22. Augusta Owen Patterson, "Maryland House of an MFH," *Town & Country* (May 1936): 85.

23. Ibid., 86.

24. Ibid.

25. Baldwin, *Billy Baldwin Remembers*, 219; Leith Griswold, conversation with author, October 12, 1994.

26. Patterson, "Maryland House," 88; Baldwin, *Billy Baldwin Remembers*, 219.

27. Baldwin, *Billy Baldwin Remembers*, 217.

28. Patterson, "Maryland House," 86; J. B. van Urk, "Good Hunting," *Town & Country* (March 1936): 42. That little "summer house" was probably the "frame shed" noted in 1814; Ladew turned it into a card room.

29. Audrey Bishop, "Maryland Fox Hunter Extraordinary," *Sunday Sun Magazine*, September 22, 1957. Ladew recalled a depression-era visit he and Molly Davis made to Ruth Twombly and her mother "at their palace in New Jersey." Mrs. Twombly, a granddaughter of "Commodore" Vanderbilt, told Ladew, in all seriousness, "All my friends are cutting down and I have decided I will have to cut down also. So I am cutting down the footmen from six feet to five foot six."

30. Baldwin, *Billy Baldwin Remembers*, 224.

31. HSL, Sage interview.

32. Baldwin, *Billy Baldwin Remembers*, 221.

33. HSL, Sage interview.

34. Baldwin, *Billy Baldwin Remembers*, 201; Helen Comstock, *One Hundred Most Beautiful Rooms in America* (New York: Viking Press, 1958), 196–97; "House for a Horseman," *Town & Country* (September 1939): 101.

35. Baldwin, *Billy Baldwin Remembers*, 224.

36. Patricia Corey, conversation with author, January 17, 1997.

37. Baldwin, *Billy Baldwin Remembers*, 221.

38. Ibid., 220–22.

39. Ibid., 220.

40. "House Parties Arranged for Harford Hunt," *Baltimore Sunday Sun*, November 11, 1932.

41. Ladew's other expatriates to the local scene evidently wished to "become Marylanders," too: John Valentine served as the hunt club's MFH from 1915 to 1921, Ambrose Clark from 1921 to 1924, Florence Lowe from 1925 to 1931, Harry Nicholas from 1928 to 1933, and Bryce Wing from 1931 to 1932; all these men and women hailed from New York or Philadelphia.

42. *Daily Sketch*, February 12, 1937.

43. Elizabeth Ober, "A Horsewoman's Diary," *Baltimore Sun*, August 15, 1938. See also "Hundreds Throng Course for Harford Hunt Club Races," *Baltimore News Post*, November 16, 1934.

44. McIntosh, *History*, 73.

45. Edward Voss became joint master in 1939 and would serve as master or joint master on and off until 1970.

46. Elizabeth Ober, "A Horsewoman's Diary," n.d., clipping at LTG.

47. Harvey S. Ladew, "Maryland in the Pink," *Town & Country* (May 1940): 54–55, 110.

48. HSL to ELG, June 30, 1968, LTG.

49. Patterson, "Maryland House," 86.

50. Baldwin, *Billy Baldwin Remembers*, 72.

51. "Sportsmen Seek State's Horsey Lands," undated clipping, LTG.

52. Ibid., 72–73.

53. Leith Griswold, conversation with author, March 25, 1994.

54. HSL to ELG, n.d., LTG. Ladew wasn't the only one to be taken in. In January 1963 Nancy Mitford wrote Evelyn Waugh, "Well a statement by Picasso was read out on France III, the serious programme here, in which he said that the public nowadays know 0 about art & as soon as he realized this, in the 20s, he decided to amass an enormous fortune. . . . Its v. interesting." Quoted in Charlotte Mosley, ed., *The Letters of Nancy Mitford and Evelyn Waugh* (Boston: Houghton Mifflin Co., 1996), 473.

55. Lavinia Edmunds, "Alice Garrett," *Johns Hopkins Magazine* (February 1993): 51.

56. *Town & Country* (May 1939): 121.

57. The Peale Museum, *Life in Baltimore, 1948*, exhibition catalog (Baltimore: Peale Museum, 1948), 21; random clipping, LTG.

58. HSL, Sage interview.

59. Bibber Dow, conversation with author, July 10, 1996.

60. His committee for the Beard and Bustle consisted of, in part, Mrs. B. H. Griswold III, Mrs. Edwin Hower, Mrs. T. Courtney Jenkins, Mrs. Peter Keyser, Mrs. Charles E. Scarlett Jr., Mrs. Joseph D. Tydings, Mrs. Edward Voss, and Mrs. John Westerlund. The "proconsuls" of the second event were simply listed as "Eastman, Griswold, Ladew, Lanahan, McLean."

61. Constable, Dow, and Griswold, Camp interview.

62. Mary H. Cadwalader, interview by author, March 21, 1996.

63. Baldwin, *Billy Baldwin Remembers*, 216.

64. Ibid., 215.

65. Valentine Lawford, *Horst: His Work and His World* (New York: Alfred A. Knopf, 1984), 133.

66. Constable, Dow, and Griswold, Camp interview.

67. Baldwin, *Billy Baldwin Remembers*, 272, 250.

68. Lawford, *Horst*, 8–9. In the late 1940s, Lawford, the fair-haired boy of the British diplomatic corps and widely viewed as a future prime minister, gave up that world to move in with Horst at Oyster Bay, where he stayed the rest of his life. Baldwin, *Billy Baldwin Remembers*, 214–15. The two combined talents in a series of articles about people and houses for *Vogue* and in several wonderfully evocative books about the 1930s and 1940s.

69. Baldwin, *Billy Baldwin Remembers*, 209. Horst wrote that Baldwin was "one of the first new friends [he] made in New York." He also observed that the decorator "had two sides: he was very elegant . . . , but then would be seen at the worst nightclubs. He was quite a naughty boy." Lawford, *Horst*, 318.

70. Baldwin, *Billy Baldwin Remembers*, 270–71.

71. HSL, Sage interview.

72. Valentine Lawford and Horst, *Vogue's Houses, Gardens, People* (New York: Viking Press, 1968), 86.

73. Pearson, "Osbert," 167. Sitwell dismissed the Prince of Wales as the "Philistine Incarnate." John Pearson, *The Sitwells* (New York: Harcourt Brace Jovanovich, 1978), 313.

74. *Journal American* (May 1943), clipping at LTG.

75. Baldwin, *Billy Baldwin Remembers*, 294.

Chapter 4 "The art of personality"

1. Jane Brown, *The English Garden in Our Time* (Woodbridge, England: Antique Collectors' Club, 1986), 37.

2. Wagley, "Pleasant Valley Farm."

3. Quoted in Betty Massingham, "The Natural Garden, 1890–1910," in *The Garden: A Celebration of One Thousand Years of British Gardening*, ed. John Harris (London: Victoria and Albert Museum, 1979), 68.

4. Anne Scott-James and Osbert Lancaster, *The Pleasure Garden* (London: Century Books, 1977), 85.

5. Robinson hated any form of pretension. He waged a years-long war with Sir Joseph Hooker at Kew Gardens over that institution's policy of using Latin names—rather than English—on plant labels.

6. The late Henry Mitchell, whose "Earthman" column ran for years in the *Washington Post*, phrased the same thought thusly: "Architecture is the mother art of gardens, not because a garden needs to be (or should be) cluttered with architectural geegaws, but because the stuff of architecture—the tension between differing volumes, the fall of light and dark, the rhythms of texture—is the essence of a garden." Henry Mitchell, *One Man's Garden* (Boston: Houghton Mifflin Co., 1992), 6.

7. Charles Elliott, "Style Wars," *Horticulture* (February 1995): 22.

8. Gervase Jackson-Stops, *The Country House Garden* (New York: New York Graphic Society, 1987), 61.

9. Garden Club of America, 1971 Distinguished Achievement Award to HSL, LTG.

10. Quoted in Massingham, "Natural Garden," 67.

11. Quoted in Jackson-Stops, *Country House Garden*, 60.

12. Brown, *Our Time*, 13–15.

13. Ibid., 34.

14. Penelope Hobhouse, ed., *Gertrude Jekyll on Gardening* (Boston: David R. Godine, 1983), 185.

15. Penelope Hobhouse, *Garden Style* (Boston: Little, Brown and Co., 1988), 195.

16. Quoted in ibid., 190. "Garden rooms also share the same 'roof,'" one landscape architect recently pointed out. Michael Staz, conversation with author, February 26, 1998.

17. Clive Aslet, *The Last Country Houses* (New Haven: Yale University Press, 1982), 297.

18. Hobhouse, *Gertrude Jekyll on Gardening*, 274.

19. Aslet, *Last Country Houses*, 297.

20. Massingham, "Natural Garden," 60.

21. Quoted in Scott-James and Lancaster, *Pleasure Garden*, 85.

22. Quoted in Hobhouse, *Gertrude Jekyll on Gardening*, 180.

23. Jane Brown, *Gardens of a Golden Afternoon* (New York: Van Nostrand Reinhold Co., 1982), 154.

24. HSL to ELG, September 23, 1947, LTG.

25. Brown, *Our Time*, 13, 24.

26. *Journal of the Royal Horticultural Society* 54 (1929), in Hobhouse, *Gertrude Jekyll on Gardening*, 287. The American landscape architect Beatrix Farrand rescued Jekyll's papers from sure destruction and donated them to the University of California at Berkeley.

27. *Lutyens* (London: Hayward Gallery and the Arts Council of Great Britain, 1981), 19.

28. Brown, *Gardens*, 14.

29. Hobhouse, *Garden Style*, 24.

30. Carole Ottesen, *The New American Garden* (New York: Macmillan Publishing Co., 1987), 194.

31. Brown, *Our Time*, 46, 54.

32. Brown, *Gardens*, 153. In all, *Country Life* covered twenty-seven Jekyll gardens, including Abbotswood (February 15 and 22, 1913), Crooksbury (September 15, 1900; October 6 and 13, 1944), Deanery Garden (May 9, 1903), Ednaston Manor (March 24, 1923), Folly Farm (January 28, 1922; February 4, 1922), Great Dixter (January 4, 1913), Hestercombe (August 23, 1919; October 10, 1980), Little Thakeham (August 28, 1909), Marsh Court (September 1, 1908; April 19, 1913; March 19 and 26, 1932; April 2, 1932), Munstead Wood (December 8, 1900), and Orchards (August 31, 1901; April 11, 1908).

33. Russell Page, "English Gardens from 1910 to the Present Day," in Harris, *The Garden*, 77.

34. Constable, Dow, and Griswold, Camp interview; Leith Griswold, interview with author, June 11, 1995.

35. Aslet, *Last Country Houses*, 297.

36. Brown, *Our Time*, 77.

37. Mary Biddulph, "Rodmarton Marton," in *The English Woman's Garden*, ed. Alvilde Lees-Milne and Rosemary Verey (London: Chatto & Windus, 1980), 31.

38. Jane Brown, *Sissinghurst, the Making of a Garden* (New York: Harry N. Abrams, 1990), 125.

39. Peter Coats, *Great Gardens of Britain* (London: Weidenfeld & Nicolson, 1976), 175. Coats (nicknamed "Petticoats" by Noël Coward) and Channon were intimate and longtime companions.

40. Pearsons, Mitchell, and Geddes, *Ordnance Survey Guide to Gardens*, 98.

41. See Graham Stuart Thomas, *Gardens of the National Trust* (London: National

Trust, 1979), 160–62. See also "Knightshayes Garden Guide," n.d., National Trust. Thanks to Judith B. Tankard for kindly providing these references.

42. Aslet, *Last Country Houses*, 297.

43. Alvilde Lees-Milne, "Lawrence Johnston, Creator of Hidcote Garden," in *By Pen and Spade*, ed. David Wheeler (New York: Summit Books, 1990).

44. Many of the words and phrases Lees-Milne used to describe Johnston could well be used for Ladew: "an avid reader"; a man who "enjoyed painting," who had "a faultless sense when it came to choosing furniture," who "endeared himself to all who knew him, . . . especially his staff," and who was an animal lover, "inseparable from his pack of little dachshunds." Ibid.

45. Ibid., 152.

46. Ibid., 157.

47. Brown, *Our Time*, 168.

48. Page, *Education*, 18–19.

49. Eleanor Perenyi, *Green Thoughts* (New York: Random House, 1981), 238.

50. Lees-Milne, "Johnston," 157.

51. Fred Whitsey, "Where Wharton Led . . . ," *Country Life* (July 7, 1994): 69.

52. Ibid., 70.

53. Lees-Milne, "Johnston," 157.

54. Ibid., 159.

55. Whitsey, "Where Wharton Led," 71.

56. Hobhouse, *Garden Style*, 190.

57. Mac Griswold and Eleanor Weller, *The Golden Age of American Gardens* (New York: Harry N. Abrams, 1991), 194. Delano was the architect of Baltimore's Walters Art Gallery.

58. Lawford and Horst, *Vogue's Houses*, 91; see also Calder Loth, *The Virginia Landmarks Register* (Charlottesville: University Press of Virginia, 1986), 15.

59. Lawford and Horst, *Vogue's Houses*, 91–92; Lawford, quoted in Coats, *Great Gardens*, 272.

60. Ottesen, *New American Garden*, 18. Diana Balmori, Diane K. McGuire, and Eleanor M. McPeck, *Beatrix Farrand's American Landscapes* (Sagaponack, N.Y.: Sagaponack Press, 1985), 78.

61. Griswold and Weller, *Golden Age*, 194.

62. Aslet, *Last Country Houses*, 296.

63. The watercolors, while today valued as much as Wharton's text, were not what she wanted; she told the publisher she would have preferred plans.

64. Quoted in Ethne Clarke and George Wright, *English Topiary Gardens* (London: Weidenfeld & Nicolson, 1988), 10–13.

65. Gertrude Jekyll and Sir Lawrence Weaver, *Gardens for Small Country Houses* (London: Country Life, 1927), 84.

66. Theresa Craig, *Edith Wharton* (New York: Monacelli Press, 1996), 39–40.

67. Brown, *Our Time*, 86.

68. George Plumtree, "Where Giants Meet," *Country Life* (May 19, 1994): 99.

69. David Plante, "A Last Fantasy in Florence," *New Yorker* (July 10, 1995): 41.

Continuing, Plante wrote that "for many young homosexual men . . . La Pietra was an entree into a world they had fantasized about."

70. Acton, *Memoirs*, 6–7; see also Alessandro Albrizzi, *The Gardens of Florence* (New York: Rizzoli International Publications, 1992), 147–49.

71. Sir George Sitwell, *On the Making of Gardens* (London: Dropmore Press, 1949), 12.

72. Bishop, "Maryland Fox Hunter Extraordinary," 14; "An Old Maryland House Re-created by Its Versatile Owner," *House & Garden* (March 1951): 108.

73. Jekyll and Weaver, *Small Country Houses*, 71.

74. Harvey S. Ladew, "An American Topiary Garden," undated manuscript, LTG.

75. Wharton, *Italian Villas*, 249.

76. Constable, Dow, and Griswold, Camp interview.

77. Ibid.; Brown, *Sissinghurst*, 55; Jekyll and Weaver, *Small Country Houses*, 99.

78. Jekyll and Weaver, *Small Country Houses*, 209, 207, 214; Richard Cole, conversation with author, June 19, 1990.

79. Jekyll and Weaver, *Small Country Houses*, xxxix.

80. HSL, Sage interview; Bob Six, conversation with author, April 10, 1997. Six added that the modest Ladew dismissed one neighbor, who kept trophies and ribbons on display, as "that terrible man."

81. Ladew's quotes and the ones in the following nine paragraphs are drawn from his manuscript "An American Topiary Garden."

82. Blow, *Fields Elysian*, 40. The hedge continues to attract hunting owners. In 1954 Rosemary Donner and her husband bought the property from Lady Blanche "because of the topiary": "We were very keen hunting people." The widowed Mrs. Donner continues to maintain the hedge, although she frets that, because of problems finding skilled people to prune it, "the hounds look more like alligators now." Rosemary Donner, letter to the author, September 8, 1996, LTG.

83. The duke of Beaufort to HSL, January 15, 1970, LTG. It was Voss's wife, Elsa, who painted the portrait of Harvey à la Picasso, mentioned in Chapter 3.

84. A September 20, 1953, story in the *Baltimore American* notes that Ladew "moved the fox hunting hedge . . . to his new home."

85. Photographs taken in the 1970s show well-developed hounds and fox but a scraggly horse and rider, suggesting that the latter had not had time to grow into maturity, as the former had.

86. Jekyll and Weaver, *Small Country Houses*, 140.

87. Constable, Dow, and Griswold, Camp interview.

88. Ibid.

89. Bob Six, conversation with author, April 20, 1997.

90. Constable, Dow, and Griswold, Camp interview; HSL to ELG, June 30, 1967, LTG.

91. He, aided by Benjamin H. Griswold III, waged continuous battle with the Immigration Department, whose bureaucrats kept threatening to deport his mainstays: "I only hope Ben can help me keep my Italian servants," he wrote his sister on August 18, 1968.

92. Constable, Dow, and Griswold, Camp interview.

93. Page, *Education*, 214.

94. Jekyll and Weaver, *Small Country Houses*, 180, 129–31.

95. J. C. Shepherd and G. A. Jellicoe, *Italian Gardens of the Renaissance* (London: Ernest Benn, 1925), 24.

96. Clarke and Wright, *Topiary Gardens*, 135.

97. Jekyll and Weaver, *Small Country Houses*, xxvi.

98. Page, *Education*, 123.

99. Sitwell, *Making of Gardens*, 21.

100. Jekyll and Weaver, *Small Country Houses*, 125; Wharton, *Italian Villas*, 238.

101. Constable, Dow, and Griswold, Camp interview.

102. Patterson, "Maryland House," 86.

103. Jekyll and Weaver, *Small Country Houses*, 141.

104. In 1970 Ladew said, "This engineer made the swimming pool for me 40 years ago I guess. It cost $2,500." HSL, Sage interview.

105. Six conversation; Elizabeth Constable, conversation with author, June 10, 1992.

106. Philippa Nicolson, ed., *V. Sackville-West's Garden Book* (New York: Atheneum, 1968), 16–17.

107. Ibid., 15.

108. Jekyll and Weaver, *Small Country Houses*, 215.

109. He also wanted a pair of white swans, some "Mandarin Ducks," and a parakeet that talked "very well." "I could take several if I like the one you send. I would like him sent to my Florida address . . . but I could easily meet the bird if he was sent to West Palm Beach air field."

110. Ladew dated the music hall at 1768. Constable, Dow, and Griswold, Camp interview.

111. Dee Hardie, "A Shrine to Beauty Can Be Maryland's," article (c. 1965) in the *Sun*.

112. Constable, Dow, and Griswold, Camp interview.

113. Constable conversation.

114. Bunny Hathaway, conversation with author, May 10, 1994. Mrs. Hathaway then chaired the foundation's Garden Committee.

115. Letter dated November 4, 1943. Ladew also ordered "7 Duquesa de Penararnda." The total cost of those 122 plants was $103.70.

116. Elizabeth Constable in Constable, Dow, and Griswold, Camp interview.

117. Pearsons, Mitchell, and Geddes, *Ordnance Survey Guide to Gardens*, 313.

118. Coats, *Great Gardens*, 125–28. Luton Hoo was also a favorite of Ladew's dear Queen Mary. She became engaged there to the duke of Clarence (he died a year later, and she was then engaged to the future George V); she made her last visit to Luton in 1950 to inaugurate the estate's open-to-the-public era.

119. Hobhouse, *Jekyll on Gardening*, 131.

120. Coats, *Great Gardens*, 252.

121. On his death, Griswold left his collection to the Walters Art Gallery.

122. HSL to Virginia Sherwood, June 10, 1970, LTG.

123. Sibyl Brown, conversation with author, July 22, 1997; Brown, *Golden Afternoon*, 51.

Chapter 5 *"Your old brother is a one!"*

1. HSL to ELG, November 3, 1948, LTG.

2. "Palm Beach Residents to Spend Half Million Dollars for New Golf Course on Lake Worth," *Palm Beach News*, March 18, 1923; Donald W. Curl, *Mizner's Florida* (Cambridge: MIT Press, 1984), 92.

3. Aslet, *American Country House*, 224.

4. Harvey S. Ladew, "Palm Beach #2," unpublished typescript, LTG. (There are two very different histories of the town.)

5. Boegner, *Halcyon Days*, 222, 148; Peggie Phipps Boegner, conversation with author, August 10, 1995.

6. HSL to ELG, April 1, 1967, LTG.

7. Ladew, "Palm Beach #2."

8. Curl, *Mizner's Florida*, 48.

9. The architect called his formal attire his "fishing clothes," because he said he attended parties to fish for clients.

10. "Rumors Rife in Regard to Polo Field Here Next Winter," *Palm Beach Times*, March 10, 1924.

11. See, e.g., "Phipps to Improve Delray Polo Field," *Palm Beach Post*, September 11, 1927; "Polo Ponies Going North for Summer," *Palm Beach Times*, March 28, 1929; and "Polo at Phipps Fields, Gulf Stream," *Palm Beach Life*, January 13, 1931.

12. "Phipps to Improve Delray Polo Field."

13. Boegner, *Halcyon Days*, 192. Boegner added that her aunt decided to become the first woman to pilot a plane solo across the Atlantic even though she knew nothing about flying; she was eventually dissuaded from this by her brother Howard and instead "generously arranged to have Amelia Earhart take her place." "Of course, this was more practical [because] Amelia knew how to fly."

14. "Polo Ponies Going North"; "Huge Sums Spent to Prepare Sports Center for Season," *Palm Beach Times*, September 11, 1927.

15. Alexandra Fatio, *Maurice Fatio, Architect* (privately published, 1992), introduction by Eric Egan, 4.

16. Ibid., 4, 3.

17. Ibid., 4, ix.

18. Quoted in ibid., 5.

19. Aslet, *American Country House*, 225.

20. Lawford and Horst, *Vogue's Houses*, 7.

21. "An Architectural Survey of Delray," unpublished typescript, Delray Beach Historical Society.

22. Pamela Murray, "Letter from Florida," *Tatler*, March 19, 1941, 422.

23. Baldwin, *Billy Baldwin Remembers*, 221.

24. The bed's curtains were made of 10 yards of Schumacher shantung #111313;

in 1953 it cost eleven dollars a yard wholesale, a figure Ladew called "expensive." Miscellaneous papers, LTG.

25. Baldwin, *Billy Baldwin Remembers*, 221, 225.

26. Sibyl Brown, Bibber Dow, and Kitty Hoffman, "'Pied-à-Mer'—Reminiscences Shared," February 10, 1983, typescript, LTG.

27. Baldwin, *Billy Baldwin Remembers*, 221.

28. Philip Hoare, *Serious Pleasures: The Life of Stephen Tennant* (London: Hamish Hamilton, 1990), 222.

29. Baldwin, *Billy Baldwin Remembers*, 221.

30. Murray, "Letter from Florida," 422.

31. Baldwin, *Billy Baldwin Remembers*, 225.

32. "Society Goes Arty: Nat Saltonstall Opens A Gallery," *Miami Herald*, December 17, 1952.

33. Brown, Dow, and Hoffman, "'Pied-à-Mer.'"

34. Baldwin, *Billy Baldwin Remembers*, 225.

35. "House of Cards," *Vogue* (April 1, 1958): 136–39.

36. "Bridge Winners in Colony Tournament," *Surf and Tide*, February 3, 1949, 12.

37. "House of Cards," 139.

38. "Atlantic Avenue, Delray Beach, A.D. 1943," *Delray Beach News*, February 26, 1943.

39. *Maryland Horse* (February 1943): 12.

40. Fatio designed a new library for the organization in 1936.

41. Letter dated September 17, 1949, LTG. He continues, "I will now give you the list of Tableaux and a few notes and comments on them. I am sure you saw most of the pictures we intend to reproduce. . . . I would appreciate it if you would write me who you think would be good for the pictures we have not already cast. . . . Magni has already painted the background for his picture and I hear it is lovely."

42. Harvey S. Ladew, "Palm Beach," *Town & Country* (March 1946): 117, 206.

43. Baldwin, *Billy Baldwin Remembers*, 226–27.

44. HSL to ELG, September 10, 1947, LTG.

45. In 1961 Nancy Mitford wrote to Evelyn Waugh, "In fact people one knew were never killed in raids . . . except Myrtle." Mosley, *Letters*, 215.

46. Blow, *Fields Elysian*, 128.

47. Later, Garrett founded the Federal City Council in Washington, an organization that oversaw the capital's redevelopment in the 1950s and 1960s.

48. HSL to ELG, November 14, 1947, LTG; Harvey S. Ladew, "Fox Hunting in Eire," *Harper's Bazaar* (March 1948): 183–85.

49. HSL to ELG, October 21, 1947, LTG; Horst, *Thirties*, 130.

50. Harvey S. Ladew, "Fox Hunting in Eire," *Harper's Bazaar* (April 1948): 183–84.

51. HSL to ELG, December 4, 1947, LTG.

52. HSL to ELG, September 2, 1947; *Property from the Collection of the Duke and Duchess of Windsor* (New York: Sotheby's, 1998), 1:512. The Windsors rented the château from April 1946 until the spring of 1949. Frederic Hugues Alfred, baron de Cabrol, was born in 1920.

53. HSL to ELG, September 2, 1947, LTG.

54. HSL to ELG, September 14, 1947, LTG.

55. HSL to ELG, September 2, 1947, LTG.

56. HSL to ELG, September 14, 1947, LTG.

57. HSL to ELG, September 2, 1947, LTG.

58. Hoare, *Coward*, 105–10. When Queen Elizabeth II was crowned, Coward and Fellowes-Gordon watched the proceedings on television. As the procession of foreign dignitaries passed, a carriage came into view which contained the quite large Queen Salote of Tonga and an unknown small man. "Who's that man next to the Queen," someone asked. "Her lunch," Coward replied. "Oh, Noel," Fellowes-Gordon laughed. "That was so funny" (401).

59. Elsa Maxwell, *I Married the World* (London: William Heinemann, 1955), 249. Maxwell felt that Fellowes-Gordon "wanted no part of the Windsors except, maybe, their heads on a medieval pike." Maxwell had to add, though, that "Dickie eventually broke down and confessed that [the Windsors] were much nicer than she had ever imagined" (251).

60. HSL to ELG, September 14, 1947, LTG.

61. HSL to ELG, September 16, 1947, LTG.

62. HSL to ELG, September 23, 1947, LTG. The palace, correctly the Palazzo Contarini-Polignac, is widely regarded as one of the gems of Venetian Renaissance architecture. Even the crusty John Ruskin, who hated most of Renaissance Venice, deemed it "exquisite." See Elena Bassi, *Palazzi di Venezia* (Venice: Stamperia di Venezia Editrice, 1976), 94–97.

63. On November 14, 1947, he wrote his sister, "I think it is amusing that you met Elsa—She is really quite charming—didn't you think so?—but, of course, an old devil." Maxwell had a well-earned reputation for making money any way she could and was not above swindling her friends. But Ladew told his sister the party giver was "making lots of money now" with her column—"so I don't think she will pull a trick on us—but she might!"

64. Lawford, *Horst*, 163, 135, 177.

65. "Well-Heeled Achilles," *Time*, September 5, 1955, 47.

66. Maxwell, *Married the World*, 128.

67. Ibid.

68. Betsy Stinson, "County Resident Describes Miss Elsa Maxwell's Luxury Cruise," *Baltimore Sun*, n.d., LTG.

69. Conspicuously absent were the Windsors, then in the middle of a six-year feud with Maxwell. *Time* reported, "Not to be outdone, with regal precision Wally . . . timed her arrival in Venice to coincide exactly with that of Elsa's guests. 'His Royal Highness and I come here,' she cooed to a reporter, 'expressly not to take part in the social life.'"

70. "Well-Heeled Achilles."

71. Stinson, "County Resident."

72. Maxwell, *Married the World*, 130.

73. Stinson, "County Resident."

74. HSL to ELG, September 10, 1947, LTG; HSL to ELG, November 3, 1948, LTG; HSL to ELG, June 2, 1948, LTG; HSL to ELG, November 13, 1948, LTG.

75. Horst, *Thirties*, 4.

76. "For reasons of hedonism, fashion, and legality, this resurgence had a strong homosexual flavour. Nancy Mitford recorded one evening that of the twelve people she had in for dinner . . . 'I was the only normal one . . . It is rather strange one must admit. Nature's form of birth control in an overcrowded world, I dare say.'" Hoare, *Coward*, 365; see also Graham Payn and Sheridan Morley, eds., *The Noël Coward Diaries* (Boston: Little, Brown and Co., 1982), 113–14.

77. Horst, *Thirties*, 4.

78. Ibid.

79. HSL to ELG, November 27, 1948, LTG.

80. The daughter of Paul and Marie Curie, Eve Curie was a noted pianist. She served with the Free French Forces during World War II and later married Henry Labouisse, executive director of UNICEF.

81. HSL to ELG, December 6, 1948, LTG.

82. HSL to Carmel Snow, December 6, 1948, LTG; HSL to ELG, November 13, 1948, LTG.

83. Horst, *Thirties*, 10.

84. HSL to ELG, November 13, 1948, LTG.

85. Horst, *Thirties*, 7, 163.

86. Ibid., 10.

87. Ibid., 5–6.

88. Ibid., 14, 162.

89. HSL to ELG, December 8, 1948, LTG.

90. HSL to ELG, July 16, 1948, LTG; HSL to ELG, July 12, 1948, LTG.

91. That reference to "Hoytie" underscores, if it needs underscoring, that Ladew continued to mix with the *gratin*. Flanner, for instance, described Wiborg as "one of the few . . . condiment sprinkling of Americans . . . seen in the Parisian upper circles." Horst, *Thirties*, 6, 131.

92. Eleanor Davies Tydings Ditzen, *My Golden Spoon* (Lanham, Md.: Madison Books, 1997), 296. Ladew sometimes referred to the cereal heiress as "Marjorie Weatherbeaten Post," HSL to ELG, April 1, 1967, LTG.

Chapter 6 *"America is going to* HELL!*"*

1. HSL to ELG, October 21, 1969, LTG; The theme of the dance was "Come as your favorite villain"; he, Bluebeard, escorted Sibyl Brown, who dressed as Lizzie Borden. Sibyl Brown, conversation with author, November 2, 1997.

2. HSL to ELG, May 25, 1970, LTG.

3. Ladew, *Random Recollections*, i.

4. Griswold in Constable, Dow, and Griswold, Camp interview.

5. "They have made me so comfortable," he wrote his sister. "Paolo, without asking me, has painted the kitchen all over with white enamel and Gina has made new curtains. . . . Paolo can also make topiary frames beautifully and drives the car well."

But the honeymoon soured—only a bit—and a few weeks later he had to admit, "The Italians have no experience about setting a table—they will put a fish fork on the table for a meat course! La vie est difficile pour moi." HSL to ELG, August 18, 1968, LTG.

6. Chrismer, "Pleasant Valley Farm."

7. Pattie Penniman, conversation with author, July 10, 1995.

8. *Baltimore Sun*, undated clipping, LTG.

9. Dee Hardie, "A Shrine to Beauty Can Be Maryland's," *Baltimore Sun*, undated clipping, LTG.

10. Constable, Dow, and Griswold, Camp interview.

11. HSL to Griswold, Fancy Hill Farm.

12. HSL to Griswold, winter 1965, Fancy Hill Farm.

13. HSL to Griswold, n.d., Fancy Hill Farm.

14. Constable, Dow, and Griswold, Camp interview.

15. Nan Black to HSL, January 25, 1968, LTG.

16. Black-HSL correspondence, LTG.

17. HSL to ELG, n.d., LTG.

18. Minutes, Ladew Topiary Gardens Foundation, LTG.

19. Carroll and Hopkins to HSL, Fancy Hill Farm.

20. In November 1973 Griswold stepped aside as chairman in favor of his wife, Leith; at the same meeting, Josephine Doak agreed to replace Hopkins as treasurer; she in turn was succeeded by Sibyl Brown in 1975.

21. HSL, Sage interview.

22. Sibyl Brown, conversation with author, July 20, 1996.

23. The committee was headed by Mrs. Nancy Martin, Mrs. George Garrett, Mrs. Sol Kahn, Mrs. Thomas Nichols, Mrs. John Schapiro, Mrs. Bonsal White, and Mrs. DeWitt Sage.

24. Louise Ingalls, "Garden Party amid Topiary," *Baltimore News Post*, June 26, 1975.

25. Constable, Dow, and Griswold, Camp interview.

26. Ibid.; Elizabeth Phillips to HSL, July 2, 1966, LTG; Dee Hardie, *Hollyhocks, Lambs, and Other Passions* (New York: Atheneum, 1985), 162. The book is a collection of her magazine columns and some current observations.

27. Nigel Nicolson, foreword to Brown, *Sissinghurst*, 7.

Epilogue

1. Ladew Topiary Gardens, Minutes of Executive Committee, November 18, 1976, LTG.

2. Ibid.

3. "Minutes," January 28, 1977, LTG.

4. "Minutes," June 18, 1973, LTG.

5. "Minutes," September 18, 1977, LTG.

6. "Minutes," April 5, 1977, LTG.

7. The following men and women constitute the Visiting Horticultural Committee in 1998: Dr. Darrell Apps, Ms. Nancy Bechtol, Mr. Thomas Buchter, Dr.

H. Marc Cathey, Mrs. John R. S. Fisher, Ms. Susan Martin, Mr. J. Liddon Pennock Jr., Mrs. Adrian Reed, Mr. Richard Simon, Mr. Marco Polo Stufano, Mr. R. William Thomas, Mr. W. David Thompson.

8. Constable, Dow, and Griswold, Camp interview.

9. "Minutes," June 9, 1977, LTG.

10. Constable, Dow, and Griswold, Camp interview.

11. "Minutes," April 19, 1984, LTG.

12. Constable, conversation with author, May 10, 1995.

13. Ibid.

14. See Christopher Weeks, "Ladew Topiary Gardens Battles the Woolly Adelgid," *Green Scene* (March 1994): 3–6.

15. Constable conversation.

16. If the foundation failed, proceeds from the "special donations" were to be divided among three other specified Maryland charities.

Index

Library of Congress Cataloging-in-Publication Data

Weeks, Christopher, 1950–
     Perfectly delightful : the life and gardens of Harvey Ladew / Christopher Weeks.
        p.   cm.
     Includes bibliographical references (p.   ) and index.
     ISBN 0-8018-6112-8 (alk. paper)
        1. Ladew, Harvey.   2. Baltimore Region (Md.)—Biography.   3. Socialites—Mary-
     land—Baltimore Region—Biography.   4. Baltimore Region (Md.)—Social life and
     customs.   5. Upper class—Maryland—Baltimore Region—Social life and customs.
     6. Ladew Topiary Gardens (Monkton, Md.).   I. Title.
F189.B153L34   1999
975.2′71043′092—dc21
[B]   98-46387
                                                                                                      CIP